THE
SALES
COMPENSATION
HANDBOOK

THE
SALES
COMPENSATION
HANDBOOK

John K. Moynahan, Editor

amacom

American Management Association

This publication is designed to provide accurate and authoritative
information in regard to the subject matter covered. It is sold with
the understanding that the publisher is not engaged in rendering
legal, accounting, or other professional service. If legal advice or
other expert assistance is required, the services of a competent
professional person should be sought.

Library of Congress Cataloging-in-Publication Data

The Sales compensation handbook / John K. Moynahan, editor.
  p.   cm.
  Includes index.
  ISBN 0-8144-0110-4 (hard cover)
  1. Sales personnel—Salaries, etc.   2. Incentives in industry.
3. Compensation management.   I. Moynahan, John K.
HF5439.7.S24   1991
658.3'22—dc20   90-56191
                                                             CIP

Printing number

10 9 8 7

Contents

Preface

Why read another book on sales compensation? Why, for that matter, should another work on sales compensation be written? These are fair questions, considering that the basics of salary, bonus, and commission design for field sales representatives and managers have been more than adequately covered by earlier publications.

This *Handbook* expands upon the previously published body of sales compensation knowledge in attempting to fill two important needs. First, more than ever before, businesses must compete in an environment where *change* is the norm, and awareness of and adaptability to customer interests are of paramount importance in the minds of sales and marketing executives. Old policies and procedures are being reevaluated, and their continuing appropriateness is being validated in the context of a changing and complex customer environment. This *Handbook*, more than its predecessors, focuses on the links between compensation systems and other sales management processes (e.g., quota-setting techniques on which the success of a compensation plan is so often dependent).

Second, this *Handbook* has been written as a *practical* guide for you, the sales or human resources manager, in developing solutions to contemporary compensation problems. The collective expertise of the team of authors (which amounts to not years but centuries of compensation experience) has been incorporated in numerous practical examples of simple, immediate improvements to a compensation program. The goal of this *Handbook*, therefore, is to provide not only an academic treatment of the basics of sales compensation design but a practical guide for verifying that your sales compensation program rewards are aligned properly with the changing needs of your business.

You will probably not read this entire volume at one sitting; and, even if you do, you will no doubt want to refer back to specific sections of the book as issues arise. The Table of Contents may be especially useful, as a quick source of where in the *Handbook* to turn for discussion of specific issues. Each of the *Handbook*'s first twenty chapters consists of a series of between three and twenty subchapters, each addressing a particular set of sales compensation concerns.

The title of each of these 152 subsections is included in the Table of Contents; therefore, you should be able to access material relevant to specific issues quite easily.

The organization of the *Handbook* moves from the general to the specific. Background chapters establish the importance of understanding the sales/marketing/organizational context before judgment is passed on any conclusion relative to a sales compensation plan. Chapters 4 through 9 address the analytical processes employed in building, revising, or stregthening a sales compensation system. Along the way, you will inevitably encounter concerns with goal and quota setting, sales force organization, and sales information systems. These critical managment processes and their interdependency with a sound sales compensation program are covered in these analytical chapters.

Chapters 10 through 17 cover the fundamentals (as well as the tricky details) of plan structure and design. All you need to know, from the various design alternatives to how to determine commission rates to the administration of sales force base salaries, is included in these chapters. There are, of course, some special situations in every sales force. One of these is the sales manager, whose compensation program is discussed in Chapter 17. There are other special sales roles, such as government, distributor, or major account roles, which call for the special techniques covered in Chapter 18. Finally, the *Handbook* would not be complete without a discussion of that unquestioned, yet controversial, goal of "equity." For a concept that no one ever opposes, equity certainly raises concerns in pay design. Chapter 19 should shed some light on the equity issue.

Plan design is a continuing process; you need to monitor the plan and decide when you need to start over with another audit leading to plan change. Chapters 20 and 21 conclude the *Handbook* by helping you identify when you need to turn back to one of the earlier chapters and start the whole process over again.

Acknowledgments

A book of this scope could not have been completed without the help of a number of individuals whose substantial contributions will not be evident to the reader. While this *Handbook* was a collaborative effort, with many contributing authors (each of whose biographies is included elsewhere in the *Handbook*), only a handful of individuals were part of the process from start to finish. Adrienne Hickey, Senior Acquisitions and Planning Editor at AMACOM, demonstrated incredible understanding, patience, and tolerance of delay. How right she was when she told me at the start of the whole process that bringing together the collective expertise of a number of authors would be far more difficult than the process of writing a book alone.

Thanks also go to Stockton Colt of TPF&C for his help in obtaining the contributions and his review of the complete draft manuscript. His invaluable suggestions strengthened the *Handbook* in several key areas.

Next, I need to thank Brian Lewis of TPF&C, whose task it was to take chapters, and parts of chapters, which had been drafted by different contributors, and make them read in as consistent a style as possible. In doing a final review of the manuscript, I realized how good a job Brian had done when it was difficult for me to recall, in many of the chapters, which of the contributors had first drafted the material.

Nancy Duden began working with me October 1, 1979, shortly before publication of my first AMACOM book; we worked together for nearly nine years after that. Typing my drafts of this *Handbook* from the original dictation is but one of many of the indispensable chores which Nancy accomplished in those nine long years, but one which should benefit the readers of this book for a long time to come.

Mike Sivilli of AMACOM picked up the editing responsibility in the final stages, and helped the final production process run more smoothly than I ever imagined it could.

Finally, I must acknowledge the hundreds of organizations worldwide who have been clients of mine and of the other contributing authors. They have given us a unique vantage point from which to observe, advise, and learn. Much of what we have learned is included in this *Handbook*. On behalf of the readers, therefore, thanks to the clients whose experiences formed the basis for all the material in this *Handbook*.

THE
SALES
COMPENSATION
HANDBOOK

1

Sales Compensation and the Management Process

1.1   Compensation and Sales Management Systems

Sales force compensation is one of a number of interrelated sales management systems. So closely connected are these systems that often what appear to be defects in the sales force compensation system are really symptoms of underlying problems in other sales management systems. When this is the case, strengthening compensation will not, in itself, improve sales force effectiveness.

Sales management systems that must be properly linked to sales compensation include:

- Selection
- Training
- Deployment and role definition
- Sales information systems
- Goal and quota setting

A company's sales management systems should conform to its business and marketing strategies and reflect how customers actually think, not how they used to think or how the company would like them to think (based on its existing internal systems).

Clearly, corporations have cultures with belief systems and behavioral norms that can powerfully affect sales management systems. Most successful companies, for example, focus on market characteristics, anticipate changes in customer thinking, and adapt their own systems to capitalize on emerging opportunities. In short, they see the customer as a partner in a mutually beneficial relationship and view changes in the external environment as opportunities, not nuisances.

Other organizations that are less market-adaptive and consequently less successful are often constrained by their own traditions—that is, their inclination to always do things the same way limits their responsiveness.

If properly designed, a sales compensation plan can serve as a powerful medium of organizational communication, enabling a company to improve the return on its investment in a most important resource: its sales talent. But if other systems send a conflicting message, a dysfunction occurs and the sales force will not behave according to management's intentions. This problem frequently develops when related management systems reflect cultural values that are no longer—if they ever were—relevant to contemporary thinking among customers. Here are some examples:

Selection	A chemical company had always recruited college graduates with chemistry degrees to staff its industrial sales force. Although the company diversified and acquired a consumer goods business, its selection procedures remained unchanged, despite the fact that a degree in chemistry (and the compensation level that background commanded) was not required in a consumer goods sales force.
Training	A telephone communications company gave its sales reps a three-week training course in basic telephony. Customer needs (and the company product line) later expanded to include far more elaborate systems. Because the training still focused on simple equipment, sales force productivity suffered.
Deployment and role definition	A grocery products company maintained the same organizational structure despite a major change in customer decision-making processes. The company assigned sales reps to geographic territories that could include independent stores, national account headquarters, food brokers, and outlets of national chains. Each distribution channel called for a different level and type of selling skill. Yet the sales role, as the company defined it, required that the rep be proficient at a number of difficult—but mutually exclusive—tasks. Thus, because of its traditional geographic-organizational structure, the company wasted much of its skilled reps' selling capacity on relatively mundane activities. This resulted in unnecessarily high sales costs.
Information systems	An industrial company's strategy called for quickly increasing penetration of the automotive industry. But sales reps preferred to concentrate on industries in which the company was more firmly entrenched. Sales managers' reports identified where products were shipped, and whether and how quickly they

were paid for, but could not differentiate sales by industrial segment. Thus, the company was unable to measure its penetration of its target industry.

Goal and quota setting
A company's sales reps received a salary plus a bonus based on how their sales volume compared to their quotas. Quotas, however, were set arbitrarily and were not based on solid data concerning market potential. Some of the company's best sales reps (in management's judgment) were not even earning the targeted bonus. Management feared losing key contributors and searched for a better compensation plan.

In all of these situations, management perceived a need to improve sales force effectiveness and tried to redesign the compensation program accordingly. Unfortunately, the problems were in sales management systems, not in sales compensation.

1.2 Customer Values and Needs

Knowing what's required for effective selling provides the key to determining how the sales role should function and how reward systems should be structured to reinforce that role. If all customers made their buying decisions the same way, there would be no need for sales staff. Companies could simply target their advertising, promotions, and other marketing strategies to meet a single set of customer requirements. Sales reps would then act as order takers or walking advertisements. Fortunately or unfortunately, all customers are not the same.

It follows, at least in those situations where sales reps do influence the buying decision, that a prime ingredient of this influence is the ability to adapt to specific customer needs. But adaptive selling is impossible without knowing how customers differ in making their buying decisions. That's why understanding the buying process and possessing whatever other information is necessary to successfully execute the sales role are essential to effective incentive design.

Unfortunately, many sales incentive design efforts start from a completely different perspective. Managers who don't understand the sales process and who view sales reps as a necessary evil look to sales incentives as a way to "make" reps do their jobs. Although they might say that an objective of program change is to help sales reps work more intelligently, in reality these managers put more weight on making them work harder. Sales incentives become a scapegoat because they're easy to change and they attract attention (and problems). If repeated changes in the incentive program have failed to get results, that's a clue that the difficulties are symptoms with causes rooted in other elements of the sales management process.

A more constructive perspective begins with the ultimate purpose of sales management: to develop loyal customers and profitable sales at low costs. The sales force *implements* the customer management process. Because the customer is where sales and profits originate, that's where any process designed to reinforce the sales role should begin.

Each customer has his or her own values and needs. The expert sales rep understands these needs—that is, he or she knows about a customer's requirements in the context of market characteristics, company/competitor products and services, and specific account characteristics. The best way for a sales manager to develop an understanding of how customers actually think is by asking the top sales reps detailed questions about how buying decisions are made and by directly observing customer decision-making patterns.

1.3   Market Characteristics (Segmentation)

Customer types, buying processes, and product applications vary dramatically. For example, although the same product might be sold to both universities and private companies, educational institutions usually have pricing needs that are much different from those of private companies. Marketers try to manage these differences by establishing "market segments," or groupings of similar accounts for strategic marketing purposes. Marketers might then use particular advertising media to reach these groups.

Segmentation can be extremely valuable in the sales effort as well. It can provide important clues as to what to find out about account and selling strategies, and it can also provide information that is vital to sales organization and deployment. For example, customer characteristics that differ substantially and a product or service that demands a lot of adaptation from one situation to another argue for separate, or at least specialized, sales organizations. If the differences in customer characteristics are greater than or even close to the differences in product technology, the organizational lines are best drawn along market rather than product lines. Information available about the number and size of customers in each market segment can also provide crucial insight into sales deployment (size of the sales organization).

Sales role characteristics must serve as the primary criteria in segmenting customers. For example, companies often establish market segments according to industry. This makes sense if the product sold, its application, and the buying process vary significantly from industry to industry. However, the sales role may be the same for similar industries but differ according to the sophistication of the account. So, for the purpose of managing the sales force, a different (or modified) segmentation from that used in the marketing process might be advisable.

Alternatively, customers are frequently classified by volume (or potential volume), with sales reps told to call more often on "A" accounts, less often on "B" accounts, and so on. But such a classification scheme (although it might help reps be more efficient) doesn't make the sales force any smarter. To match selling skills and customer needs effectively, customers should be classified according to their decision-making processes: for example, how will the buyer *use* the company's product? And what variables will the buyer consider in choosing vendors? Figure 1-1 summarizes some of the segmentation alternatives.

Selling specialized products (e.g., medical equipment) usually requires the ability to communicate technical information to a sophisticated customer. The sales rep will, of necessity, develop a narrow product specialization. Therefore, a number of reps may have to call on a single customer—a situation that demands careful account management. If, on the other hand, distributors play a major role in decision making, they might provide a reason for segmentation. The sales organization can accommodate differences in the products purchased, the competition, or

Figure 1-1. Sales force segmentation alternatives.

Specialization Strategy	Situations Where Most Applicable
Product	• High degree of technical issues determine sales to sophisticated buyer. • Little commonality occurs along other dimensions (e.g., industry).
Large account	• Buying process changes drastically based on the size of the organization (e.g., "national" organizations). • Large, multisite accounts want coordinated sales approach.
Industry	• Nature of product, product application, or buying decision differs significantly from industry to industry. • One or more industry segments have tight-knit relationships, unique business jargon.
Distribution channel	• Product must be sold not just to the end user but to others at various points in the distribution channel. • Nature of sales role varies (e.g., selling electronic components to end users differs from encouraging a distributor to spend more time on the same products).
Customer/vendor relationship	• When personality issues represent the most important factors in buying decision. • When skills in different parts of the sales relationship (e.g., securing new accounts vs. maintaining old ones) differ, and a graceful transition is possible.

the service required. A less conventional criterion for segmentation might be the customer/vendor relationship itself.

The sales force may also be partially, rather than totally, segmented. This is common when segmentation is based on account size. Partial segmentation can fit other situations, too, such as uneven geographic distribution of customers, which may warrant industry specialists in dense territories and generalists in sparse ones.

Specialization enhances sales force effectiveness, but it is not without trade-offs. Specialization often increases travel time, which decreases the time available to spend with customers. In addition, travel is expensive, as is the more complex management of a segmented sales force. Is this greater cost worthwhile? If the probable benefits outweigh the cost and if similar benefits cannot be achieved by less expensive means, the answer is yes.

Examining a specialized approach, however, is almost always worthwhile, because the process helps identify the best selling approaches for each market segment. Even if the economics do not justify a specialized organization, disseminating segment-specific information can help sales reps develop strategies that are more closely tied to account characteristics. The information can also help in training and troubleshooting problem accounts.

Companies with a market focus obtain the information they need to

Figure 1-2. Strategic vs. product information.

MedElect, a manufacturer of medical devices, introduced a new product, accompanied by a great deal of technical product literature (and trade advertising). The device sold poorly in most territories, although a few reps did well. Why didn't all do well? Here's what MedElect discovered:

- Although most of the company's other products were sold to individual practitioners, the new device, used primarily in hospitals, was bought by hospital purchasing committees. The reps that had experience selling to hospitals were more comfortable and more successful selling to them than were the reps without that experience.
- The new device had several possible applications. In the most obvious of these, it competed with a number of other products. Although it was arguably a "better mousetrap," the competitive products worked satisfactorily. So why would a hospital risk using something new, and increasing its inventory, when existing products sufficed? The successful reps focused on the applications where competitive products either did not exist or worked poorly—and where the new device filled a real need. The other reps, struggling with a new product in a less familiar environment, focused on the more obvious applications, which were easier to understand, because they didn't realize this decision made the sale more difficult.

---

formulate business strategies by examining *customer* rather than internal characteristics. Figure 1-2 illustrates the value of a customer rather than a product perspective on sales information.

Once the company understood what was happening, it took two steps to present the new product better. The first was to specialize the sales force: In geographically concentrated markets, different reps covered the old and new products. The second step was to provide more information to the entire sales organization about those product applications where the company had an advantage. The company also advised reps on how best to explain product advantages in the marketplace. With these changes, product sales improved significantly.

2

Corporate Cultures, Personalities, and Value Systems

2.1 Corporate Cultures

The vice-president of customer service and marketing of a major gas and electric utility pounded his desk and declared:

> We must change our culture to be successful in this market-place. Our business is being deregulated, and this utility must understand the needs of its customers. It must use its new sales force efficiently as the first line of communication with those customers.

Surrounded by numerous photos of himself with former U.S. presidents and other celebrities, the patriarch of a family-held winery discussed his company's approach to the market and its internal values in this way:

> Wine is a direct complement to good food, and it should be sold in that manner. We are not selling boxes of wine bottles. Our role in the marketplace is to teach consumers, hotel managers, and maître d's that our white and red wines are perfect matches for fine gourmet meals.

> We value knowledge and loyalty among our employees. We treat them like family, and we expect open communications. We hire only the best, pay above industry levels, and expect that the quality of their performance will reflect the quality of our product. There is no need to advertise because the quality of our sales force sells the product.

Faced with an increasingly competitive market in which all disk drives look the same, the sales and marketing vice president of a computer equipment company contemplates change:

For several years now we have been the lowest-cost producer of computer disk drives. Because of this advantage we have done well, but only because our sales force pushes those drives into every market nook and cranny. We are, of course, concerned with the customers' applications for our product, but our key goal is to keep that Far East plant humming.

We must be different from our competitors; they are closing the cost gap on us. We must get closer to the customers to better understand how they might use our disk drives. Our culture will have to change. We might also have to change the type of salespeople we hire, and maybe the compensation program as well.

These vignettes, involving executives of three different companies with different sets of values and markets, demonstrate that corporations have personalities. These personalities, which are generally referred to as corporate cultures, evolve subcultures for particular functions. In the case of the sales force, a subculture attempts to align sales actions and behavior with the values of the company. Companies also develop sales management programs, for example, incentive compensation schemes, that support and communicate corporate cultural values. But, as the previous examples show, marketplace developments and the resulting evolution in corporate culture suggest that parallel changes are required in the systems that control and monitor the sales force.

The principal components that shape corporate cultures include:

- Internal competition among employees
- Operating independence
- Creativity and innovation
- Respect for the individual
- Self-confidence
- Informality
- Openness of communications
- Employee and customer participation
- Customer service
- Propensity for action and change
- Focus on analysis and planning
- Decentralization of organization and decision making
- Orientation to risk
- Quality emphasis
- Security and seniority

To be successful, a company must understand, develop, and communicate its corporate values and beliefs effectively. In addition, it must use these values as the foundation for hiring, managing, and controlling the sales force. The key vehicle for communicating culture to the sales force is the sales incentive compensation program. As a result, the structure of the incentive program is critical; it must communicate values and goals accurately and encourage appropriate behavior.

2.2   Corporate Cultures and Pay Systems

Let's consider some typical corporate cultures and the sales compensation systems they usually employ.

The Manufacturing or Technology Culture

A company with a strong manufacturing or technology focus normally concentrates on product quality, features, efficiency, and production. The CEO of such a company is frequently a graduate of the production, research, or engineering function of the company (or one of its competitors), and the style of the organization is characteristically low-key, conservative, and participative. Manufacturing- or technology-driven companies often take a somewhat detached view of the customer.

Sales reps recognize that nonselling roles in research or production are more highly valued. For this reason, many often see sales as a place to "do some time" on the way to other positions.

The incentive compensation schemes commonly found in such companies are usually risk-averse. The sales rep receives only a base salary or a salary plus a very modest incentive award. The incentive is usually "backed into" to ensure that the salesperson receives exactly the amount of planned incentive dollars. There is little true variability in the selling situation.

This compensation method does not allow the company to reward specific selling efforts of strategic importance. Consequently, retaining star sales reps becomes difficult, especially if competitors are offering variable compensation on top of salary.

The Numbers Culture

A numbers-driven company focuses heavily on revenue, accounting, and growth. The CEO usually comes from a finance or engineering background and has a style that is often autocratic, intense, and controlling.

In a numbers-driven culture, the customer takes second place to the internal goal of "getting the numbers," and the sales force is viewed as a cost center rather than an investment. The sales force must create market demand consistent with the company's goal. Not surprisingly, sales rep behavior reflects the intense pressure to reach management's aggressive sales or profit goals, which are often formulated with little or no counsel from the sales force. This results in high turnover, especially among the better salespeople.

Pay programs in such companies invariably entail significant risk, in the form of commission plans where the salesperson receives a preestablished percentage of the revenue or profit sold. Usually no salary is provided. This scheme reflects the company's philosophy, which says that if the numbers don't come in sales reps don't get paid.

Such an arrangement disposes the sales force to seek the quick and easy sale. This makes it difficult for the company to direct selling efforts toward other strategic goals, such as selling to selected customer groups or pursuing relationship-building roles that will not result in an immediate sale.

The Market Culture

In a market-driven company, the chief executive often hails from the marketing function. Marketing is given a high priority, and senior executives participate actively in formulating strategies. Market-driven companies focus on achieving market-based strategic goals. Such organizations recognize the importance of knowing their current and potential customers. In the market-based culture, selling is a respected function that carries high stature. In today's highly competitive environment, where a few large companies often vie for a limited number of customers, many companies are adopting this cultural form.

Pay systems in the market-driven culture tend to be risk-oriented, but to a lesser extent than in the numbers culture. The company usually provides a small base salary supplemented by some form of variable compensation to provide motivation and direction. The variable component often takes the form of multiple bonuses that vary in proportion to the sales rep's performance against defined, objective goals. Salespeople can earn the bonus by attaining specific market-related goals.

These bonuses might concentrate the sales rep's effort on selected customer groups, particularly high-profit product lines, or special selling efforts with long-term significance to the company. Incentive compensation programs are easier than commission plans to structure in ways that meet the needs of the company's customers as well as the company's strategic and cultural values.

2.3   Reconciling Culture and Market

As the business world grows more competitive, companies are increasingly challenged to ensure greater consistency between the characteristics of their markets and their corporate cultures. They must also ensure that sales management systems focus on customers' needs, not on their own.

The first step in strengthening the link between the customer and the company culture is to understand customers' specific needs. These "needs" might include such factors as delivery speed, availability of terms, technical support, on-site repair, and special labeling as well as customer segmentation and the company's competitive strengths and weaknesses. By analyzing the market, you might learn, for example, that your culture and therefore your sales management programs are inconsistent with each other.

The second step, because of this stronger bond between market needs and culture, is to require complementary sales management systems to communicate and reinforce these values, as shown in Figure 2-1.

To understand the importance of these relationships, let's return to our three corporate culture models (the manufacturing, numbers, and market companies). By examining the buying habits of their customers, you can learn a great deal about consistency among customer needs, company values, and support programs.

Figure 2-2 lists common characteristics shared by the customers served by these companies. You will note that their general buying habits vary as widely as the three cultures do from each other.

Figure 2-1. Influences on sales management systems.

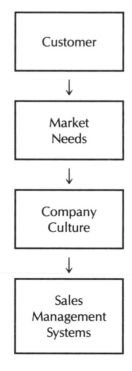

Figure 2-2. Linkages between culture and selling environment.

Company Culture	Characteristics of Selling Environment
Manufacturing/technology	• There is repetition of sales. • Products are substitutable. • Salesperson's role is minor.
Numbers	• Selling cycles are short. • Incidence of sales is predictable. • There is a high number of transactions.
Market-based	• Incidence of sales is unpredictable. • Selling is indirect. • Sales are "one-of-a-kind." • Sales situations are multifaceted. • Customer is seeking solutions, not products.

Customers of manufacturing/technology companies require little sales support and buy on the basis of price, quality, or other factors not controlled by the sales rep. Little true interaction with this customer base is required and, as we have seen, little customer service is provided. Customers in the numbers culture need more attention. Sales calls must be numerous and predictable, but actual demand may be a function of market growth rather than sales rep effort. Customers of the market-based companies require significant sales force support, in such projects as exploring potential applications for products and solving customer problems. The sales force and the anticipatory, strategic activities of management should align with these needs. In summary, your success in the marketplace is a function of reconciling your values and systems with the needs and demands of your customers.

Experience has shown that if customer needs and cultural values are not in alignment, sales management systems will reinforce values that are inconsistent with those of your customers. This can impair the effectiveness of your sales organization. The symptoms of sales management systems that are failing to reinforce values appropriate to their markets are listed in Figure 2-3.

To judge whether your culture and sales management systems are consistent, ask yourself the following questions:

■ Do your management information systems capture the appropriate information about your customers, their buying habits and practices, and account profitability? Similarly, can you or do you track each sales rep's frequency of calls and use of selling time? In short, do your systems provide information that supports marketing and sales decision making?

Figure 2-3. Symptoms of dysfunctional sales management systems.

System Component	Symptom
Goal and quota setting	• Sets unattainable quotas. • Provides no motivation to exceed quotas. • Offers insufficient dollar awards.
Management information	• Contains little customer-related data. • Is unable to track performance. • Fails to identify profitable customers or products.
Incentive compensation	• Applies awards inconsistent with productivity. • Fails to focus selling activity. • Generates uncompetitive earnings.
Training	• Permits weak sales management skills. • Produces poor product knowledge. • Provides incomplete assistance with customer applications.
Sales classification	• Fails to distinguish more important prospects. • Encourages misuse of selling time. • Fails to track how selling time is actually used.

▪ Is your sales force organized to reflect properly the buying practices and processes of your key customer segments? Is it effective for your salespeople to call on multiple buyers at the same account or should you specialize the sales force by customer or customer segments? Do your sales managers have the appropriate spans of control?

▪ Do you set reasonable and equitable goals and judge fairly the sales rep's performance against them? Does the sales force participate in the goal-setting process? Are they a source of information for the process? Do you have too many goals that result in small, meaningless payments? How relevant are goals to true market opportunities?

▪ Are you recruiting and training sales reps whose skills match the needs of your customer base? Do your salespeople have the technical skills necessary to understand customer applications and recommend appropriate company products? Are sales managers receiving enough management training to support your selling tactics?

▪ Are you providing the sales force with definitive career paths and the training and knowledge to progress from one level to another?

▪ Do you give the sales force a system to classify both prospects and existing customers? Do you help the sales force allocate selling time according to the strategic importance of the prospect or customer, its buying habits, and competitive penetration?

- Does your compensation program reward the achievement of specific strategic goals? Do actual incentive earnings truly reflect sales force productivity and goal achievement? Does the plan design encourage the sale of more strategically important or profitable product lines?

2.4   Cultural Change

As market characteristics change, many companies are recognizing that their cultures are no longer consistent with their customers' needs. Some of the major external factors driving market changes today are:

- Government-directed deregulation (in, e.g., the financial services, telecommunications, and trucking industries)
- Significant changes in the competitive environment (e.g., the rise of Far East competition in the marketing of computers and peripherals)
- Evolution of technology
- Consolidation, acquisitions, and mergers of competitive companies
- Evolution in the company's life cycle

Once your company concludes that cultural change is necessary, you will find that the sales incentive compensation program can be an important agent in making that change. With it you signal to the sales force that certain values and behaviors are required for success and that by conforming the force will serve both the customer and the long-term success of the company.

In developing such a compensation program, consider the following design principles:

- *Defining and balancing performance measures.* Measures might include volume, profit, selling milestones (such as getting a product specified into a customer's engineering drawing), product line activity, or customer market share. The company's marketing priorities will dictate the number and balance of these factors. By carefully structuring performance measures, you can focus selling efforts on your competitors' weak spots and shape selling behavior to serve the specific needs of your customers.

- *Variability of the sales force compensation.* How much variable compensation you use in your program will depend on how much your salespeople influence customer buying decisions. A careful study of the interaction between customers and salespeople will reveal the nature of their relationship. Do the salespeople influence only volume, or can they affect other aspects of the sale (e.g., which customer group is targeted or which product lines are sold)? Where it is appropriate, compensation programs should encourage and reward the high-risk selling efforts of highly influential salespeople who have a significant impact on closing the sale. Higher variability in earnings will signal to the sales force the importance of successful proactive selling.

■ *Frequency of award calculation and payment.* Customers have a rhythm in their buying, and this pattern should be a key design factor. Some selling situations, such as sales to government entities, require long selling cycles with frequent customer contact that might not result in short-term volume. In the fashion industry, by contrast, the buy decision is made only semiannually.

■ *Consistency with corporate strategy.* Objectives set for your sales force must be parallel with, and communicate, the company's marketing and financial goals. To reinforce a cultural change through the compensation program, you must clearly delineate your goals and incorporate them directly into the compensation program. At issue are such goals as revenue or profit growth, new products or markets, product or customer emphasis, and qualitative versus quantitative selling tasks and selling costs.

A sales incentive compensation program can act as an agent of change. It directs and molds the actions and attitudes of the sales force through incentive measures. A carefully designed incentive program can ensure proper sales force focus on market needs, the successful achievement of company goals, and continual reinforcement of new values.

3

Preliminary Self-Diagnostics

3.1 Should Sales Reps Have a Separate Compensation Plan?

Should sales reps be paid differently from the way other employees are paid? If a company gives bonuses to its sales staff, shouldn't it give them to everyone? Human resources specialists, who deal with such issues as compensation equity among employee groups, frequently raise these questions. A rational examination of the uses of sales incentive compensation, however, will indicate why a company should pay its salespeople differently from the way it pays other employees.

From the company's point of view, a separate compensation program for sales reps makes sense if one or more of the following conditions is present:

1. *The sales management process needs reinforcement.* Compensation serves as a channel of communication between sales management and the field. Without day-to-day supervision, many sales reps will set their own priorities and ignore management's directives to focus on the more difficult tasks (e.g., securing new accounts and selling profitable products). A compensation plan designed specifically for sales reps provides a strong economic motive to follow the company's priorities.

Sales management, the translation of abstract (usually numeric) goals into account and market-specific tactics, is an art. It requires skill and hard work on the part of managers, which will be wasted if sales reps disregard the company's wishes. A variable pay system that underscores the message that accomplishing specified performance measures will lead to increased total compensation can *strengthen* the sales management process in two ways:

- By recognizing the importance of sales reps to the company in attaining its financial goals and by providing the reps with financial rewards for their achievements
- By forcing sales managers to improve their goal-setting skills because the achievement of those goals will affect their subordinates' pay

2. *Sales reps can "create their own value."* In certain businesses, the sales rep's value to the organization resists conventional measurement. The market and the product are such that the sales rep is worth whatever he or she proves to be worth, as measured by some index of productivity (usually volume). The product is indistinguishable from alternatives and the "value added" that gives competitive advantage derives from the creativity and salesmanship of the rep. In such selling situations, the sales rep's productivity cannot be accurately rewarded through a predetermined salary (although salary may be used for part of the pay package to ensure the steady flow of subsistence-level income). Certain industries, e.g., encyclopedia sales, retail stock brokering, and individual life insurance, possess these characteristics and therefore deliver most if not all of the sales rep's pay through commission. But in many other industries, sales jobs (or sales roles with particular market segments) may have these same characteristics.

If management is uncertain about whether reps can create their own value in its business, it should consider the following criteria:

1. Does the sales rep have to persuade the customer of his or her need for the product, process, or service?
2. Do numerous, often indistinguishable, alternative sources of the product, process, or service exist?
3. Are these alternative sources formidable competitors that aggressively seek the same business from the same customer/prospect base?

If all three conditions are present, then the sales rep can indeed "create" value for him- or herself, and the company must offer some form of incentive compensation so that income delivered reflects income deserved on the basis of productivity.

3. *Incentive compensation is a competitive necessity.* Competition for sales talent includes all of those organizations that could employ the sales force, without significant retraining, to sell their products or services. Thus, the competition comprises not only direct industry competitors but also external companies whose selling tasks are similar. If competitors characteristically layer an incentive compensation opportunity on top of the sales rep's base salary, then it behooves any competitive sales force to do so as well.

The presence of incentive compensation will cause the distribution of earnings to widen. A company that pays salary but no commission in a labor market where its competitors offer both will probably pay salaries that are slightly higher than average, thus ensuring the loyalty of mediocre performers. But such a company will probably not be able to offer salary levels, even to its best performers, that match the total of salary and incentives offered the best salespeople in the labor market. Nor should you want to elevate salaries to such a level; for in our society, it is difficult from a human relations standpoint to rescind a salary increase given in a prior year. Salaries tend to go up, and only up. Because a salary increase is usually permanent, its present value (and hence its cost to the company) greatly exceeds that of a comparable payment of incentive compensation, which, to be received in the future, must be re-earned through sustained productivity.

4. *The company has limited resources.* Turning part of sales compensation expense into a variable cost is particularly critical to companies that have limited resources. An entepreneurial start-up venture may not have the capital resources to offer competitive base salaries. In such cases, even if industry practice and management preference are to pay salary alone, economic necessity dictates that sales reps be required to "trade off" some secure base salary income for the opportunity to outearn their salaried peers in other organizations, should their sales performance merit significant commissions or bonuses.

Most organizations will find it advantageous to deliver sales force compensation, or a significant portion thereof, in variable pay. Only those organizations that have an exceptionally strong sales management process and extensive resources, and whose competitors also pay base salary, can safely avoid developing a separate remuneration system for the field sales force. Certain basic industrial sectors such as chemicals, metals, petroleum, steel, and carbon have been able to use salary exclusively. But even in these industries, with the emergence of special markets and applications, and as a result of diversification into new ventures, sales incentives are working their way into company compensation packages.

3.2   The Sales Rep as an "Investment"

Is the sales force a cost or an asset?

A sales organization is neither a necessary evil nor a cost to be minimized; rather, it represents an investment on the part of the company that offers an opportunity to improve the company's return.

A sales rep is, in a sense, an investment in selling capacity. The individual has available at his or her disposal approximately 2,000 working hours per year (40 hours × 50 weeks). To maximize the return on its investment in salespeople, a company must make optimum use of the sales rep's time.

Among the factors that affect a company's return on its investment in sales force capacity are:

- The number of field sales territories
- The extent to which available selling time is used for selling rather than for administrative tasks
- The credentials required of incumbents (indicating market rates of pay)
- The effective categorization of accounts, to guard against redundant sales calls
- The costs per territory of benefits, expenses, and perquisites
- The cost of incentive pay relative to underlying productivity

Although reorganizing territories and controlling costs can help improve the return on investment in sales capacity, compensation plan designers usually lack authority to make changes in these areas.

The rules of the "economic game" embodied in the incentive compensation plan must focus on yielding more productivity per dollar spent. And this is done by aligning the recipient's economic well-being with the allocation of time that most benefits the company in meeting its objectives.

Faced with myriad responsibilities and more tasks than he or she can possibly accomplish, a sales rep will allocate time according to the path of least resistance. Tasks that provide positive reinforcement will receive more than their fair share of time, and those that are distasteful in any way will not receive sufficient attention (see Figure 3-1). Their neglect can be easily rationalized: After all, there aren't enough hours in the day to do everything.

In the absence of an economic motive (such as a commission or a bonus incentive), the sales rep will understandably devote the bulk of

Figure 3-1. Typical time allocation according to sales task characteristics.

Excessive	Insufficient
Task Characteristics	
• Pleasant	• Unpleasant
• Familiar	• Unfamiliar
• Easy	• Difficult
• Gratifying	• Frustrating
• Nonthreatening	• Competitive
Examples	
• Maintain existing relationships.	• Introduce new products.
• Sell familiar products.	• Take accounts away from
• Concentrate on existing customers.	competitors.
• Secure an order today.	• Set stage for future volume.
• Prospect for new customers.	

his or her time to the more appealing aspects of the job. Unfortunately, in terms of strategic results, the most important sales tasks for the company are difficult and frequently require the sales rep to endure repeated rejection in the pursuit of success.

The incentive compensation plan serves as a mechanism to alter the allocation of time that might otherwise occur, by aligning the rep's economic interest with the accomplishment of tasks that might otherwise be neglected. Therefore, the design of the compensation plan can serve to increase the return on the company's investment in sales capacity.

How often have you heard a sales rep lament, "I am so busy taking care of my accounts that I don't have time to get new accounts or sell the newer products"? At the same time, management is usually striving to find ways to get more new accounts and introduce its new products successfully. If you look closer at this scenario, invariably you will find a compensation plan that rewards the rep comfortably for what he prefers to do, not what is in the strategic interest of the company to accomplish. Valuable selling capacity is being wasted, and the company is not securing the best return on its investment in its sales capacity. Changing the compensation plan could have a significant impact. By making comfortable levels of pay contingent on attaining the more relevant goals, the sales compensation manager can give reps the opportunity to become more valuable to the company and increase their compensation. The company's return on its investment in selling capacity will improve, its sales costs may decrease, and its sales capacity will be better utilized.

3.3   Matching Plan Design to Company Goals

If sales managers are asked if their compensation plans are effective, some will answer, "Absolutely"; about the same number will respond with a no; and most will shrug their shoulders and say, "I'm really not sure. I think it's okay."

"Okay," however, is not good enough. Sales reps represent an important investment for a company, one that should yield a very favorable return. "Absolutely," on the other hand, sounds a lot more like what most of us would demand if we were footing the sales compensation bill.

What constitutes a sound compensation plan? The first step is to prepare a list of *general* objectives of a good incentive plan. Most lists would include at least some of the following:

- To reward sales accomplishment
- To motivate
- To direct the sales force
- To make the rep work harder and smarter

- To attract and retain talented people
- To encourage poor sales talent to leave the company
- To create a "win-win" situation for the company and the sales rep
- To not overpay for the easy part of the job
- To pay for more than just current sales, e.g., to recognize preparations for future sales, recognizes profitable sales, encourage and reward the sale of new products
- To help sales managers manage
- To be simple and understandable
- To remind the rep that he or she is a member of a team as well as a lone ranger: that the rep must help in joint selling and in training and that he or she must be cooperative and do all the reports

The next step in developing a sound compensation plan involves identifying, in as great a degree of specificity as possible, five to ten of the most important objectives for the particular sales organization. Then the current plan can be evaluated by assessing how well it accomplishes each objective:

☐ Very well
☐ Moderately well
☐ Little or not at all

Note that each objective could mean different things to different companies. For example, depending on the situation, "helps sales managers manage" might mean:

- To allow a manager to assign territories/accounts in a way that doesn't have a direct windfall/deadfall effect on the sales rep, so that she can optimize the sales force's use of time
- To allow a manager to set sales priorities and to calibrate plan payouts to recognize the uniqueness of his geographic region—what is easy and what is difficult to sell
- To keep a rep from becoming indifferent to the difficult aspects of the job because she has already reached her economic point of indifference (earned plenty) on the easy part of the job (easy customers or market segments)

Focusing on a company's specific sales and marketing objectives permits sound value judgments in the evaluation of a sales compensation plan.

3.4 Uncovering Danger Signals

As we have seen, one way of measuring the effectiveness of a sales compensation plan is to examine whether it is accomplishing the company's stated objectives. Searching for specific problems that might indicate a suboptimal plan represents another approach that allows a more thorough audit of the plan.

After identifying and describing such problems, the sales manager should assess them vis-à-vis improvement opportunities. In any evaluation, however, you should proceed on the basis of the following premises:

- No sales compensation plan is perfect, and not all problems are important enough to fix.
- A sales compensation plan should not try to monitor and direct each and every action of a salesperson.
- A sales compensation plan should direct the major efforts of the rep and reinforce his or her successes.
- Sales compensation plan inertia can be a powerful and destructive force that helps preserve inadequate plans. Just as companies regularly revise their sales and marketing strategies to address changes in the marketplace, so, too, should they review the appropriateness of their compensation plans.

Nevertheless, senior sales management must take care not to appear too impulsive in changing compensation plans or salespeople may lose confidence in their judgment. A company that has uncovered problems must sense when to overhaul a compensation plan and when to administer minor repairs.

Turnover and recruiting problems represent the two most readily quantifiable indicators that a sales compensation plan is in trouble. These issues are covered in Sections 3.5 and 3.6. There are, however, several other signs that relate to the entire sales management structure.

Perhaps the most important analysis that a sales manager can perform is also one of the simplest, and often the most overlooked. A central underlying objective of any sales compensation plan is to direct and reinforce the sales force to accomplish those sales-related activities that are called for in the company's strategic sales and marketing plan. By comparing this strategic plan to the sales incentive plan, significant inconsistencies should become apparent. For those companies without a strategic plan, the task is barely any more difficult. The sales managers as a group should chart the sales and marketing objectives that need to be realized, as shown in Figure 3-2.

In this case, the sales incentive plan neglects to cover pricing decisions or new product introductions, except as they might be reflected in higher sales revenue. Such a sales incentive plan, interestingly enough, might be screaming to the sales rep to do the following:

- Accept lower prices, which, if combined with higher unit sales, would increase total revenue—irrespective of whether this revenue results in lower total profit margins.

Figure 3-2. Sales and marketing objectives.

Sales and Marketing Strategy Priorities	*Sales Compensation Priorities*
Sales volume	Sales volume
Profitability of sales (pricing maximization)	———— (Only covered to the degree that higher price of selling will cause higher sales revenue.)
Product mix	Product mix
New product introduction	———— (Only covered to the degree that new product selling will result in higher sales volume.)

- Let other reps introduce new products, while he spends his time selling the existing volume product line (which will maximize individual gain—compensation—today) and selling new products only when they have established market appeal. Unfortunately, if everyone followed this path, new product introductions might never be successful.

A second analysis that can be performed involves investigating territory assignment and associated compensation opportunity. If there is a mismatch between plan earnings and hours worked, a company is receiving a suboptimal return on its investment in its sales force. Whether a company is utilizing its sales reps' time effectively can be determined as shown in Figure 3-3.

This analysis alone may show that rep A is underworked (even though she controls some of the most important accounts) and that rep C is overworked (or at least can't possibly be calling effectively on all the accounts to which he is assigned). If the sales incentive plan compensated rep A well in excess of competitive levels and compensated rep C well below competitive levels, it would be clear that the company was incurring an opportunity cost. If some of rep C's accounts were transferred to rep A, wouldn't the company achieve better account penetration? Perhaps the sales compensation plan is getting in the way, linking account assignment with resulting pay opportunity. By more properly allocating resources, a manager might, in fact, be raising rep A's "overpaid" status and further deteriorating rep C's "underpaid" status. Such an analysis, therefore, may reveal a significant inconsistency between the incentive plan and the territory assignment process.

A third analysis revolves around the credibility of goal setting. A sales incentive plan, its earnings risk and potential, takes on meaning

Figure 3-3. Analysis of use of sales rep time.

Rep	Large Accounts[1]	Medium Accounts[1]	Small Accounts[1]	Travel Time	Total Calling Time
A	$10 \times 24 \times 3 = 720$;	$20 \times 12 \times 2 = 480$	$100 \times 4 \times 1 = 400$	300	1,500 hours
B	$2 \times 24 \times 3 = 144$;	$40 \times 12 \times 2 = 960$	$100 \times 4 \times 1 = 400$	500	2,004 hours
C	——	$80 \times 12 \times 2 = 1920$		500	2,820 hours

1. Number of accounts times the required number of calls per year times the number of hours per call.

only when reps know their territory and the goals (quotas) expected of them. Although reps will always complain about their goals, a historical analysis showing what percentage of reps achieved what percentage of goals provide a fair representation of the distribution of results to quotas. You would expect some sort of bell-shaped curve, with perhaps 80 percent of the sales force achieving between 80–85 percent and 115–120 percent of quota.

If the majority of sales reps substantially overshoots quota and the incentive plan is highly leveraged, the plan may be contributing to an overpay problem. If the majority are well under quota and the plan is highly leveraged, then the plan may be underpaying the sales reps. Or, in these same situations, if pay leverage is insufficient, the plan might in fact be acting less as a motivator than as a vehicle to correct (minimize) the ills of the goal-setting process. As far as goal setting is concerned, and however it is accomplished, one would hope that 80–85 percent of sales reps would qualify for some amount of sales incentive payout. If fewer are qualifying (if the plan threshold is too high), much of the sales force won't be motivated to sell most effectively and intensely. If virtually all reps qualify, payouts may be too easy, with insufficient negative feedback given to the reps who are not really making the grade.

Sales strategy, account assignment, and goal setting all run deeper than sales incentive plan design and, as the primary controls of sales management, must be addressed first. Yet all are inextricably linked with sales incentive plan design. Analysis of these first three should identify significant cracks in the sales management architecture. If the edifice is basically sound, compensation plan design can act as supporting cement. If they are not found to be sound, you will have to reexamine the foundation itself.

3.5 Turnover as a Symptom

"Excessive" turnover frequently provides the first signal that something is wrong with a company's sales compensation plan. Although turnover is observable and would appear to present a clear message to management, it is not as obvious an indicator as you might think. In fact, sales managers who are experiencing serious defections need to examine the nature of the turnover closely. Specifically, they should determine:

- The level of turnover.
- The types of people leaving. Are they recruits or veterans? Are they sales leaders or poor performers, reps from all regions or from specific locales? And at what career stages are they leaving?
- The factor(s) causing the turnover. Are defections pay-related? If so, is the principal reason base salaries, incentive opportunities, or total cash compensation? Or is turnover due to sales organization and career path concerns; sales burnout, stress, or territory coverage; or inadequate sales management direction, concern, guidance, or communication?

If pay is responsible for the loss of sales reps, is it a problem or a blessing? Perhaps the compensation system is merely weeding out underachievers. The following exhibits illustrate a pattern of sales force turnover experienced by a typical high-tech company.

Figure 3-4 shows an analysis of turnover by service. Is the company losing "recruits or veterans"? Similar analysis might be done for other types of sales reps, e.g., direct versus distributor, and at different levels.

Each bar represents a group of equal service employees. The height

Figure 3-4. Sales turnover analysis (field sales positions).

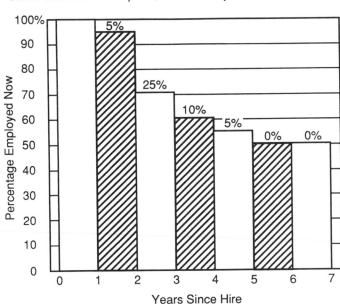

of the bar indicates the percentage of employees remaining for that group of the total hired. The number above the bar shows the turnover from one year to the next. For example, the third bar shows that of the employees with two to three years of service, 70 percent have remained with the company, a decrease of 25 percent from the prior year's retention. The exhibit fairly clearly points to years 2 through 4 as the danger zone: This company retains most of its veterans (turnover is only zero percent to 5 percent a year) and its recruits (turnover is also zero percent to 5 percent) but not those in between.

Unfortunately, in most sales organizations, it is the two-to-four-year group that is most productive (and most vulnerable to being raided). This analysis would suggest that management give additional attention to this group of sales reps. Although we now know more about where turnover is occurring, we don't yet know why.

Figures 3-5 and 3-6 analyze compensation trends over time to help answer the question of why turnover is concentrated in the second through fourth years.

Figure 3-5 shows compensation progression for salespeople with less than four years of service. By indexing pay (dividing actual pay by pay at hire) makes it apparent that pay increases decelerate around the second year, encouraging employees to consider opportunities outside the company. Why does pay progression slow down after two years? Many companies provide more frequent reviews during the first year or

Figure 3-5. Pay progression analysis (sales reps with less than four years of service).

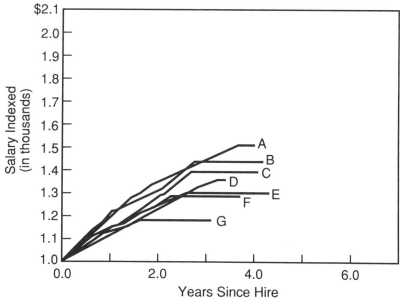

two of a rep's tenure, with the expectation that incentives will kick in after this point. Sometimes they don't.

The curve flattening in this particular company was caused by a salary increase moratorium. Figure 3-6 shows the same kind of analysis but for salespeople with five to seven years of service. Here, pay increases continue unabated through their fourth year but then flatten out. The reason why the curve flattens out in the last few years for both populations, of course, is the salary increase moratorium. Employees who have been with the organization for five years before the moratorium can view it with some perspective. Employees with shorter tenure, however, can't.

What does this analysis suggest for the compensation program? There isn't a "systemic" impediment to pay progress—the moratorium was a onetime event. But it might not hurt to consider some tenure-based focus in incentive design or other rewards. For example, the incentive might not be applied to employees with less than a year of service (a "compensation" solution). Alternatively, the company might spend extra effort to find career growth opportunities within *our* organization (a "career path" solution).

Which is the right answer? It still is not clear, because the qualitative turnover analysis should be supplemented by talks with sales reps and managers. But these charts do give a better idea about what questions to ask in those discussions.

To summarize, to understand turnover data:

Figure 3-6. Pay progression analysis (sales reps with five or more years of service).

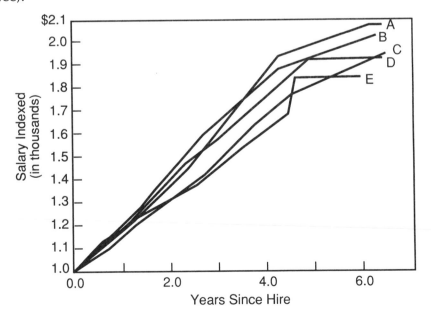

1. Break the figures down into their component parts, analyze them, and make them tell a logical, qualitative story.
2. Analyze where various groups of individuals have gone, to detect any patterns or reasons for leaving: to competitors or to different industries? to positions requiring similar selling skills or ones that represent a complete orientation?
3. Follow the money. If it is a sales compensation problem, then money should have something to do with it: in either the sales compensation program itself, the assignment of accounts/territory, or goal setting, all of which are inextricably linked to sales compensation opportunity.
4. Compare these levels of turnover to levels experienced in prior years for comparable positions and to what industry competition is facing. There are industry segments where 10 percent turnover is high and those where 25 percent is low, so understanding of the context is critical to assessing turnover data.

3.6 Recruiting

Turnover problems can cut across all levels of the sales staff or focus narrowly on new recruits. Sales managers must be prepared to analyze recruitment procedures as diligently as they explore general turnover issues. In particular, they should investigate:

- The frequency of recruiting failure.
- The positions that experience the most difficulties. Are they entry-level or midcareer? Are all geographic areas affected or only certain locations?
- The background of recruits. Is the company recruiting candidates with sufficient selling skills, experience, and background?
- The sources where recruits are obtained: competitors or unrelated industries.
- The reasons given by candidates who turn down offers of employment. Is it compensation or something else, e.g., training opportunities, career development, position characteristics, or "chemistry"? If compensation is the critical factor, is it a question of salary levels, incentive opportunity, or total cash compensation?

In studying these problems, the sales manager should do the following:

- Analyze the employment records of different types of recruits. The company may not be recruiting sales staff from the right sources or at the right levels.

- Compare current and past recruiting experience with that of your competition (by position level and geography), keeping in mind that pricing movements affect supply and demand everywhere, including the labor market.

3.7 Compensation as a "Cost of Sales"

When a company's cost-of-sales ratio appears excessive compared to industry norms, the sales compensation program almost always comes under review. Improving the return on investment can lower this important ratio, but it is important to remember that there are other causes of an excessively costly sales force.

In addition to being an ineffective expense control device, treating the sales force as a cost to be minimized implies that sales reps are a "necessary evil." Such an attitude will adversely affect the morale of a sales organization. In a financially driven corporate culture where management tends to focus too narrowly on ratios, the sales force can find itself constantly on the defensive, playing the part of the numerator in an ongoing quest for a lower ratio.

There is, in fact, only one sure way to reduce the cost-of-sales ratio: namely, to increase the denominator (sales). But the sales compensation program may already be doing as much as possible to motivate reps to achieve maximum sales. In fact, many sales compensation programs already rely too heavily on current volume measures and *ignore* other indicators of sales effectiveness that may provide a more complete and accurate measure of a sales rep's worth to the company and to himself.

Therefore, revising the compensation program by reducing sales reps' pay is not a constructive approach. Although paying sales reps less would reduce the numerator in the cost-of-sales ratio, it would also lower the quality of the sales force by rendering the company either less competitive or uncompetitive in the market for sales talent.

In an indirect way, however, changes in the compensation plan can affect the cost of sales, because the process by which a plan is developed will often highlight previously overlooked opportunities for more efficient deployment of sales resources. Consider the following example:

> A grocery products company was concerned about rising sales costs. An audit of the sales compensation system indicated that sales reps were often obliged to spend their time playing a number of different roles (national account manager, closer, maintainer, order clerk, facilitator, broker manager, and shelf stocker). Only a few of these roles required significant expertise. By redefining roles, the company was able to replace high-priced sales reps with lower-paid, in-store merchandisers. This increased enormously

the time key sales reps could spend on major accounts and enabled the company to reduce head count, boost pay for high-performing reps, and achieve an overall reduction in the sales-cost ratio.

In short, companies concerned about costs of sales should spend less time worrying about "controlling" what a sales rep spends in traveling from point A to point B and more time considering such important questions as the optimum numbers of calls on accounts in various categories and the credentials (which in turn have implications for competitive compensation levels) needed to fulfill the sales role. Altering the number of territories, or the organizational or staffing characteristics, can have a significant impact on the numerator of the ratio—and it is toward these opportunities that management's attention should turn. For the principal cost of sales is not the pay the reps earn, but the existence of a given sales territory.

3.8 Qualitative Diagnostics

Every sales manager involved in the sales incentive design process has an obligation to put himself in the shoes of the sales rep and to understand the environment in which the sales force operates. This is not as easy as it would appear, despite the fact that the sales manager was once a sales rep himself. There are five steps a sales compensation manager can take to help avoid incentive plan problems:

1. *Pay attention to feedback from sales reps.* Take seriously the views of the sales staff on pay levels, the incentive plan (and its relationship to other sales management tools), and the underlying sales culture. To maximize the effectiveness of its compensation strategies, a company should listen carefully to what its reps are saying. If their points are well taken and can be incorporated into the compensation plan, management should do so. If management has good reasons for not adopting a particular recommendation, it should provide the sales staff with an explanation.

2. *Read the incentive plan the way a sales rep would.* Remember the way it felt when you were in the field. The incentive plan is simply an economic game imposed by management on salespeople. Because of the spatial freedom of sales reps, the incentive plan, in effect, serves as an absentee manager. The game, as practiced by someone in the field, is remarkably simple: "Maximize your earnings, according to the following rules." Reps quickly learn how to post their best scores under a sales incentive plan. Remember the accounts you worked and the relation-

ships you established with them. How would you have maximized your earnings under the plan? Under this scenario, will the company also achieve a "win"? Goal congruence is essential to a win-win strategy.

3. *Create paths for career advancement.* Career "pathing" represents the determination and implementation of a logical series of job progressions taken by individuals who succeed in their responsibilities. With promotions should come greater income and, with each position, a logical progression in the use of incentives—the desired mix, associated risk/reward, and the elements (and the weighting of each) in the incentive plan. Does the plan give logical signals? Do the incumbents agree?

4. *Be attuned to the culture, understand it, and use it.* Link the various reward elements with the known value system, or work to change those values. Some companies have very powerful value systems. Although the incentive plan may send one signal, the underlying culture may be sending a stronger one. For example, does the culture, or the awards associated with it, trigger promotional decisions or qualify an individual for the President's Club? Steady sales may be the way to maximize earnings, but if the route to recognition is to "land the big one," then a certain portion of reps may attempt to win at that game, overriding the intent of the incentive plan.

5. *Evaluate how well the plan (and associated sales strategies and tasks) is conveyed to the field and how well administration of the plan is carried out.* Have you ever actually picked up a copy of the plan that the sales reps receive and read it cover to cover? Can you understand the plan?

As to plan administrative issues, do you know what printouts the rep receives and how easy or difficult it is to track performance with incentive calculations? How closely is the timing of performance tied to rewards? When there are calculation difficulties or plan interpretation problems, can the rep get a straightforward, reliable, and timely explanation? Is credibility lost at every turn in the road?

A sales force is an expensive human asset. Know your sales force as you would know your customers, and treat your salespeople with respect.

3.9 Correlation Analysis: Performance vs. Pay

One of the most interesting analyses that a sales manager can perform is to combine management's qualitative assessment of sales rep performance with the quantitative measure of performance delivered by the compensation plan, i.e., earnings. In fact, this analysis involves three studies: management's assessment versus salary, incentive, and total pay (base salary plus incentive).

The sales manager can conduct this analysis fairly easily. Pay histories are a matter of record. The manager gathers earnings data from the period selected for study (usually the most recently completed quarter or year; sometimes a number of periods are used).

In performing the analysis, the sales manager should look for two types of findings. First, are there any (or many) "out-liners"—individuals whose qualitative rankings far exceed or fall well short of their relative pay scale positioning? The situation of these individuals, who would be over- or underpaid, provides a starting point for hypothesizing as to why the plan is not working. What is it about the qualitative assessment that has been overlooked by the pay system, and what elements of the pay system have contributed to these aberrations? Do these problems represent individual situations that should be rectified (or justified), or are they signals that call for the restructuring of the pay system (primarily incentive plan)? Also, besides pay system blame, this investigation could well point to irregularities in goal setting, territory (account) assignment, and particular windfall/deadfall situations.

The second type of findings involves groups of individuals. For example, how does qualitative performance relate to pay for the top paid 10 percent or 20 percent of the sales force versus the middle 20 percent or 30 percent and the lowest 10 percent or 20 percent? You might *also* be advised to pull certain groups out of the sales force for additional separate analyses. Some of these might include national account reps, major account reps, sales/service personnel, first-level managers, newer versus more tenured reps, or reps for different locations. In each analysis (for each grouping, by salary, incentive, and total compensation), you should seek answers to the following questions:

- Is pay differentiation (upward or downward) sufficient to reflect the varying levels of contribution of high and low performers? If the plan acts to ignore performance variation ("low" performers earn as much as or more than "high" performers), a significant problem exists.
- Which, if any, pay elements are causing problems (i.e., need to be addressed)?

Whether this analysis is done formally or informally, the results can be enlightening and often surprising. Many organizations assume that because they have an incentive plan, the best performers will invariably get the best pay. But it isn't necessarily the case. For example, Figure 3-7 shows pay versus billings for a company with a largely salary-based compensation program that has a discretionary incentive plan. The company didn't use a commission program because it wasn't the best match to job characteristics, and rightly so. All agreed, however, that over the long term there ought to be a relationship between the larger

Figure 3-7. Sales compensation vs. billings.

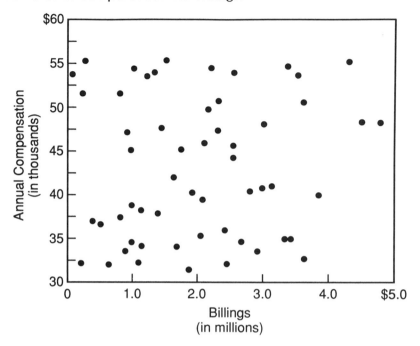

(more important and more difficult) territories and sales compensation. In fact, they *believed it already existed*. The facts show otherwise, however.

Figure 3-8 provides basically the same analysis for a different company, which used a volume-based bonus with some additional performance kickers. The analysis, however, indicates that profit contribution for each territory was the more important measure.

Although the results aren't as bad as in the prior exhibit, there are still a few disparities. More important, the quantitative analysis shows the cost of using incorrect performance measures, not just in inequitably allocated compensation dollars but in sales reps following the wrong signals.

Another clue is a simple qualitative ranking of salespeople (by whatever subjective measures managers decide to use) compared to compensation. Figure 3-9 illustrates this kind of chart in an organization with a reasonable but not perfect relationship of pay to performance (if perfect, all of the points would lie on the straight line).

In all of these analyses, it's probably most important to see that the top-ranked people are the top paid. If so, and there aren't any nonpay problems, that's cause for relief. If there are problems (e.g., in sales force turnover, accomplishing marketing objectives, and so on), the difficulties might lie more in management's direction than in sales execution or compensation. Regardless, the development of a forced ranking of pay and performance almost always generates a constructive dialogue, with

Figure 3-8. Last year's pay vs. profit contribution (actual and "fitted").

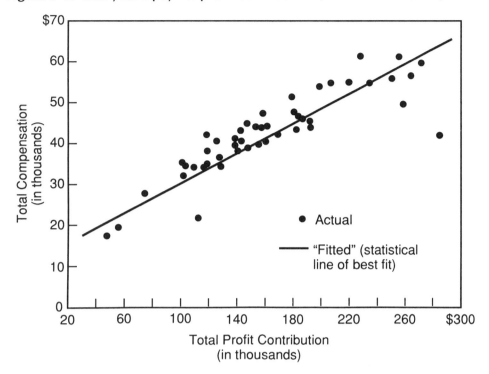

an increased understanding of what's important (and what hypotheses need to be further tested).

3.10 Should You Have One Plan or Many?

Compensation planners love the concept of equity. Unfortunately, many companies confuse equity with uniformity, creating sales compensation plan problems for themselves. For example, if the nature of the sales rep-customer relationship differs among the company's divisions (or among sales roles within a given division), it follows that the indicators of sales success will also differ.

When properly designed, a sales compensation plan reinforces the accomplishment of specific, sales-controllable, observable results. If those results vary from unit to unit, then the compensation plan, to be "equitable" to both the company and the sales staff, must reflect the particular results relevant to each sales force. Thus, if diverse roles exist throughout sales forces, equity and uniformity are mutually exclusive goals and the company must have multiple compensation approaches to match its multiple sales roles.

Those involved in plan administration generally do not like multiple

Figure 3-9. Subjective correlation analysis.

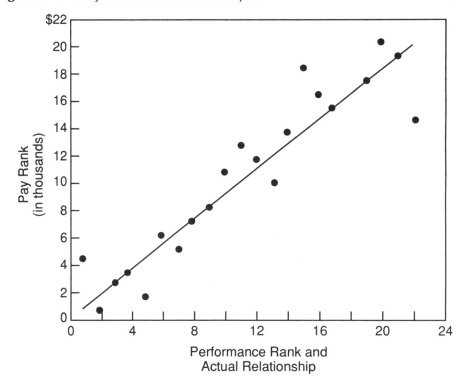

compensation approaches. Although a desire to reduce administrative workloads is understandable, a bias toward fewer (or even no) sales compensation plans is often directly at odds with the diverse market presences that determine the company's present and future success. Sales compensation plans should reinforce the management process, not restrain it.

To be successful, a company must know its marketplace and organize its resources around how customers actually think. Yielding to administrative convenience ignores the world as it is. And in many cases, those encouraging the use of a single plan have no familiarity with or responsibility for marketing. A sales compensation plan is a well-recognized sales management technique; line managers need the authority to manage as befits the needs of their particular business. Requiring diverse businesses to conform to a single pay model is shortsighted and contrary to the best interests of the organization.

Figure 3-10 illustrates situations where a multidivisional company might employ a single sales compensation approach without jeopardizing its ability to manage and direct its sales force. Figure 3-11 describes situations where a multidivisional company should employ different sales compensation plans.

Far more common, however, are business situations in which each

Figure 3-10. Situations permitting a single, uniform, multidivisional sales compensation plan.

- Sales reps tend to move on to other functions as their careers progress.
- A great deal of mobility exists between divisions within the sales function.
- Sales reps do not have a strong and direct impact on short-term volume in any division.

Figure 3-11. Situations requiring different plans for different businesses.

- A skilled sales rep is mot valuable in a field position, and, if successful, is likely to have account responsibility indefinitely.
- The selling skills sought by the various divisions are sufficiently different that it would be unusual for a rep to transfer across divisions.
- The nature and extent of sales rep influence differs from division to division. Some reps have a greater impact on short-term volume than their colleagues do; others may exert a longer-term, more indirect influence on both volume and nonvolume-related results.

---

sales force's role should be examined separately, with pay reinforcing influence points specific to the particular business. Some plans may resemble others (and indeed some divisions might have identical plans), but equity would be achieved by giving each participant the opportunity to be well paid for his or her skills, as applied in a particular context.

3.11 Other Influences on Plan Design

Most of all, a sales compensation plan must "fit" comfortably into a company's business situation. There is no single "right" answer to the design issues, but an understanding of the impact of such factors as sales role definition, company values, and marketing strategy will facilitate management's selection of the optimum pay approach: the one that "fits" the best.

Sales Role Definition

After examining the various roles that a sales rep plays, the sales manager can define specific approaches to compensation to match the success factors accompanying each major sales role. A compensation plan must calibrate sales value in terms of success factors applicable to the particular sales role. Figure 3-12 gives examples of the variety of roles

Figure 3-12. Sales rep roles and "success factors."

Sales Role	Representative Title	Success Factors
Prospector/closer: Identifies and closes sales within a territory.	• Sales representatives • Account executive • Sales executive • Marketing representative	• Current revenue • Current gross margin • Number of new accounts • Territory profit
Account manager: Develops and maintains relationships.	• National account manager • Industry account manager • Senior account manager	• Volume increase • Increased market share • Account profitability • Execution of account plan
Technical sales: Provides continuing technical support.	• Sales engineer • Field engineer • Technical sales representatives	• Retention and growth of business in assigned accounts
Facilitator: Coordinates product delivery and availability.	• Sales representatives • Account manager	• "Distribution fill" • Market share • Special products sales volume • Implementation of promotions

a sales rep can play and "success factors" that could form the basis for part or all of the rep's incentive opportunity.

Company Values

A company's history determines its particular set of values, which in turn shape its management systems. Companies, like individuals, have distinctive personalities, and these personalities are reflected in the unspoken, but powerful, norms of behavior that are acceptable in a particular corporate environment. There are three principal types of corporate societies:

1. The manufacturing-oriented society
2. The financially driven society
3. The market-based society

Each of these societies can function effectively in any kind of business, provided that the systems that emerge from them do not create sales behavior at odds with customer expectations. Customers are partners in a mutually beneficial business process and, most often, have the option of taking their business elsewhere. Therefore, it behooves top executives to structure management systems (including sales compensation systems) that encourage and reward behavior customers recognize as not only in the company's interest, but in their own as well.

Change can create a need to revise a company's management systems to remain compatible with an evolving business environment. Such outside forces as regulatory bodies can impose change on an organization as in the deregulation of the financial services and telecommunications industries. Change can also occur as an industry matures. For example, in the infancy of the computer business, many companies sold packaged software that was purchased as commodities; today, customers creatively combine hardware and software to solve their unique business requirements. Finally, acquisitions can result in new environments that mandate a change in a company's culture. Thus, a value system that was appropriate for a bulk chemical company might not serve the interests of the customers of that parent company's newly acquired electronics division. Figure 3-13 illustrates the manner in which the orientation of company values will influence the design of its sales management systems.

There is no one preferred approach to corporate personality. The approach that is right is the one that aligns the interests of the company and its customers in the most harmonious fashion. If, for example, continuity of presence with a customer is likely to produce greater confidence and a more solid, long-term business relationship, it would not be appropriate to use the typical career management approach of a manufacturing-oriented society, which "rotates" an individual through the sales function as part of overall career development. The market-based position, namely, that sales is an integral part of the management process and that the sales career track can lead to high-level positions in the company, is one that is better suited to the needs of the marketplace. A company that overrides its own historical preferences to reshape its systems in response to customer needs will greatly improve its chances of success.

Marketing Strategy

The compensation plan must also support the marketing strategy; ideally, it should serve as a tool for implementing that strategy. Too often, the sales compensation plan designer becomes caught up in the detailed workings of the plan and loses sight of the need for the plan to serve the strategy. One of the most frequently encountered problems in sales compensation is a plan that promotes sales force behavior counter to the strategic marketing direction. For example, a plan may encourage the

Figure 3-13. Orientation of "company values."

	Manufacturing	Finance	Market
Selection	• College graduates, technical degree	• MBAs, quantitative background	• Sales aptitude
Training	• Product knowledge	• Company procedures, internal demands	• Pure selling skills, customer characteristics
Career management	• "Rotation" through sales; sales reps are substitutable one for the other	• Heavy turnover tolerated; growth in account volume required	• Sales can be a career; hierarchy based on increasing importance of account management
Compensation plans	• Low risk • Perhaps salary only	• Heavy risk • Top-down goals • Low salary • Short-term volume oriented	• Risk reflects prominence of sales in market • Flexible, adaptable • Linked to relevant, account-specific goals

sales rep to emphasize markets or products that are not strategic priorities or to work toward goals that are not consistent with competitive positioning. Furthermore, the compensation plan is the principal medium of communication with the sales force. Sales reps scrutinize the plan description more closely than they do any other message from management. Accordingly, the priorities communicated by the plan must conform to the strategy. In short, marketing strategy should drive compensation plan design.

To integrate strategy in sales compensation plan design, the sales manager must first understand the concept of marketing strategy. This can present a problem, because the word *strategy* is probably one of the most misused words in business communications. And although all companies have a strategy, many are unable to articulate that strategy in a way that is useful to the compensation plan designer.

Essentially, a marketing strategy should represent a statement of the focus of a company's business. Every enterprise must set priorities

Figure 3-14. Marketing strategy and compensation plan design.

Marketing Strategy Emphasis	Compensation Emphasis	Illustrative Measures
• Survival • Revenue • New accounts	• High-risk • Straight commission • Frequent payouts	• Percentage of revenue • Percentage of gross margin • New account bonus
• Protect base • Growth revenue	• Salary/commission • High-risk • Frequent payouts	• Percentage of revenue • Percentage of revenue in relation to quota
• Manage accounts • Secure new accounts • Broaden penetration	• Salary/bonus • Moderate risk • Commissions on selected products/ markets	• New account bonus • Bonus on revenue as percentage of goal • Percentage new-product revenue
• Sustain and solidify existing relationships	• Salary/bonus • Low-to-moderate risk • Account management	• Account-specific longer-term goals as well as current revenue goals
• Develop customized "solutions" for customer needs	• Salary/bonus • Infrequent (annual) payout • Project focused	• Percentage of expected project profit • Account-specific goals • "Milestone" goals

stating how resources will be allocated and directed, and the marketing strategy provides that direction. The marketing strategy must always define three areas:

1. *The market segments on which the company will focus its efforts.* Market segment focus specifies those customer groups that the company expects will generate most of its sales and on which it will concentrate most of its marketing resources. The compensation plan should reward the sales rep for developing and maintaining sales to those priority customer groups.

2. *The principal products the company will sell to those segments.* Product focus considers those products that, because of profitability, growth expectations, or other reasons, have been selected for concentrated sales effort. The compensation plan must be designed to reward the rep for selling those products.

3. *The way the company will position itself against the competition.* Positioning against the competition covers a number of areas:

Figure 3-15. Criteria for determining the best approach.

	A Single Plan	Several Plans	Complete Autonomy
Number of sales forces	• One or few.	• More than one.	• Many.
Management style	• Autocratic, centralized, highly controlled.	• Groups of businesses operate with autonomy.	• Highly decentralized, participation.
Nature of business	• All businesses have same general industry characteristics.	• Customer characteristics vary among groups of sales forces, e.g., industrial group, consumer group.	• Significant differences in customer characteristics from business to business.
Mobility of sales force among divisions	• High mobility; skills transferable from one sales force to another.	• Limited mobility; transfers may occur within groups of sales forces, but not across groups.	• Virtually none; sales skills generally not transferable among divisions.

level of service the company intends to provide its customers; quality/price relationships versus the competition; product innovation versus a follower position; distribution channels; and other such elements. Again, the compensation plan must support this positioning. It must reward the sales rep for behavior needed to sustain the position, such as customer service levels, type of customer communication, and technical support provided.

The sales compensation plan can reinforce a good marketing strategy; however, it cannot transform a poor strategy into a good one. Often the market analysis used to develop a sales compensation plan will uncover a poor strategy; that is, in analyzing the situation the plan designer may identify flaws in the marketing strategy that make it unacceptable. For example, the strategy may:

▪ Not recognize the basic user requirements for the product and not provide for required technical and service support

- Fail to understand the buying process or how its differs among customer groups
- Mistake a mature market for a growing market and emphasize development of new accounts rather than greater penetration of existing accounts
- Overemphasize key high-profit products at the expense of other products when the customers require a broad-line supplier

The compensation plan designer can often identify these problems but should not attempt to correct them through compensation plan design. The sales compensation plan is only one of a number of programs implementing the marketing strategy, all of which must be coordinated to support that strategy. Figure 3-14 illustrates the linkage between marketing strategy and compensation plan design and identifies measures of sales success, which are linked to the marketing strategy.

Management can shape sales compensation plans, consistent with its culture, to fit the specific needs of its varying sales roles. An effective program will apply to many sales jobs, whether it is packaged as multiple plans or as a single plan with multiple varieties. The "best" approach depends upon a combination of business and market characteristics. Figure 3-15 lists criteria for determining the most appropriate compensation plan.

4

Guiding Principles/Objectives

4.1 Defining the Sales Task

A company's overall business strategy and its customers ultimately define the sales job. One without the other is insufficient to tell us what we need to know about a given job's key roles and tasks. Business strategy governs the products and services, technologies, market segments, distribution channels, and distinctive competencies that the company must develop or emphasize and the types of customers it must attract and keep. The customers themselves, each with specific vendor requirements and selection criteria, govern the attributes a sales force must exhibit to be successful. Some of these attributes can be inferred only from the customer's conduct, organizational structure, and purchasing practices, and no existing vendor sales force may meet certain criteria.

Where customers are stable and essentially committed to a vendor, because such factors as regulation and economics restrict competitive entry into the vendor's marketplace, there may be no need for a true sales function. Given demand and no alternative sources of supply, a business will have a relatively assured customer and revenue base and will tend to grow as that base grows. Organizations of this type need service personnel and perhaps a public relations function, but few of them need salespeople unless there is a need to focus on additional services or products for which there is no established demand.

In other words, there is no need for a sales function if there is no need for advocacy. The customer must have alternatives to consider, including the alternative of doing nothing, before a sales force is appropriate. In addition, the vendor organization must derive some practical value from using personal selling to deliver the sales message, as opposed to using media or direct mail advertising or automated telemarketing. Use of sales reps is usually necessary when the organization has few other ways to identify prospective buyers or when person-to-person advocacy plays a key (and cost-effective) role in getting or keeping business. If advocacy plays a key role but the cost of direct sales is prohibitive, organizations typically turn to alternatives such as advertising or telemarketing. If advocacy is not a strong factor in determining buyer choice but the organization still needs a sales representative "in the loop," use of a sales-service is often appropriate.

In organizations where there is a need for the sales function, the variety of actual sales tasks can be immense, even within a given industry. But most can be categorized as either customer identification or customer development. The table of traditional sales force activities in Figure 4-1 illustrates this basic point.

Even in organizations where significant market research, lead generation, and lead qualification precede the actual sales process, there is usually some customer identification work left to be done by the sales force itself. Thus, although a sales rep may not be required to conduct customer identification activity, he or she often has the opportunity to uncover additional decision makers or individuals who influence the sales process or to find new accounts that weren't targeted by prior research.

Although most sales tasks can be categorized as relevant either to customer identification or customer development, some sales positions have little responsibility or opportunity for one or the other of these general activities. A familiar example can be helpful in clarifying this key point. A merchandising sales rep for a consumer package goods manufacturer usually has little responsibility for prospecting, at least in more mature markets. Instead of finding new accounts or gaining a competitive share of an existing account's volume, the rep's developmental activities might include gaining temporary display space and acquiring incremental or better permanent shelf space to improve product performance. This sales rep provides a key interface between the customer and the vendor, delivering product management service rather than product information (i.e., product advocacy). This sales job also reflects the company's business strategy. Other ways of bringing products to market in the consumer package goods industry include the use of distributors, brokers, jobbers, and fully dedicated direct salespeople.

Although it is easy to say that the customer tells a sales organization what it needs to know about the tasks that should be performed, it is

Figure 4-1. Traditional sales force activities.

Customer Identification	*Customer Development*
• Joining local networks	• Presentations/proposals
• Cold calling	• Demonstrations/tests
• "Cross-referencing" to find the "real" buyer	• Order/delivery oversight
• Lead follow-up	• Follow-up and line growth
• Trade show participation	• Training and consulting
• Local market analysis	• Service/relationship management
	• New accounts and products

not easy to read the "script" that a customer provides the sales representative. Consider a sales organization that calls on dealers only. The organization makes no direct sales and does not use distributors; the dealers take inventory directly from the manufacturer and sell directly to the consumer or end user.

In this situation, what can we expect that the dealer will want from the manufacturer? In general, dealers need to turn inventory at adequate margins and with few such problems as product failures under warranty and inventory stockouts. Dealers also want as much support as they can get from the manufacturer, including discounts, floor planning, advertising, product enhancements, and dealer training.

Given these concerns, we can expect a dealer to want a manufacturer's representative to represent his or her products well and to represent the dealer's needs and terms to the manufacturer. The communication runs in both directions because the dealer must work with the producer to sell the producer's product. But the dealer is a customer as well as an intermediary. As a customer, the dealer will expect all the service and consideration that any customer will expect. The salesperson must therefore perform the following tasks:

- Ensure that inventory commitments are met
- Negotiate special pricing arrangements and discounts
- Support and execute any cooperative advertising programs
- Train dealer salespeople and participate in trade shows with the dealers
- Ensure that all product/service support requirements are fulfilled
- Assist the dealer sales force with lead development and collaborative selling directly to the end user or consumer
- Achieve minimum acceptable volume and margin levels from each dealer
- Maintain high levels of dealer satisfaction with the producer
- Obtain dealer sales across the entire product line
- Ensure accurate and thorough product representation by the dealer sales organization

Although most of these tasks are compatible, some are inherently adversarial and must be reconciled skillfully and carefully by the producer sales force. For example, the producer may be reluctant to negotiate special pricing or even to invest further in dealer training if the dealer sales organization tends to misrepresent the product to the final buyer, or if the dealer isn't providing balanced support for the entire line of products.

The definition of the sales task is therefore the result of an array of practices (i.e., commitments) and objectives (i.e., expectations). Both the buyer and the seller have commitments and expectations. To forget that the buyer shapes the sales agenda is to forget that the buyer is a customer, with the privilege of voting in favor of another supplier. To forget that the strategy—however implicit or informal it may be—defines the customer is to relinquish active management of the business to contingent influences.

4.2 The Influence of the Buying Situation

As just indicated, the degree to which personal persuasiveness or advocacy is critical to achieving business success defines the sales job for each product/market segment. In some situations, the conduct or values of the buyer render it virtually impossible to conclude a sale without substantial person-to-person advocacy.

In true competitive bidding situations, for example, the involvement of field salespeople is often indispensable in setting the bid specifications before the release of requests for proposals (RFP). This preselling process obviously increases the number of RFPs received and the probability of getting the business. In addition, the proposal process itself frequently requires that the principals meet to review and revise the details of the proposal. This is a highly interactive process, where the customer's needs and wants and the seller's capabilities and approach emerge gradually.

In general, the more creative, entrepreneurial, and unsupported the sales process, and the more improbable, untested, and unknown the product or service being offered, the more persuasiveness or advocacy is critical. Conversely, the more routine, established, and supported the sales process and the more straightforward, proved and visible the product or service, the more the sales process consists of managing a customer relationship. This often involves heavy sales force emphasis on performance assurance, i.e., on assuring that the seller is performing as required by the customer. Why? Usually because the customer is a preferred buyer and has become a "major" or "national" account, or because the industry has matured and suppliers must seek competitive advantage by providing quality service.

In addition to considering the relative independence of the supplier sales force and product/market maturity, we must also examine the buyer's setting. Three factors provide a fairly comprehensive portrait of buying situation influences on the sale job:

1. *Buyer stratification*—the steps and layers in the buying process
2. *Buyer sophistication*—the buyer's experience and the criteria it uses
3. *Buyer concentration*—the number and density of buyers

An increase in unintentional buyer concentration, due to such factors as urbanization, will alter the travel patterns of the sales force.

Frequently, sales force productivity rises as a result, or at least as less cream is "skimmed." As intentional buyer concentration increases, each buyer's leverage in the transaction tends to increase, and the supplier must deploy skilled, focused, and motivated sales reps to meet this challenge. Further, the activities of these sales reps must be highly customer-oriented and supported by the entire supplier organization.

Increased buyer stratification makes the selling message more involved and usually extends the length of the sales cycle. If buyers are especially risk averse or are very consensus oriented in decision making, the salesperson will have to touch many bases in the right sequence and at the right level of teamwork with the customer. Increased stratification tends to result in sales force job design and organizational structure similar to that found in situations where there is intentional buyer concentration and dissimilar to situations where there is unintentional concentration.

Increased buyer sophistication naturally requires a parallel increase in selling sophistication if the supplier is to remain competitive. Any mismatch between the resources of the buyer and those of the seller can quickly result in lost business. Buyer sophistication does not, in itself, demand increased sales time, but it may require a formal segregation of some sales tasks, with senior sales reps or account managers assigned to more challenging and usually large customers.

The matrix in Figure 4-2 illustrates how the interplay of the three buying influences with the two key selling influences, i.e., product/market maturity and sales force independence, shapes sales tasks. As each of the factors on the left increases, the sales tasks listed in the column headings are commonly affected as shown.

Figure 4-2. Interplay of buying and selling influences.

Influencing Factors	Advocacy	Relationship Management	Sales Cycle	Team Selling	Call Frequency
Maturity/uniqueness of products offered	M	M	M/H	M/H	M/H
Maturity/similarity of products offered	L/M	H	M	L/M	M/H
Selling independence	H/M	H	L	L	M
Intentional buyer concentration	H	M	M/H	H	M
Buyer stratification	H/M	H	H	M/L	M
Buyer sophistication	H	M/H	L/H	L/H	L/H

H = High   M = Moderate   L = Low

The matrix is only a general guide to assist in the detailed analysis of an actual selling situation. Overall, however, it suggests the following rules of thumb:

- The length of the sales cycle, the degree of relationship management, and call frequency tend to be positively related to, and to increase with, the size and complexity of the sale.
- Active advocacy (i.e., "pure selling") tends to increase with product differences and to decrease with higher product/market maturity.
- Increases in intentional concentration, stratification, or sophistication all make greater demands on the attention, skills, and commitment of the sales force.
- Increases in sales force independence are often characterized by more opportunistic and shorter-cycle selling.

The matrix also suggests that the interplay of internal and external factors is complex, and that "reading the script" to determine the right tasks in their optimal sequence for each sales situation is as difficult as it is critical.

4.3 Factors Affecting the "Value" of the Sales Representative

Education and experience obviously affect the value the sales rep brings to the sales process. But a sales rep also has the opportunity to create value based on the characteristics of the product/market he or she serves.

A buyer's perception that a sales rep provides little value may jeopardize product acceptance. If the product is clearly superior and acceptably priced, and the buyer has an immediate or substantial need for the product, the purchase may occur anyway. But the narrower the gap among competing products, the greater the need for excellence in customer service and product advocacy.

Consider the computer paper industry. Without embossing, logo printing, or special enhancements, computer paper would seem to be a true commodity. Although there are different varieties of computer paper in a range of grades, sizes, and performance characteristics, most suppliers offer their customers a complete line of choices. Customers thus find it difficult to prefer one supplier over another on the basis of traditional criteria, i.e., product characteristics and product line breadth.

Manufacturers of these products obviously want to avoid a strictly brokered buyer-supplier relationship that might reduce their margins or seriously weaken their control over the revenue/demand side of the business. How do these manufacturers avoid such consequences and remain successful? They sell. The salesperson becomes part of the product, and the value he or she adds is the reason the buyer selects this supplier over another. When this happens, the supplier becomes a vendor and the buyer becomes a customer.

The salesperson who becomes part of the product or service is usually well positioned to gain or at least maintain ground. The salesperson must establish the relationship, be responsive to the customer's needs—while guiding how the customer determines those needs—and be effective in ensuring that the customer acts in the desired ways. In practical terms, this usually involves providing the customer with information; helping the customer identify real needs and alternatives; and overseeing delivery, installation, and invoicing.

As the skills necessary for a given sales position increase, the tasks performed by the salesperson tend to become an important part of what the customer is purchasing: The sales role itself brings a required value to the process (see Figure 4-3). This role might be consultative, with the salesperson acting as an advisor, or responsive, with the salesperson demonstrating skill in understanding what the customer is demanding.

4.4   Behavior Modification

Human beings faced with a finite amount of time and an apparently infinite number of tasks will allocate time according to certain priorities

Figure 4-3. Salesperson as source of value to vendor and customer: a guide.

		Product Differentiation		
		High	*Moderate*	*Low*
Vendor Differentiation	*High*	Clarify, stress, and redefine the differences	Stress vendor differences and/or product strength	Stress vendor and rep experiences, methods, and depth
	Moderate	Stress product and highlight vendor strength	Active advocacy and competitive service response	Highlight vendor strength, excel with rep service
	Low	Stress product strengths and uniqueness	Stress product strength, excel with rep service	On-call service and alertness to every need

that may not match the strategic needs of the business. When this happens, managers usually search for some way to redirect sales force behavior.

Conventional approaches to modifying sales force behavior include:

- Redesigning jobs
- Restructuring the organization
- Realigning territories
- Reassigning accounts/prospects
- Modifying performance rules/scorekeeping
- Reassigning or terminating employees
- Redesigning or strengthening performance appraisal
- Reassessing recruiting profiles/methods
- Redesigning compensation

Redesigning and restructuring the organization is usually difficult and disruptive for both the company and its customers. Performance appraisal changes are often dismissed because they are seen as "soft" and too remote in their impact vis-à-vis the immediate business need. Alterations in the recruiting profile sometimes receive the same treatment, although they should not.

Changing the compensation plan is, by far, the most common approach to changing behavior. The compensation plan is usually seen as the covenant of the sales organization. It is thought to embody the rules by which the sales force plays a unique and critical "game" for high personal and corporate stakes. To the extent that the pay plan does perform this function, it is certainly one place to look for the solution to behavioral problems. If a review of the rules suggests that the answer lies elsewhere, and it frequently does, the next logical step is to look at the actual players.

Perhaps the most common misalignment between sales force behavior and the strategic agenda of the company involves product mix: The sales force isn't selling the preferred amount of a given product relative to other products. Figure 4-4 reveals how significant and complex this issue can become.

Although the actual and preferred mix of product revenues in Figure 4-4 is different for each product sold, as it often is in multiproduct businesses, the differences are most serious for products A and B.

What principles should you consider in redirecting sales behavior to reduce sales force (or customer) emphasis on products A and B and increase emphasis on products C and D? First, you must remember that customers are currently purchasing products and services in the existing mix and at existing levels. If you do not want revenue levels for A and B to decline, then total revenue must increase, almost exclusively for products C and D. But if you want actual revenues for products A and B

Figure 4-4. Percentage of total product revenue.

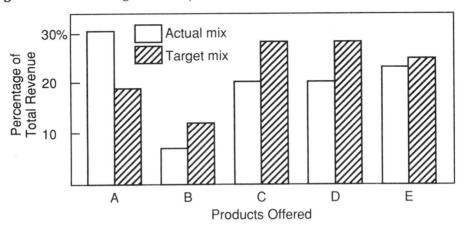

to decrease while revenues for products C and D increase, you must make more fundamental changes in customer and sales force behaviors.

Suppose that products A, B, C, and D "interact"; that is, one can serve as a substitute for the other. In this situation, the job of changing product mix is particularly challenging and usually requires changes in pricing, promotional/advertising support, and manufacturer support, as well as changes in sales incentive compensation, before real changes in purchase/selling patterns will result. When products do not interact, it is easier to rely on changes in the incentive plan (and other economic arrangements with the sales force) to modify the product mix.

Although a wide range of incentive design architectures is available to encourage salespeople to sell in the preferred mix, every successful technique reflects awareness of the interplay among the following factors:

- *Relative difficulty of the sale*—the number of times more difficult (ten times, for example) it is to sell product A than product B.
- *Relative return on the sale*—the number of times more rewarding it is to sell product A than product B.
- *Minimum return on any sale*—the minimum incremental return necessary for a salesperson to sell one more unit/dollar of the least saleable product.
- *Principle of sufficient difference*—the difference in the economic return sufficient to make the salesperson actively prefer/pursue A over B. Increasing the economic return on the sale of product A to the point of parity with product B, allowing for the relative difficulty of each sale, only makes the salesperson *indifferent* to whether he or she sells A or B.

Empirical studies conducted by social scientists, economists, and decision theorists tend to support these rules of thumb, but there is as yet no comprehensive theoretical or empirical model of sales force choice behavior. Nonetheless, experience suggests that rules or models of this type are often helpful in extracting information about the factors that underlie sales force behavior and how those factors interact.

Sales force conduct obviously includes far more than product mix management. To provide a short list, it also includes behavior that can influence profit margins, total gross profit, market share, market share by product (i.e., the number of times larger the share of one competitor is than that of another), account penetration, number of new accounts, types of accounts, length of customer commitment, selection of a purchase versus lease or rent option, customer willingness to assume special charges such as one-time production costs and freight expenses, and so on.

The critical point at this juncture is that sales behavior is at least as multidimensional as the tools available to manage it. Sales behavior is not a tool, objective, or variable. It is the net consequence, in the field, of all the tools, objectives, and variables in play. Figure 4-5, a short list of key sales behaviors and the tools most commonly used to shape them, helps demonstrate this key point.

4.5 Categories of Sales Tasks

Now that it's been established that most sales activities can be categorized as either customer identification or customer development, it's useful to break these categories down further, as follows: obtaining new accounts, keeping old accounts, selling special products, improving the penetration of existing accounts, and managing a profitable territory.

Obtaining new accounts can be thought of as increasing the *vertical penetration* of a business, while improving the share of an existing

Figure 4-5. Key sales behaviors and traditional tools.

Sales Behavior	*Traditional Tools*
• Basic selling competencies	• Formal training, mentoring, OJT
• Market and account focus	• Territory and account assignments
• Sales task/account focus	• Job design
• Level of sales independence	• Organizational structure
• Sales volume or profit	• Periodic performance objectives
• Product mix of sales	• Weighted/differential incentives
• Profit orientation	• Incentives linked to margins/profits
• Account development	• Incentives linked to new accounts and account growth

account's volume can be thought of as increasing *horizontal penetration*. The importance of each of these strategic thrusts varies according to the type of business involved, the maturity and diversity of the marketplace, and the level of competitive activity.

Businesses that must acquire accounts to grow, because the purchasing power of a single account may be close to the size of a single purchase, will clearly emphasize vertical penetration (see Figure 4-6). In general, the more mature, less diverse, and less openly competitive the marketplace, the more a business is likely to focus on gradual or incremental horizontal penetration. Such a business pays only moderate attention to vertical penetration because great investments of time, energy, and money are necessary to win accounts away from current suppliers. Businesses in industries with few potential customers emphasize horizontal penetration.

Keeping old accounts is closely related to expanding the level and type of business with an existing account, but it is sufficiently different to constitute a separate sales task. Keeping old accounts requires doing what accounts expect as a condition for *continuing their purchases* of a given vendor's products or services. These activities usually include (1) providing on-site problem-solving assistance, (2) tracking down misplaced orders or incorrectly specified orders, (3) conducting on-site training sessions for new employees who may be unfamiliar with the vendor's products, (4) overseeing the delivery or installation of a product or system, (5) simply being available and responsive, and (6) representing enough of the customer's special needs and interests to the vendor's senior management to convince the customer that the relationship is reasonable.

Figure 4-6. Sales strategy and the account structure of the marketplace.

| Share of Total Accounts in the Market | High Percentage | Strategic Focus of Businesses With Few Prospective Large Customers | Ideal Market Position |
| | Low Percentage | Weakest Market Position | Strategic Focus of Businesses With Limited Prospects for Increased/Large Number of Customers |

| | Low Percentage | High Percentage |

Share of Each Existing Account's Business

Selling special products is a common and frequently challenging aspect of sales force accountability. A sales force will usually be enthusiastic about new products that enhance existing products, and for which there is pent-up demand. But a sales force may be indifferent to or even resist new products that are unrelated to existing products, if salespeople doubt that the market is ready to accept the product and/or believe the economic return for the selling effort is inadequate. New products that compete with older, established products will be welcomed if the older products are losing market position and if the newer products are truly superior. But these products may prove difficult to introduce if the sales force sees little gain and considerable aggravation associated with the effort.

The key to the successful introduction or expansion of special products is to position them with the sales force as either a winning or an indispensable initiative for the company and the sales force.

Managing a profitable territory can mean many things and may or may not be important to the employer. Salespeople who either are or act as independent contractors are basically in business for themselves. The employer typically compensates such reps with a commission earnings schedule that is tied to either volume (i.e., units), revenue (i.e., net sales), or profit (i.e., gross or contribution margin). In such arrangements, the employer is only incidentally concerned with the salesperson's profitability as a separate "business" and relies on that salesperson to manage his or her own expenses.

To the extent that the sales force is directly reimbursed for its out-of-pocket selling expenses, management will often be interested in the control of those expenses. And to the extent that the sales force can influence the profit margin generated by a specific sale, management may be interested in linking sales compensation to that margin.

4.6 "Typical" Time Allocation

A typical sales rep will allocate time according to familiarity, convenience, personal acceptance, and ease. This does not mean that salespeople invariably take the path of least resistance or invariably optimize the expected value of their undertakings by applying prior probability estimates to possible outcomes. It does mean that the salespeople are usually alert to efficient behaviors within the context of the "game" they are playing. Because this is exactly what most managers want their salespeople to do, the key is to channel this instinct in directions that work for the company and for each sales rep.

One way to look at the allocation of a salesperson's time is to segregate it into generic categories applicable to virtually every sales organization. Figure 4-7 depicts the average "scores" (survey responses) provided by sales representatives in a large-print advertising sales force.

This sales organization spent considerable time detailing and revising advertising layouts to meet customer expectations. The sales force was also heavily dependent on incentive compensation and especially dependent on getting new accounts. The survey shows that, on average, sales reps devoted only 41 percent of total time to selling and another 25 percent to such activities as travel and customer service, for total customer time of 66 percent. The sales force spent an estimated 34 percent of total time, or all of the time of every fourth salesperson, on "other" activities.

Sales force frustration with this arrangement becomes very clear in the results displayed in the second column of the exhibit. Rank-and-file salespersons expressed a strong preference for spending less time on administrative duties and internal coordination/customer service and far more time on selling to prospective customers. Their proposed restructuring of sales tasks increased customer time to 82 percent, with only 10 percent spent on customer service/internal coordination.

This profile of actual versus ideal time allocations is not uncommon. Most salespeople prefer to spend less time than they currently spend, no matter how much time they currently spend, on administrative matters. And new business-oriented salespeople generally resist some of the "duties" associated with maintaining existing business. To give salespeople increased leverage in their workday, it may be necessary to improve sales methods and practices (to get greater efficiencies from the sales force) and to redesign some of the jobs in the organization so that some sales support roles can be defined and staffed.

Figure 4-7 Allocation of actual and preferred time.

Sales Activity	Percentage Time Currently Spent	Percentage Time Should Be Spent
Selling to existing customers	31%	39%
Selling to prospective customers	10	23
Customer service and internal coordination	16	10
Administration, staff meetings	21	7
Travel	9	10
Receiving and providing training	9	7
Providing supervision	4	4
	100%	100%

In addition to these generic and rather static characterizations of sales force time allocations, we also need to briefly describe a frequently effective "model" for understanding time allocations *at the margin, i.e., at the point where salespeople are making very active trade-offs between alternative sales behaviors and business results.*

The algebraic description of how time tends to get allocated at the margin, when allocation decisions are consciously made by a salesperson, can be developed as illustrated in Figure 4-8.

Although it is extremely rare for a sales organization to calibrate the values of these variables, a process that requires professional resources and the use of expertly structured questionnaires and focus groups, it can be done. The framework outlined in Figure 4-8 is a variation on the classic utility model. It uses prior probabilities, or Bayesian statistics, to weight the returns and costs that a salesperson believes are associated with each possible activity. It is valuable to the sales manager because it provides a way of looking at the attitudes and behaviors of the sales force that can produce extremely robust results. It is another rule of thumb for

Figure 4-8. Modeling the choice of activity 1 over activity 2.

Stipulations

C	Each activity can be assigned a *cost*.
R	Each activity can be assigned a *return*.
P	Each *return* has a *probability of occurrence*.
T	Each cost has a *probability of occurrence*.
M	Any activity must provide a *minimum expected return,* net of costs, for that activity to be undertaken.
NER	For one activity to be preferred over another, a minimum positive difference of 15% in *net expected return* (NER) is required.

Model Names

- Return and probability [cost and probability] for activity 1 are, respectively, $R1, P1, C1,$ and $T1$.
- Return and probability for activity 2 are, respectively, $R2, P2, C2,$ and $T2$.

Equation for Net Expected Return (NER)

$$NER = (P)(R) - (T)(C): \text{ i.e., expected return net of expected costs}$$

Condition for a Net Expected Return That Will Lead to Action

If $NER > M$, then $NER - M$ is positive. If $NER - M$ is positive, there is sufficient return to the salesperson for the action to occur.

Test for Activity Preference

Does either NER1 or NER2 exceed the other by 15 percent or more? If so, a "preference vector" for the action with the larger NER can be expected.

predicting and managing the sales force. Future studies will certainly strengthen and modify such frameworks.

A concrete example of the application of this framework will be helpful. Suppose that a sales force is thought to have the following beliefs: (1) the minimum net expected return (NER) required for any additional sales effort is $100, (2) the return on selling to a new account is $500 and the probability of getting a new account is 25 percent, (3) the expected return from getting one more order from an existing customer is $200 and the probability of that result is 55 percent, and (4) the cost associated with making one more sale will be $16.50 and the probability of that cost is 90 percent.

The NER for getting a new account is therefore $110, because the expected return is $125 (i.e., 25 percent $\times$ $500) and the expected cost is $15 (i.e., 90 percent $\times$ $16.50). The NER for making another sale to an existing account is $95 (i.e., NER = [55% $\times$ $200] − $15). Thus, only one of these activities provides adequate net expected return sufficient to give the sales force reason to make an additional sale; that is, getting a new account is the only activity with an NER that is greater than the required minimum of $100.

4.7   "Strategic" Time Allocation

Given sufficient information about accounts and markets, a company can develop a strategic model of sales force deployment. This model attempts—generally intuitively—to:

- Prioritize customers, prospects, and products on the basis of financial and market development criteria.
- Identify the specific selling behaviors, for example, goals and activities, that will support the priorities of the business.
- Identify the relationships between jobs and functions that are required to support targeted results.
- Match the skill set of the salesperson to the sophistication and expectations of the customer.
- Equalize the marginal selling cost with the expected marginal "profit" (gross profit or contribution) derived from selling.

The strategic allocation of sales force time is a theoretical ideal rather than a reality, but there are few alternatives to trying to achieve it. Failure to align the selling effort with what the market requires can be very costly in an environment of decreasing product life cycles and increasing competitive agility.

4.8 Compensation Risk

No-risk compensation is salary (or incentive income) the sales rep is assured of receiving, regardless of performance, as long as employment continues. Risk compensation is income that the sales representative may not receive. In most cases, it is incentive compensation that varies with sales results. But some sales compensation programs also permit rollbacks of base salaries and reductions in draw levels if sufficient performance failures occur.

The degree of risk built into a sales force compensation program should parallel the degree to which the sales force can influence business results, everything else being equal. This is the most widely accepted principle of sales compensation and perhaps the most intuitively obvious. But other factors, such as the length of the sales cycle, the required base salary, and the company's ability to track individual sales achievements, are also important in determining the appropriate level of compensation risk.

4.9 Degrees of Risk

Low-risk compensation is the compensation a sales rep is virtually assured of receiving unless performance is so low that it triggers an unusual compensation adjustment. Moderate-risk compensation covers the full range of incentive compensation that competent performers can confidently expect to receive. High-risk compensation is "speculative" income that is clearly tied to extra personal attainment and even to chance—company-sponsored sales contests, for example.

In most sales organizations, the percentage of earned income that is actually at risk is lower than either the compensation program or the framers of the incentive plan would suggest, because a significant portion of the incentive income stream is usually "disguised base salary," i.e., incentive income that is really assured and not at risk.

4.10 Illustrations of Low-Risk and High-Risk Plans

In a low-risk compensation plan, the overall distribution of earnings, either within the group or by individual, will vary little from year to year. In a high-risk plan, total cash levels may vary considerably.

The relationships depicted in Figure 4-9 illustrate a key point: Compensation risk is high only when the variance in *total earnings* is high. Even though incentive income may vary significantly, *total* income does not vary unless incentive income represents a major portion of the total income stream of the sales rep.

Figure 4-9. Illustrative sales force earnings variance.

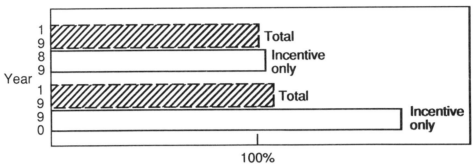

True high-risk compensation plans include straight commission plans for sales reps with limited experience in unproven territories, and plans with substantial incentive opportunity tied to quota attainment on a strict all-or-nothing basis. Lower-risk plans deliver a larger portion of total earnings in the form of base salary or a nonrecoverable draw and base incentive earnings on a performance continuum.

4.11   Some Misleading Statistics

Attempting to determine the degree of risk present in a compensation plan by examining the proportional relationship between base salary and incentive compensation can be tremendously misleading. Consider companies A, B, and C, with the following average compensation levels for a common sales position:

	Base	Incentive
Company A	$30,000 (75%)	$10,000 (25%)
Company B	$30,000 (80%)	$ 7,500 (20%)
Company C	$25,000 (55%)	$20,500 (45%)

Which company offers the least compensation risk for the job in question? Company B, where base is the largest portion of total compensation, might appear to offer the least risk. But company B also pays the lowest total compensation. So *total compensation risk* certainly appears to be the greatest at company B, even though the "leverage" at company B, i.e., the percentage of total pay that is incentive, is the lowest.

Compensation at the company offering the highest total pay (i.e., C) might appear to involve the least risk because C's salespeople have shown that they can earn more. But only $25,000 of the income stream at C is base salary, and a sales rep at C could end up with less than a rep at A or even B. The company (A) offering the highest base salary ($30,000) and a total income ($40,000) that is higher than that of B ($37,500) and lower than that of C ($45,500) may also offer the least income risk. If A's $10,000 incentive income stream is more dependable than the $20,500 program that C offers, there may be less risk at A. This amounts to saying that there is less risk at A if the *long-run income stream* at A is greater than that at C and perhaps more predictable.

Thus, compensation risk cannot be determined solely by using the base salary-incentive mix, either actual or targeted. We must also consider the probability that the rep will receive incentive income, the value (high-to-low) of the incentive income stream, and the variance in base salaries. The greater the probability of the stream, the higher the value of that stream, and the lower the negative variance of that stream vis-à-vis expected income, then the lower the incentive risk. Similarly, the higher the starting and midpoint salary rates, the more defined the base salary administration process, and the greater the linkage between performance and salary action, then the lower the base salary risk.

The principal meaning of risk is *not receiving some expected level of incentive income*. One way to characterize this risk is to determine what portion of the sales force fails to receive the income. If 50 percent of the sales force does not reach the expected incentive income (EII) level, for example, we will probably conclude that incentive risk is high. Another way to characterize risk is to measure the average magnitude of any shortfalls. If those sales reps who do not reach the EII level miss it by only one percent, we may want to revise our initial conclusion and say that the incentive risk is low. Finally, we can also characterize risk by looking at the range of shortfalls to see how far off the mark it is possible to be. Under this definition of incentive risk, the further off the mark it is possible to be, the greater the risk involved. Confusion usually surfaces when discussions of risk include all three of these characterizations.

A mathematical description of perceived incentive risk, developed by Edward A. Francisco* in 1985 on the basis of hundreds of sales force interviews, appears to cover most situations. This description is a working model (see Figure 4-10) that should be further tested and refined.

Let's take a concrete example to see how this would work. Assume that 10 percent of a sales force has missed the EII by an average magnitude of 15 percent, and that the largest shortfall from EII is 50 percent. Assume also that the importance weights for *a*, *b*, and *c* in the model in Figure 4-10 are 1.00, 0.25, and 1.00, respectively. The model therefore suggests that the perceived level of risk will be closely related to the computed "risk score" of 2.75 percent (i.e., [(1.00) 15.0% + (0.25) 50.0%] × [(1.00) (1/10)]).

Assume that a second sales force has the same importance weights,

*A contributor to this handbook.

Figure 4-10. Perceived incentive risk.

Perceived level of incentive risk	[varies with]	{(a) (average shortfall) + (b) (largest shortfall)} × (c) (fraction of sales force not reaching the EII level)

a, b, c = "importance weights" that reflect the role of each factor in determining the perceived level of risk
EII = expected incentive income

an average shortfall of 10 percent, a maximum shortfall of 30 percent, and that 70 percent of all salespeople are missing their EII. Our model suggests that the perceived risk in this instance will be related to the score of 12.25 percent (i.e., [(1.00) 10.0% + (0.25) 30.0%] × [(1.00) 97/ 10)]). Given these weights, the model predicts the greatest perceived risk where the percentage of those missing the expected income level is high and where the margin of the miss is great.

4.12   A Universal Plan Model

All sales compensation plans fit a general algebraic model. Total cash compensation (TCC) is equal to the sum of assured income (A) plus incentive income (I), sometimes reduced by a "validation" factor (V) applied to base salary. The incentive piece of the compensation plan is one or a series of earnings opportunities that depend on the achievement of certain performance results.

$$TCC = A + (I - V)$$
$$I = OR_1 + OR_2 + \ldots OR_n$$

O is an earnings rate and R is a result; so,

$$TCC = A + (OR_1 - V_2) + (OR_1 - V_2) + \ldots (OR_n - V_n)$$

A validation factor is necessary in plans where some or all of base salary or other guaranteed income must first be "covered" by computed incentive earnings before any incentive income is actually paid. The most common validation mechanisms are draws and thresholds. A draw is a cash advance against expected incentive earnings. It can be either *recoverable* or *nonrecoverable*. A recoverable draw is a strict cash advance that is forfeited if sales results are insufficient to generate enough calculated incentive to "cover" the draw. A nonrecoverable draw is a guaranteed minimum level of income for a specific period of time, such as a week or a month. If sales results are insufficient to cover the draw, the difference is not deducted from current or future income. The very important way in which a nonrecoverable draw differs from base salary is that in the former case the incentive is earned only after the draw is validated or covered, whereas incentive is received "on top" of a base salary. Figure 4-11, a depiction of base salary, draw, and a simple incentive, illustrates the key relationships involved.

4.13 Prominence in the Marketing Mix

The level and mix (assured percentage vs. variable percentage) of sales compensation are closely allied to two relatively independent factors:

- *The prominence of the salesperson* in the mix of all the marketing variables that collectively create the "message" heard by the buyer
- *The barriers to entry into the sales job,* i.e., the specific knowledge, experience, and personal contacts that are required to do the job

Prominence is a measure of the salesperson's influence on the buying decision. It is not an absolute measure. It captures the *relative influence* of the salesperson compared to the influence of pricing, advertising, product quality, sales organizational structure, the level of customer service, the proximity of the sales force to the ultimate user or consumer, and so on. When prominence is high, the salesperson is heavily involved in differentiating his or her company's "offer" from offers presented by other companies.

Differentiation takes one of seven classic forms: (1) advocacy (i.e., active "selling"), (2) problem identification, (3) solution development, (4) consultative problem solving, (5) administrative problem solving, (6) providing service, and (7) sales style and conduct. When prominence is low, the salesperson is unable to exert much positive influence on the *prospects* for business. Many jobs can exert substantial negative influence on the prospects for business by not permitting a company to fulfill the

Figure 4-11. Essential relationships between base salary, draw, and incentive.

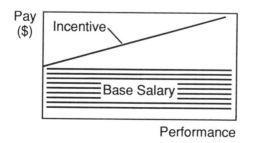
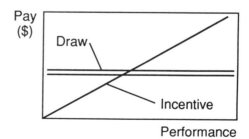

expectations of its customers. However, a limited number of jobs in most companies are designed to *improve the prospects for business*. A low-prominence sales job is one that can make only modest contributions in this regard.

The list of twenty-one key factors in Figure 4-12 attempts to capture details of the market situation, sales role definition, internal sales methods, and product characteristics that have been found to affect prominence. It is not comprehensive and there is some overlap among the factors. In addition, none of the factors has been weighted for importance, although some are clearly more critical than others. Nonetheless, extensive field experience with this diagnostic suggests that it is very effective in distinguishing between high- and low-prominence sales positions. In the above illustrative rating exercise, the average rating is 3.5, indicating a sales position with a clear and important role in the marketing mix. Because these scores tend to collapse toward the mean of 3.0 with averaging, it is important to note that 4.0 is a very strong score, indicating high prominence, and that 2.0 is a very low score, indicating negligible prominence.

Figure 4-12. Indicators of sales prominence: a quick diagnostic.

Low Prominence (1)	High Prominence (5)	Illustrative Rating
Heavy advertising/promotion	Little advertising/promotion	4.5
Low market share	High market share	3.0
Defined customer base	Undefined customer prospects	4.5
High product acceptance	Low product acceptance	4.0
Homogeneous needs	Many market segments	1.5
Mature/stable market	Emerging market structure	5.0
Low price competition	High price competiton	3.0
Closely supervised role	Independent role	4.0
Member of a sales team	Individual contributor	3.5
Strong company image	Weak company image	3.0
Repetitive sales message	Creative sales message	3.0
Indirect support selling	Direct commitment selling	5.0
High administration required	Low administration required	3.0
Little/no repeat contact	Relationship as the key	2.0
High support by staff	Low support by staff	4.5
Specifications filling	Systems selling	3.0
Low upside influence	High upside influence	5.0
High postsale service	Low postsale service	3.0
Simple products	Complex products	3.0
Slow technological change	Rapid technological change	4.0
Clear choices for buyers	Me-too product environment	3.0
	Average rating	3.5

4.14 Three Key Indicators of Prominence

Prospecting, the creativity of the sales process, and the competitiveness of the product are three key indicators of sales force prominence. A product that can readily be sold to a predefined and stable group of customers in an easily forecasted industry, with a well-known and widely respected product name and brand and standard features, functions, and benefits, requires little if any prospecting, creative selling, or selling to overcome objections. Although such a product may require some field support, it will require little sales advocacy. Thus, any salesperson assigned the product will have a low level of prominence relative to other factors in the marketing mix.

If the product must be *sold* in a person-to-person setting and the *selling situation* requires the salesperson to demonstrate spontaneous creative skill—or a skill that is not easily replaced by another marketing tool—in *establishing a competitive profile* for the product, then the prominence of the salesperson is high.

4.15 Examples of Sales Prominence

High- , medium- , and low-prominence sales jobs are easy to recognize. A telemarketing sales rep or the classic door-to-door salesperson who seeks to sell an unadvertised and unknown product is very prominent in the success of the business. This salesperson must frequently overcome the extreme reluctance of a prospective customer, and the job usually requires a substantial tolerance for negative response. The salesperson's challenge is to make the customer receptive to the form and medium of the contact, the product or service category, and the specific brand.

A department store sales counter clerk may be minimally important in the process that leads the customer to make a purchase. The prominence of the job tends to increase to the extent that the product lends itself to consultation and the clerk is expected to advise the customer. Yet even at the extreme, where the counter clerk's role is to move the customer "up the line" to higher-profit selections and to answer an array of questions and even demonstrate the product, this sales job can only achieve moderate prominence relative to sales jobs in other industries. In retail, the store and its location, merchandising philosophy, advertising commitments, and pricing practices usually play a larger role in the customer's decision to walk into the store, approach a specific counter, show interest, stay long enough to make a purchase, and buy the items that offer the best return to the store.

High-prominence sales positions are usually found in businesses where few resources are available to manage or support a field sales effort, or where the only practical access to the buyer is through direct, personal selling. Many sales positions that involve professional selling to sophisticated commercial customers, where in-depth knowledge of how and why the customer buys is critical, are very prominent in the overall mix of marketing elements. As a result, the mix of assured and variable compensation opportunity for these positions is usually skewed toward the variable component. Because the skills and industry experience required to be a successful participant in the professional sales arena can be significant, however, there is also a need for the pay package to reflect the market value of these resources.

4.16   How Prominence Varies

The prominence of a sales job in the marketing mix should be understood as a dynamic concept. Prominence varies as the point of customer contact, the product mix, the sales message, the sales role, and the type of customer vary. And because there is usually some change in all or some of these factors in a given business, the prominence of a given sales job will usually change over time as well.

Because prominence is essentially a function of account control by the salesperson, anything that tends to alter the level of control also alters prominence. A few common examples will illustrate this key point. Once the buyer has decided to purchase selected components from a specific supplier, the supplier must deliver what has been promised and perhaps attempt to broaden the business relationship to include other components. While the contract terms are being hammered out, the salesperson representing the supplier is usually very prominent in the closing and the profitability of the sale.

After the contract is signed, however, the nature of the sales role for the account will usually change. Part, if not all, of the work on the account will now involve *servicing* the needs and requests of various individuals and departments of the buyer.

At this point, the prominence of sales declines and the prominence of postsale support increases, with other supplier functions becoming involved in steering the level and quality of the business with the customer. Sales force control over the relationship has usually been reduced.

If the supplier relies upon the same field position to close deals as well as to provide postsale support, the prominence of the sales job may change even further as more of the salesperson's attention is focused on account maintenance and less on new account development. Problems of declining sales force motivation and high costs of sales often emerge as management realizes that the compensation program, which was probably designed to aggressively support entrepreneurial selling, has not kept pace with changes in the content and prominence of the sales job and is too rich for a role that is largely maintenance oriented.

Another example of how changes in account control can affect the prominence of a sales position may further clarify this critical linkage. Although route salespeople representing manufacturers in the consumer packaged goods industry usually fill low- to moderate-prominence positions in product sale and distribution, this situation can change rapidly with changes in strategy or technology. If, for example, the traditional task of the route salesperson has been to familiarize store managers with the latest trade allowances and promotions and to position the product in the baked goods aisle, then any new management expectation that this job will *also* sell nonbaked goods may lead to a change in sales force control over strategy implementation.

The merchandising principles and economics that work in one part of a grocery store may not work in another part. Further, eye-level shelving promotional displays differ from storefront merchandising racks and bins. Motivating route salespeople to learn new principles and to persist in presenting something new to the same store managers who will approve or disapprove additional space for the core product line can thus be a challenge. Recognizing this challenge amounts to recognizing a "prominence spike" for the sales force; the sales force suddenly has an increased level of control over a facet of strategy, broadening business to other areas of the store, if only to the extent that the sales force can block the success of the effort. Special sales incentive programs with a defined life span can be used to reflect such prominence spikes during the early stages of implementing a new product or modifying merchandising strategy.

4.17 Implications of Prominence for Compensation Plan Design

Prominence is the key concept in the design of effective sales force compensation programs, as well as organizational roles and structures. It is also a complex concept. Prominence is neither easily measured nor easily identified. And because different sales roles will be more or less prominent in the marketing mix of a specific business and the same roles may have a different prominence in a different business, skilled observers occasionally disagree about a specific job's prominence.

These considerations are important when we try to define the implications of prominence for compensation design. Prominence is a helpful tool, but it is only as sharp as its user and it is far from sufficient for telling us how to structure a compensation plan for a given sales position. Taken alone, higher prominence suggests a closer linkage between sales results and pay because higher prominence means more control over, and direct responsibility for, those sales results. At the extreme end of the scale, this logic in turn suggests that the income of very high prominence sales jobs should be variable only (i.e., no assured income), and only when the required sales results have been achieved, because any assured compensation would act to protect the incumbents from the effects of their work.

At this extreme, we would be tempted to conclude that the pay of a high-prominence job, such as selling integrated telecommunications systems to expert buyers who routinely negotiate acceptable terms and prices, should be straight commission only. It is notable, however, that this is almost never true. There are at least three reasons for adopting another design:

1. If sales cycles are long, a straight commission plan can result in extended periods without any income.
2. New or unavailable technologies can disrupt the salesperson's ability to offer a competitive product or system.
3. The salesperson's skills and experience will command a minimum alternative value in the marketplace.

Thus, high-prominence sales positions may receive substantial levels of assured income, either in the form of a base salary or a nonrecoverable draw. But it is also possible for high-prominence positions to receive no assured income. This commonly occurs where few acquired skills and little experience are required, and where the salesperson can close sales frequently and quickly. The proper mix of assured and variable income cannot, therefore, be stipulated on the basis of prominence alone.

In general, however, the dollar amount of variable pay opportunity will usually increase with increasing prominence. This means that high-prominence positions commonly require significant incentive opportunity and that low-prominence positions commonly have little if any incentive opportunity. The total level of compensation will be determined by market practices and the need for a base salary. It is important to note that the converse is not true; the absence of significant incentive opportunity does not prove that a position has low prominence in the marketing mix. National account managers (NAMs) are frequently very visible and influential in the execution of the sales strategy and are more important to the success of the business than many other factors. Yet most NAMs are given only moderate incentive income, primarily because it is usually not appropriate to tie substantial variable income for such a global sales role to conventional yardsticks of sales performance, such as revenue and profit.

4.18 Barriers to Entry and Barriers to Exit

The second most important factor that should influence the design of a sales compensation program is the presence of barriers to entry into the job. A barrier to entry is a qualification the candidate must meet to be considered for the job. The greater the number, specificity, and value of these qualifications, the greater the barriers to entry.

In general, as barriers to entry increase, the available labor pool decreases and the new hire's minimum economic value increases, if only because the employer's requirements bid up the value of the labor supply. In addition, the skills and experience required of high-barrier sales reps probably command some kind of guaranteed income, because these individuals often have access to alternative employers and labor markets.

Barriers to exit also reflect the salesperson's valued skills and experience. These are barriers erected to retain qualified and seasoned employees who might be tempted to accept a competing offer. Barriers to exit are designed to reduce the appeal of such offers by providing some combination of competitive total and assured cash compensation, recognizing performance with noncash awards, and promoting star performers to higher or more prestigious positions. Erecting barriers to exit is particularly important if a business invests heavily in training and developing its salespeople. Key skills are seldom found in new recruits and may not be developed in new salespeople at all in many smaller and less organized companies that would welcome a competitor's well-trained salesperson.

4.19   Barriers to Entry and Prominence

It's essential to understand four basic combinations of barrier and prominence relationships when reviewing or crafting a sales compensation plan. These relationships are high barrier/high prominence, high barrier/ low prominence, low barrier/high prominence, and low barrier/low prominence. Each of these relationships represents a product/market/rep scenario that should prove instructive throughout the review or design process. Figure 4-13 illustrates the common characteristics of these relationships.

A high-barrier/high-prominence sales position clearly requires demonstrated sales skill and perhaps some scarce technical knowledge in situations where the business relies heavily on the success of the sales rep in achieving its goals. The most extreme case of high prominence occurs where marketing is a critical activity for the business and where the sales force assumes a leading role in that activity. Where marketing is critical, the product must be sold in terms of meeting and even creating a need. Where the sales force is critical, the marketing message is usually too complex, or the demographics of advertising channels too broad, to permit reliance on less direct methods.

A low-barrier/low-prominence sales position represents the opposite end of this spectrum. Most low/low positions require no previous train-

Figure 4-13. Common characteristics of basic barrier/prominence relationships.

Barriers to Entry

		High	Low
Prominence	High	• Expert/experienced rep • Product, company, application must be sold	• Minimally trained rep • Heavy prospecting • Multiple suppliers
	Low	• Technically skilled rep • Complex product, need seen, few suppliers	• Minimally trained rep • Familiar products • Established customers

ing or related experience. The risks incurred by the business in putting an inexperienced recruit in low/low jobs are usually minimal because the customer base is stable and the products are familiar and standard, requiring limited explanation or applications work by the salesperson.

4.20   Implications of Barriers to Entry, Barriers to Exit, and Prominence for Plan Design

The spectrum of low to high prominence sales positions ranges between positions that only facilitate orders to positions that create markets. Similarly, the spectrum of low to high barrier sales positions ranges between positions that do not require any relevant training or experience to positions that demand highly educated, expertly trained, and industry-experienced salespeople.

In general, as barriers to entry or barriers to exit increase, the level of fixed income, in the form of a base salary or nonrecoverable draw, also increases. Similarly, as prominence increases, the amount of variable compensation tends to increase. The actual mix of fixed and variable compensation that is appropriate for a given position is largely determined by an analysis of the interplay between these two design factors, barriers and prominence, as they act to raise or lower total compensation and the level of income risk to the salesperson.

Figure 4-14 portrays this interplay and emphasizes the importance of judgment in arriving at the correct mix of fixed and variable compensation for any position. As barriers increase, we want to raise the base salary (or nonrecoverable draw), but as we do this we reduce the percentage of pay that is variable and we raise the total level of pay. If

Figure 4-14. Implications of barriers and prominence for total compensation.

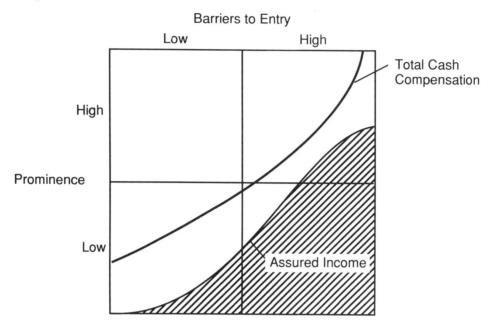

we are constrained by market practice or internal budgets to limit total pay, but still want to raise the base to reflect the role of barriers to entry, we are committed to reducing the "leverage" of the pay plan, i.e., the percentage of pay that is variable. This tends to be troublesome if the position in question is also highly prominent. It's easy to find other examples that illustrate the dynamic and complex behavior of these two factors.

The depiction of the basic variables in Figure 4-14—prominence, barriers to entry, and total cash compensation—should be viewed as a rendering rather than an exact depiction of the most important relationships in sales compensation. The point of this graphic, and many others that have been developed in recent years, is to show that assured income and total compensation rise as barriers and prominence rise, but not linearly and not at the same rate. Actual rates of change vary with the real circumstances of an actual business situation.

5

What Do We Do Next?

5.1 Overview of the Analytic Process

Companies work hard to adapt their sales and marketing strategies to the needs of the marketplace and to exploit their specific competitive advantages. Yet when it comes to the design of a compensation program, few organizations develop individualized plans. In most cases, their plans are arrived at through:

- Compensation quilting—tinkering with an established plan without addressing critical compensation issues
- Compensation plagiarism—substituting a competitor's program and mechanics, irrespective of the rival's differing marketing elements (product, price, promotion, and physical distribution)
- Compensation shortcutting—sweeping difficult problems under the rug and hoping that the sales force will not notice the dust

Compensation design, however, follows the principle that the quality of the output is directly proportional to the quality of the input. Designing or redesigning a sales compensation plan involves a complex process that includes:

1. Defining the sales role
2. Studying the "people" competition
3. Determining the competitive pay range
4. Relating external data to internal practices and policies
5. Selecting a target salary/incentive mix
6. Designing the incentive component
7. Testing, communicating, and implementing the plan

Although the steps are sequential, they interrelate and overlap. Organizations will find certain steps more relevant to their particular needs than others. Steps 1, 5, and 6 relate closely to the company's internal environment, objectives, and strategy; steps 2, 3, and 4 focus on the collection, analysis, and application of external data. Although step 7 often follows plan implementation, it is integral to the development process and to the plan's success. Each of these steps will be discussed in detail on the following pages.

Defining the Sales Role

What is the role of the salesperson in the marketing mix? What duties, responsibilities, and impact does the rep have? Answers to these questions are not always obvious. You should consider interviewing a representative cross section of salespeople and making a sampling of joint calls with them to obtain information for various sales levels and market/product segments. Also, analysis of existing sales data and background information will aid in the role definition process.

Studying the "People" Competition

When asked to name the competition for salespeople, how often have you simply rattled off a list of your business rivals? It's a good start but too narrow a definition. Enlarge the process to consider which companies' sales jobs, regardless of products sold, share similar responsibilities, skills, and buying impact. A market-based indicator of these qualities is a "Where Got, Where Gone" analysis. Determine where your salespeople (at various levels in the organization) have come from and where defectors have gone.

Determining the Competitive Pay Range

In determining the competitive pay range, you should obtain data from the "Where Got, Where Gone" sample on the overall pay range offered. W-2 data provide an excellent source. Yet the overriding rule is "Take what you can get," including:

- Highs, lows, medians, single data points, etc.
- Starting salaries, incentives, and total pay
- Magazine quotes, hiring, and turnover interviews (from published surveys)

With these data, array a pay distribution—high to low. Ultimately, you will be designing a sales incentive plan that will offer a range of earnings opportunities, more for higher performance and less for lower, that parallels the marketplace practice.

Relating External Data to Internal Practices and Policies

There are two critical steps in this process. First, segment the distribution of competitive pay; i.e., break it into bands (dollar ranges) that fit the hierarchy of sales positions found in your organization. A competitive range of $30,000 to $70,000 might, for example, "translate" into:

Rep level 1	$30,000–$40,000
Rep level 2	$37,000–$52,000
Rep level 3	$45,000–$65,000
Major account executive	$55,000–$70,000

Second, determine your company pay philosophy. Is your intention to pay at the average or median levels, the twenty-fifth percentile, the seventy-fifth percentile, or the top of the market? (Choices can vary depending on the position.) The segmented ranges above would need to reflect the position chosen. For example, if you wanted to attach a 15 percent above-market premium to the level 3 rep, the revised range would be $51,750 to $74,750.

Selecting a Target Salary/Incentive Mix

You might first view this selection as ranging from all-salary to all-incentive. Upon further reflection, however, the likely choices will narrow considerably. The subject has been discussed fully in Chapter 4; the guiding principles to observe are:

- Salary must be high enough to attract a qualified pool of potential hires. This aspect is, to a large degree, market driven within bounds for the "Where Got, Where Gone" group. Also, as might be expected, the greater the required experience, technical skills, and education, the higher this component of pay typically is.
- Incentives must be attractive enough to provide motivation and direction appropriate for the degree of impact the position has on sales results. The company must be able to track individual performance both in terms of accuracy and timeliness.

Still, there should be plenty of flexibility. And you should remember that how the incentive is structured will have an effect on the amount of de facto risk (real incentive) in the program. An 80 percent salary/20 percent incentive mix, where the incentive "cuts in" at 80 percent of quota, creates more risk (has less "fixed pay") than does a 60 percent salary/40 percent incentive, where the payout accrues from the first dollar of sales.

Designing the Incentive Component

Nothing is more fun for a sales manager than the design of the incentive component, and nothing is more critical to the company and the sales force in terms of the message that the plan delivers and the actions that it directs and reinforces on the part of the sales force. The key points to remember are:

- Don't rush; think it through.
- Don't oversimplify. The plan(s) should reflect the sales tasks demanded.
- Think of the ideal plan(s) and save important pragmatic considerations for later in the process.

Basic design issues include the form of the incentive, its threshold for activation, its limits or restrictions, the salary/incentive mix, the incentive period, and the performance measures.

The sales rep's role and impact and the market's characteristics drive the form of the incentive. It can be a bonus (defined as the opportunity to earn a percentage of salary or a set dollar amount or range), a commission (a percentage of a business result), or a combination of both forms relating to different aspects of the sales job. The incentive portion itself can accrue at a constant rate throughout or can accelerate or decelerate as performance increases over various goal or performance levels.

Determining an entry-level threshold—a performance level at which the incentive plan will cut in—is critical. This will affect the degree of true risk in the program as well as the leverage (potential reward) that may be expected. This threshold level should be set low enough so that the great majority of representatives (85 percent or 90 percent) can get into the incentive game (i.e., earn some incentive). At the same time, a company's philosophy will often dictate a culturally acceptable minimum threshold level.

Equally important is the determination of the high water mark the incentive plan is likely to generate. Even if there is no formal maximum or "cap," the plan's mechanics, when combined with territory assignment and the goal-setting process, will certainly suggest the range of realizable earnings to the various players. As far as caps, they are the enemy of all sales forces. Yet they can and do make sense in certain windfall situations, most notably on a per account or product basis and often structured as a "perforated cap," allowing some of the windfall to flow through. Thus, psychologically, reps feel that no matter how well they have done, there is always a way to make an additional dollar.

The time period of the incentive is also important. It should conform to the rhythm of the sales cycle and yet also motivate the sales force. When a time period is too long to retain the focused interest of the sales force, you can introduce progress payments. Often, annual, semiannual, or quarterly plans have quarterly or monthly progress payments.

Perhaps the most critical choice you must make involves the selection and relative incentive weights of the plan components, that is, the productivity measures. Two common mistakes to avoid are erring toward oversimplification (not considering performance factors outside of pure overall volume) and blind allegiance to uniformity (every territory should be subject to the identical incentive plan). Creative strategic thinking and a measure of flexibility are the keys.

You must address a variety of other issues in a company-specific vein, including split credits; windfalls; special plan treatments covering promotions, transfers, and special assignments; house account treatment; definition of a sale; eligibility criteria; effects of terminations and resignations; and implications of benefit programs. Sales contests must also be evaluated and staged to blend meaningfully into the overall incentive strategy.

In incentive design, you can and probably should start out with a blank sheet of paper. By being thoughtful and creating an economic game that links a sales rep's financial success, within proper limits, to the measurable, strategically sought sales results over which he or she has control, you can create a "win-win" scenario. As a result, the sales force will be able to recognize a plan that is fair and motivational and that provides a sense of needed direction.

Testing, Communicating, and Implementing the Plan

This last step, if improperly taken (or ignored), is a certain spoiler. You must evaluate how the plan will affect various individuals as well as its likely costs and expected overall results. Unfortunately, there is no control experiment to show conclusively the results of a new plan. But sound, logical assumptions will help point the direction. This testing can be done informally (on a case-by-case, what-might-have-happened basis), subjected to overall assumptions and computer simulation, or accomplished through the use of a pilot project on the part of the sales force.

In introducing a plan, you must decide how to accomplish the transition: all at once, on a phased-in basis, or with the use of grandfathering or other transitional safety net procedures.

Properly communicating a new program deserves the highest priority. The sales rep must understand why its features have been designed, how it works, and how (realistically) he or she can win. The plan should be written clearly and examples provided. Clarity allows you to pack more design into the plan and have the plan remain fully understandable. In addition to the text, meetings, slides, and videotape presentations can all play a vital role. So, too, can having a set of preanswered, likely Q&As.

Administration must be handled properly. Make sure that payouts are made in a timely fashion and that the sales force can understand the report on which payouts are based. Also, have a specific person to whom sales reps should inquire (and receive prompt feedback from) on specific problems or plan interpretation and calculation issues.

Finally, a sales compensation plan, unlike a diamond, cannnot last forever. Each year, think through your sales-related strategy, see how it has changed, and reassess the validity of the sales compensation program. You are, after all, sending a message to your sales force. Your sales compensation program ranks among the primary reasons why they work for your company. It greatly affects what they think of the company and how they will direct their focus. So make sales compensation work for you.

5.2 Allocation of Responsibilities

Generally, the best way to proceed with a review of a sales compensation program is with a reasonably sized study team or task force. Although such a group should comprise individuals with differing areas of expertise, it must be able to act as an interactive body as decisions go forward. A typical configuration might include:

- Two to three headquarters sales marketing managers
- One to two human resources/compensation managers
- One data processing/MIS representative
- One finance manager
- One to two external advisers (sales compensation consultant/sales manager/management consultant)

The sales marketing contingent would be responsible for prioritizing the sales strategy(ies) to be accomplished and for isolating those activities and results that are falling short. They should also rank the performances of field reps. As the process goes on, these individuals will need to have a strong say in the proposed program. They are, after all, the ultimate managers of the field force.

The human resources/compensation group will gather the competitive pay data (sometimes supplemented by the "Where Got/Where Gone" analysis provided through the district/region sales organization), pull together internal pay data, and interpret the results of the pay program in light of the range of performance. In the design phase, human resources would take an active role in sound compensation design and ensure that the task force evolves programs that fall within the company's available parameters. At the same time, it is incumbent upon this group to recognize that sales incentives are a unique blend of sales and compensation and most often require considerable fresh thought and intentional differentiation from more traditional compensation systems. The human resources function should also provide an overview of such associated issues as hiring, turnover, and career development and should participate in transitional plan changeover and communications issues.

Data processing must be candid about what information required to track plan performance and to trigger plan payouts may or can be provided. It should not create obstacles and delays. By and large, if the information is important enough to track for the purpose of measuring sales compensation, then it certainly is important to track in order to measure the accomplishment of sales strategy.

Finance also must not play an obstructionalist role. On the other hand, it is highly important to know what the company can afford at various levels of performance and what its cultural biases regarding payouts are—to provide a reality test.

The role of the external adviser (consultant) can include all of the above (depending on how the consultant is used vis-à-vis the inside study team) but can and usually does involve some additional responsibilities. The consultant offers three significant advantages:

1. Specialized expertise and fresh ideas
2. Confidentiality (regarding information gathering)
3. Nonpolitical partisanship (greater freedom of expression)

The consultant has a distinct advantage in obtaining honest answers from the field sales force in the interview process. This is also true of customer interviews and, to a certain degree, for interviews with headquarters executives.

In sorting through the available input (interviews and background analysis), a consultant offers a wide array of relevant experience to help pinpoint problems and lead the task force in an inductive, creative process that culminates in an appropriate solution. You should keep in mind, however, that the consultant will never know your business and its nuances as well as you do. Consultants must be harnessed. You must be heavily involved, contributing to and buying in on the solution. Ultimately, it must be your plan.

Consultants need hold no punches. Use them to lay the groundwork for the difficult sell, and if need be, to take the lead in selling the plan to senior management.

There is no single, absolute course for you to take in structuring the team, in the relative roles that are played or in the role of the external resource. It's a matter of what works for you: the depth of the problem, the openness, the commitment and expertise of the task force, and the company's underlying culture. Needless to say, budgets and timing constraints may be important as well, but it should be underscored that a sales compensation program that functions well has enormous sales and profit leverage and improvement potential.

5.3 Steps in Sales Force Analysis

Let's assume that you are given the task of auditing or redesigning your sales compensation program within three months. The greatest source of data for conducting a sales force compensation analysis comes from interviews with the sales force and with field sales managers. Nevertheless, a thorough analysis of sales-related data and written materials can help pinpoint trends, problems, and opportunities in preparation for these interviews. Such data, which already exist and can be accessed rather easily, include:

- The sales/marketing strategic plan, to identify important objectives.
- The sales compensation plan(s), to indicate the economic selling message that is being delivered to the sales force. The message can then be compared by sales position, geography, market, and product line to the strategic imperative.
- Internal data (oral or written) that speak to your competitive position by market, geography, and product line.
- Customer feedback on your strengths and weaknesses vis-à-vis your selling activities.
- Competitive pay data (salaries, incentives, and total compensation).
- Internal pay data (salaries, incentives, and total compensation).
- Rankings of sales force personnel (segmented by position), indicating performance assessment by managers versus pay element ranking. You can perform countless analyses on these data to identify problem areas.
- Hiring/turnover data.

Armed with this information, you may begin the interview/discussion stage. The interviews should include such headquarters executives as the sales and marketing vice-presidents, the national sales manager, and the human resources vice-president, who can provide much-needed direction in terms of the overall objectives of the company/division and of shortcomings in the sales compensation program. Senior executives will have their own impressions of the problems and opportunities committed and/or not addressed under the existing program. Figure 5-1 indicates the topics to cover.

At this point, you may have processed a considerable amount of information and could probably prepare a written document on the sales

Figure 5-1. Topics for headquarters interviews.

- Company strategy, goals, and objectives: near-term and three to five years out, overall and by division
  - —sales, profits, return on assets
  - —position of company in each business segment
- Factors affecting the company's ability to reach each business segment
  - —pricing, quality, production factors, sales reps, advertising, external factors (weather, housing units, economy)
  - —overall, across enough territories or division, degree to which these factors balance out
- Organizational structure vis-à-vis attainment of objectives
- Quality of current sales management process and planning process
  - —territory loading
  - —planning—top downward or bottom upward
  - —planning—accuracy, short- and long-term
  - —goal clarity
- Prevailing attitudes among sales force and field sales management
- Perception of current compensation programs
  - —including level and form
  - —including expense and car policies, etc.
- Compensation programs—ideas for change
- Problem areas in sales management or sales
- Suggested sales force interviewees (number per division, representative districts, sales force priorities)
- Career pathing
- Competitor survey companies, especially where sales influence is roughly similar

---

compensation program's strengths and weaknesses. Don't rush to conclusions. It's still early, and you have yet to gain input from the field. Keep in mind that the sales reps' impressions of their relative ability to affect the sales process (vis-à-vis other factors) and to have their impact accurately measured and assessed may vary considerably from those of executives at headquarters. And most important, their interpretation of the overall sales compensation program and the incentive plan in particular—the message it sends and the direction they take—is critical. The company must deal with the perceptions of the sales force, accurate or not.

5.4   Sales Force Interview Topics

You conduct sales force interviews to expand your understanding of the sales force's efforts and their perception of and reactions to the reward systems and related management processes. To accomplish this, the interviews must be candid, confidential, and nonthreatening.

The sales manager must therefore ask him- or herself if task force members are capable of keeping the information confidential. If not, would a third party provide that assurance? Incidentally, although individual interviews generally provide better-quality information, group interviews (typically two to four people) can produce a "safety in numbers" openness when interviews are conducted internally.

Second, you should inform the sales force of the process about to be undertaken, explaining the role of, the preparation for, and the "rules" of the interview. (A suggested announcement memorandum appears in Figure 5-2.) To reinforce the openness of the process, invite noninterviewees, on a confidential basis, to submit comments on the subject.

(text continues on page 84)

Figure 5-2. Suggested announcement memo.

TO: Sales Force

FROM:

SUBJECT: Sales Compensation Study

We have retained the management consulting firm of _____ to work with our management to review the present sales compensation plans, to identify opportunities for strengthening the existing incentive approach, and to recommend any modifications that will make the compensation plans totally consistent with the company's marketing strategies and goals.

The study will be conducted by _____ and a company task force, comprising _____ and _____ .

The consulting firm and the task force must thoroughly understand the roles of the organization, products, markets, sales strategies, opportunities, and field sales force in achieving sales and profit goals. Therefore, we shall invite a representative cross section of sales executives, district sales managers, and sales representatives to discuss these issues with the consultants in a confidential interview expected to last about ninety minutes. No preparation will be required. The consultants are interested in hearing your contribution to the company's profitability and your reactions to programs and possible modifications.

(continues)

Figure 5-2. *(continued)*

These interviews will be conducted during [*months*] in [*cities*]. Our internal staff will make the arrangements.

The consultants would also be pleased to read any written comments that others in the sales force would choose to submit regarding sales compensation. These may be sent directly to:

_____

_____

_____

_____

The company recognizes that your participation in this review is essential. I know that we can expect your full cooperation.

Field Interview Discussion Areas

   I. Interviewee's Background
- Professional history
- Educational/experiential credentials
- Territory locations
- Reporting relationships
- Perceived future career path

  II. Territory Characteristics
- Major accounts
- Prospects
- Key products/applications/opportunities

 III. Time Allocation
- Basis for priorities
- Call frequency standards
- Typical day/week/month

  IV. Account/Market Characteristics
- Interviewee's perception of categorization of decision makers
- Factors causing difficulty/ease of sale to account
  —Account characteristics
  —Product characteristics
  —Competitive characteristics
  —Other factors (identify)

- What is the minimum education/experience needed to manage each type of account/prospect?
- What characteristics make an account/prospect easy/difficult to sell?
- How and when do you know you have been successful with each product/market combination?
- How much of your time and effort is spent helping shape the needs of customers/prospects?
- What competitive pressures are present in each product/account combination?

V. Measures of Success

- Indications (examples: volume growth, overquota, market share)
- Difference of indicators' validity by product/market segment
- Time frame for each indication
- "Contaminants" to each indicator

VI. The Company "Value" System/Field Perceptions

- Perceived "standards" of performance

    —Goals/quotas
    —How set?
    —How communicated?
    —How measured?
    —Fairness/unfairness

- The pay system

    —Salaries: how set? administered?
    —Incentive compensation
    —The measures
      - Fair and appropriate; which ones?
      - Potentially unfair; depending on what?
      - Suggestions for improvement
      - Definitely avoid; which ones?
      - What time frame is fair for each?
    —Related compensation elements: sales contests, recognition program perquisites, cars, benefits, etc.; strengths, weaknesses

VII. Other Issues

   Note: For field sales managers, follow the same discussion areas, but from *both* of the following perspectives:
   - The manager's entire area of responsibility
   - On behalf of his or her subordinates (how these systems/measures could be strengthened to help him or her to be a more effective manager)

You can begin each interview by giving the participant an overview of the interview guide, which can be used as a checklist of topics to be covered. As the interview moves toward its conclusion, the guide will help you to avoid missing important discussion areas. Furthermore, this technique encourages open-ended interviews and allows you to let the interview "flow" around the key topics in a way that makes the interviewee comfortable in telling his or her story.

5.5   Sample Questionnaires

Interviews with sales reps should provide the critical information necessary for analyzing the sales compensation plan. After all, these are the people who translate strategy into action and who respond to the various systems involving goals, measurement of success, rewards, organization and deployment, hiring, selection, career development, and training.

What subjects should be discussed in the confidential meetings with sales reps? The two interview guides that appear in Figures 5-3 and 5-4

Figure 5-3. Interview guide no. 1.

I. Introduction

Cover the individual's background, career with the company, and present assignment (sales force, territory location, number of accounts, product line for which responsible).

II. Definition of Field Sales Role

The next series of questions will document the relative prominence of field sales in the marketing mix for each product/market segment, identify the segments in which prominence is the highest, and determine the appropriate indicators of performance (incentive parameters) in such segments.

- Ask the rep to describe his or her territory in terms of:
    - —Number of accounts
    - —End-use categories
    - —Size (current business and/or potential)
    - —Geography to be covered
- Does type and/or size of account make a difference in terms of what the rep does with an account (activities), whom rep calls on, how much time rep spends, and so on?
    - —If so, have rep describe in general terms what the different categories or segments may be.
    - —If not, do such factors as how accounts are organized to buy, whether they are new or mature, type of products used, and so on, make recognizable differences?
    - —If so, ask rep to describe these categories.

[*NOTE: At this point, follow the line of questioning below for each category identified above, one category at a time; if no categorization evolves, follow questions below for all accounts as one category.*]

- Whom does the rep typically call on in an account? Ask rep to describe the:

  —Frequency of sales calls
  —Purpose of sales calls
  —Individual(s) called upon
  —Type of message to each individual

- Does the rep have a plan or strategy for an account? For a call?

  —If so, ask for specific examples
  —If not, have rep suggest some possible examples.

- What are the key factors that influence volume of sales and to what extent?

  —Growth in customers' business
  —New applications
  —New products
  —External economic factors (specify which ones)
  —Rep's own skill (How is it manifested?)
  —Other

- What are some of the opportunities to increase business? (Ask for examples.) How does the rep identify them? (Ask for examples.) How does the rep capture them? (Ask for examples.)
- What are the key determinants of "the buy" and how does the rep cope with each?

  —Price (impact of and posture on price concessions. Explore the rep's real latitude and crossover point between holding price and losing the order).
  —Quality.
  —Service (explain).
  —Innovation.
  —Other.

- If appropriate, ask the rep to describe how he or she cracked a new account. (Also, how long it took—time span, number of calls, and so on)
- How does the rep's approach differ between a well-sold and undersold account? (Ask for specifics.)
- What are the easiest products to sell? Why? The hardest? Why?
- Are there any seasonal characteristics?
- Who are the key competitors? What are their strengths or presumed edge? How does the rep combat them?
- Has the rep recently lost any significant business? What and why? What are the chances of regaining it?
- What is the time frame within which success is measured?
- How does the rep know at the end of a year (or other period) that he or she has succeeded (or failed) with an account? What measures would the rep use?
- How does an account typically distribute its business? Exclusively? Two or

(continues)

Figure 5-3. *(continued)*

> more? By items? By supplier? Or does it vary by user and application? If so, how?
>
> - What is the skew of volume in his territory? (The percentage of customers accounting for x percent of volume?)

III. Planning, Priorities, and Inspection

The following series of questions will permit you to understand the field sales management process and the information base concerning major accounts/markets needed to support that process.

- How does the rep determine how often to call on accounts? How does this differ by category (defined above)? Why does it differ? Should it differ? On balance, how often should an account of a given type or in a given category be called on?

[*NOTE: In a large account, each person to be seen could and probably should represent a separate call. Explore this.*]

- How long is a typical sales call (by category), including wait time? Does it vary by type? Why?
- How many hours a day does the rep figure he or she has to sell (be with or wait for a customer)?
- How many calls per day does the rep typically make? Does the rep's call frequency or pattern vary by time of year? If so, how?
- Does the rep plan his or her calling pattern (itinerary) in advance? How much in advance? How does the rep do it? What does travel time typically amount to?
- What relationship does the rep see between time spent with or at accounts and results achieved? Should more time be spent with certain accounts? If so, what kinds of accounts? How would extra time be spent?
- How does the rep and his or her manager analyze accounts? What are some examples of plans, strategies, objectives, ideas that come out of the process? (Get copies of what is written down.)
- Is the process a useful one? How could it be improved? Could it or should it be done more than once a year?
- How well can the rep determine an account's total potential? How well can the rep estimate what he or she will sell to an account during the next year? During the next quarter? (Explore this issue.)
- Does the rep or can the rep get the information (from the company and from the account) he or she needs to plan for and sell the account? What could be improved? How? Comment on process of getting, keeping, and transmitting account information.

IV. Current Compensation Plan

- Ask the rep to describe the current compensation plan and how it works. (Explain that this is to see if there is any misunderstanding.) What are its weak points? What are its strong points?
- How does it compare with past plans the rep may have worked under? (Ask for specifics.)

- Does the rep feel his or her level of earnings is appropriate for his or her job? Does the rep specifically relate his or her earnings to his or her results? How?
- What would the rep do differently if he or she were paid solely by salary, if it was appropriately high?
- If the rep did not work for the company, where else could the rep's skills be used in a field selling position?
- To what extent does the present incentive plan focus the rep's attention on specific products/markets? Could this be done better?
- What determines the profitability of the rep's territory? What elements of profitability can the rep influence? How, if at all, does the present plan reward the rep for those actions that contribute to improved profitability?
- How is the expected or quota level of volume determined?
- Could the rep set (with his or her manager) more specific goals that would be a better (or more complete) reflection of his or her performance than the above? What would these measures be?
- To what extent does the present plan encourage the rep to obtain the highest possible price for an order? Who has the authority to vary pricing to meet competition? Can the rep influence a customer to stay with him or her when the price is uncompetitive? How?

V. Conclusion

Ask for any other comments on any aspect of the compensation program (this could include car, expenses, benefits, contests, recognition programs, promotion opportunities, and so on) or management/information processes that could be helpful to the critique of the existing sales compensation program.

---

cover a great deal of relevant territory. Each has a slightly different emphasis and style of questioning. Both represent core documents that must be adapted to your company's particular circumstances.

The sales compensation project manager should prepare such a document and use it to structure the interviews and keep them focused. During any given interview, however, make sure that you go with the flow of the conversation, while aiming at two key topics:

1. What does the rep do? To whom? How? How does he or she measure his or her accomplishments?
2. How does the rep feel about the effectiveness and fairness of compensation and other (formal or informal) reward systems? What suggestions does he or she have?

As each interview proceeds, be selective and follow certain points and issues from the questionnaire to their fullest. You will not be able to cover all topics in depth with any given rep. If you have selected a suitable cross section of the sales force to interview, by the end of the process you should be able to address each point raised in the questionnaire.

(text continues on page 90)

Figure 5-4. Interview guide no. 2.

I. Introduction

Cover the individual's background, career, and present assignment.

- Ask the rep to describe his professional history. When was he or she hired? What jobs did he or she have prior to this one? What is the rep's present responsibility?
- What is the rep's educational background? Does the rep have advanced degrees or postgraduate study credits? If so, were they essential for his or her present job or for any prior jobs?
- Ask the rep to describe his or her territory, both geographically and from the standpoint of assigned accounts and prospects. How does the rep get the information needed to capitalize on new account opportunities? How does the rep obtain information needed to maintain and develop relationships with existing accounts?
- Who is the rep's immediate supervisor? Ask the rep to describe the formal and informal channels of communication and information exchange between them. What kinds of formal/informal planning and evaluation systems does the rep have with respect to time allocation, establishment of performance goals, and results reviews?
- What are the rep's future career opportunities at the company? What aspects of the rep's present position will help the rep qualify for those future positions? In what ways, if any, does the rep feel frustrated about capitalizing on future career growth opportunities?

II. Territory Characteristics

- What are the major accounts in the rep's territory? How does the rep determine when an account is a "major" one?
- Are there situations in the territory where there are multiple decision makers within a single account? Are they ever so independent that one might view a single corporate customer as consisting of numerous separate accounts, depending on the product or application? If so, have the rep describe these situations.
- What major prospects exist in the sales rep's territory? Where does the rep get information about new prospects?
- How does the rep assign priorities among existing and prospective accounts? How does the rep approach prospects? Does the approach differ, depending on the type of prospect? If so, ask the rep to describe the differences.
- What aspects of the rep's prospecting responsibilities are most enjoyable and fulfilling? Which aspects are most frustrating and unpleasant?
- How does the rep know when he or she is making enough progress with a prospect to justify investing more time to turn the prospect into an account?
- Are there particular products/applications/ opportunities that provide the rep a particularly opportune reason for soliciting new accounts?

III. Time Allocation

- How does the rep prioritize the multitude of sales activities?
- What kinds of systems (e.g., call reports, call frequency standards, account

classification criteria) does the rep use, either on a formal or an informal basis, to help allocate time most effectively? Ask the rep to describe these systems and provide illustrations, if possible.

- How does the rep determine the optimum call frequency with respect to an existing account? Is there a point (e.g., four calls per quarter) beyond which additional sales calls cannot be expected to contribute to improved results? How does the rep determine this point of diminishing returns? Does it differ by type of account or decision maker, or by other characteristics?
- Ask the rep to describe the typical week and month. What kind of planning does the rep do prior to the start of the week or month? What kinds of adjustments does the rep typically have to make as a result of unforeseen circumstances?
- Are there opportunities that allow the rep to use his or her time more efficiently? If so, what are they?

IV. Account/Market Characteristics

- For each category of product and type of account, ask the rep to identify those observable results that indicate success (volume growth, surpassing quota, improving market share, securing an order for a different type of product, and so on).
- Over what time frame can success most accurately be measured? How does it differ by type of account? (For example, with respect to some types of accounts, it may take months for an observable indication of success; on others, success may be measured in a matter of weeks.)
- What external, uncontrollable influences can influence the rep's chances of success in each product/market combination?

V. The Company "Value" System/Field Perceptions

- What factors influence the corporation's evaluation of sales rep performance? These could include meeting sales goals and quotas, securing internal recognition, formal performance evaluation and merit increases, sales incentives and contests, and so on. Which of these processes are most important? Which have the least impact on the rep's perception of how well he is doing?
- How are sales goals and quotas established? Does the process vary by product or by such other factors as category of account? To what extent does the rep have input into the quota-establishment process? What kinds of information do the rep's superiors need to establish appropriate sales goals and quotas? Where do they obtain this information?
- What improvements can be made to the process by which sales goals or standards are established to make them fairer?
- Regarding the rep's overall level of compensation, have him or her describe how his or her salary is established, reviewed, increased, and administered. How does the incentive plan work? What are the program's strong points and weak points?
- In evaluating the rep's pay competitiveness, with what kinds of positions in what other companies would the rep compare his or her compensation? How competitive is the company's overall program?
- How do (or would) different incentive rates on products or equipment motivate

(continues)

Figure 5-4. *(continued)*

him? (Ask for specific answers.) How does (or would) the rep do it? Suppose the incentive rate was the same on all units. What would he do differently? How would the rep do it? (Or how could the rep tell where to do it?)

- How does the rep relate his or her efforts and achievements to the amount of incentive payment and/or salary increase he or she receives? How is the rep's performance assessed? How should it be assessed? What factors should influence incentive payments? Why? How would they be measured?
- Ask the rep to comment on any strengths and weaknesses perceived in the indirect elements of compensation (perquisites, company cars, employee benefits, and so on). How may these systems be significantly improved?
- If the company develops a revised incentive compensation for his position, what measures of performance should be included in that program? What measures are so potentially unfair that they should be avoided? What is the best time frame for measuring performance in each of these categories?

VI. Other Issues
- What aspects of the job, career opportunities, or management process should the company consider in evaluating the incentive compensation program?

At the conclusion of the interview stage, the study team will work with the data provided.

5.6   Competitive Compensation Analyses

To evaluate the competitiveness of a sales compensation program, a sales manager must first consider his organization's internal compensation program, pay philosophy, and incentive compensation climate. Just as every company has a distinct corporate culture, it also has an established pay philosophy and incentive compensation climate. Some companies include a formal statement of compensation policy in their corporate human resources policy statements or in compensation plan documents. In organizations that have no formal policy, common practice usually determines informal policy.

Market-pricing philosophies and basic business strategies often influence pay philosophies. For example, a company that aspires to be a "premier market leader" would try to recruit "premier" talent and would expect to pay accordingly. Similarly, a company whose goal is to be a "no frills" provider of "generic products for less" would normally try to get the most mileage possible from every compensation dollar paid.

A company's pay philosophy is typically defined by a pool of competitor compensation programs to which employees' pay is compared and by the desired position of a pay program vis-à-vis those competitors. This pool can comprise business competitors, companies in the regional employment environment, companies of similar size, and human resources competitors (the "Where Got, Where Gone" file).

After reviewing your own compensation program, you should establish your target competitive pay level profile, whether it is as an average payer in your regional employment environment or as a seventy-fifth percentile payer in a pool of premier Fortune 500 companies. The next step is to identify your organization's incentive compensation climate, that is, your company's attitude toward leverage and its aversion to risk in establishing total compensation levels. Both of these factors affect the mix of fixed versus variable compensation (compensation mix) and the amount of leverage that can be built into your sales compensation plan.

Some companies believe in encouraging a high level of performance by supporting a "pay for performance" philosophy that withholds a portion of pay (that is, places it at risk) until that performance is obtained. Unless sales reps meet the required performance level, they will not receive their total targeted pay. Similarly, performance above the established goal typically results in a reward of additional pay in excess of the target level, leveraging the pay available to top performers.

After identifying your organization's pay practices, you will be in a much better position to review the pay programs of competitors.

Competitive Compensation Surveys

The successful development (or updating) of a compensation program requires dependable competitive data. Unfortunately, few competitors will happily supply you with the information you need to design an effective sales incentive program. Aside from the question of helping a business rival, completing compensation surveys takes time and effort. Resistance to requests for such information, therefore, is not surprising.

Fortunately, sales managers can obtain competitive compensation information in other ways, for example, by purchasing a published national survey or conducting a custom survey. Each of these options has advantages and disadvantages.

Several large national compensation surveys appear annually. Executive Compensation Services, Inc., the Dartnell Research Institute, the Research Institute of America, the Conference Board, and major consulting companies provide some of the most comprehensive surveys. Industry associations also produce industry-specific surveys. These studies are usually available to any organization willing to pay the price. Surveys of this type, however, sometimes require a purchaser to submit compensation data on its own sales force for the survey data base. Given the difficulty in obtaining competitive data, many companies find this option appealing.

Published compensation surveys allow quick access to compensation data at a relatively low cost. Such sources typically contain standard data on salary and incentive payments and some minimal data about sales positions and individual sales volumes. They paint a broad picture of compensation practices.

Most companies, however, do not want to rely solely on published surveys for comprehensive reviews of compensation practices. Their reasons generally focus on the timeliness of the data and the diversity of companies that make up the data bases in these surveys.

Surveys are typically conducted annually, with a delay of six to nine months between data collection and publication. Therefore, they contain incentive payout information based on the previous year's sales performance. Much of the data is thus outdated. Furthermore, published surveys provide very little discussion of the data displayed in their standard formats or interpretation of information on incentive plan payments or operations. And without an understanding of how and why incentive plans work, to help put the particular year's incentive payouts in perspective, it is very difficult to interpret data on incentive plan payouts.

Many published surveys contain a very broad base of participating companies, representing practically every industrial category in the Standard Industrial Classification Codes lists, from the largest to the smallest. This raises questions about the usefulness of such surveys for particular companies.

When selecting a sales compensation survey, remember that sales compensation varies primarily by industry and then by company size and location. Therefore, you should look for surveys that utilize industry breaks of the data collected.

Some published surveys also provide access to their data bases for custom studies. This allows you to select special subsets of the participating companies to perform individualized analyses. Similarly, some surveys contain information on incentive plan design, administration, and salary management practices to further aid in interpretation of the compensation data provided.

Conducting a Custom Survey

Custom surveys, on the other hand, permit sponsoring companies to select the competitors they want to target for participation. These surveys also enable you to determine what information will be sought and to direct the data analysis to ensure that you will receive all the information you need to design your sales compensation program. The main disadvantages of conducting a customized survey involve time, effort, and cost. You must consider carefully whether the higher-quality data obtained from a custom survey justify the investment of time and money.

Customized surveys must be designed to collect only essential information. They must also collect accurate information in a manner that minimizes the efforts of the individuals providing the data. For this reason, many companies hire consultants to perform this function. Furthermore, the use of "impartial" or "disinterested third parties" often encourages competitors to share sensitive data.

Identifying Your Competitor Group

The selection of competitor companies represents a critical step in designing a compensation survey. Many competitive pay philosophies contain a "select standard competitor group," which simplifies this process. If yours does not, the previous discussion on pay philosophies will help guide you in making the selection.

Defining Information Required

The information that you require from competitors should relate to the following factors:

- The organization of the company and job roles
- The design of its incentive plans
- Basic pay information

It is important that you collect information describing the organization of competitor sales forces. You must be able to place the data received in context.

Begin by asking yourself about the industry of the sales force in question and the products that are sold by the employees covered by a particular sales plan. How is the sales force organized (e.g., by products, size of account, or geographic region)? Does it sell its products to dealers, brokers, end users, or a combination of these customers?

You must also inquire about the organization's expense and automobile policies as well as sales reps' access to company insurance and other employee benefit programs. Expense policies can range from no reimbursement for sales expenses, to reimbursement from incentive earnings, to total company reimbursement. Car policies can vary from a company-provided car, to shared travel expenses, to no company contribution to travel costs. Similarly, some companies provide their sales forces with complete access to benefit programs; others offer no benefits at all.

Position-Specific Data Requirements

The first step in sales position-specific data collection is "job matching" to standardized position descriptions. Information requested may include:

- Title
- Reporting relationship
- Number of incumbents
- Personal account responsibility (if any)
- Salary range (minimum, midpont, maximum)
- Salary data (low, high, average, twenty-fifth, and seventy-fifth percentiles)
- Incentive data (low, high, average, target, maximum, twenty-fifth, and seventy-fifth percentiles)
- Total compensation data (low, high, average, target, twenty-fifth, and seventy-fifth percentiles
- Individual sales volumes (low, high, average, target, twenty-fifth, and seventy-fifth percentiles)
- Number of sales reps supervised (low, high, average)

You must, of course, balance the desire to obtain as much information as possible with the need to keep the survey from becoming unreasonably long, so as not to discourage participation. This concern will influence your decisions on which elements to include, how to collect the data, and what support to provide to participating companies in their data submission process.

"State of the art" surveys today often provide computer assistance with data submission through the use of PC data entry diskettes. Such diskettes usually are preprogrammed with prepared screens, instructions, special function keys, and data tables that serve as electronic data entry forms. This helps to simplify data entry of incumbent pay information into data tables that use special function routines to identify or calculate such required statistics as high/low cases, averages, and percentile levels. These diskettes also prevent participants from having to enter manually such standard information as survey job codes, job titles, and so on.

Incentive Plan Design Requirements

The same concerns that apply to the selection of position-specific data apply to identifying information requested on the design and administration of incentive plans. You must request only information that is absolutely needed and collect it as painlessly (for participating companies) as possible.

The use of a structured (multiple-choice) questionnaire will prove quite helpful. (Designing the questionnaire, though, requires careful planning to anticipate appropriate responses.) Experience has shown that participants are more willing to choose from several possible responses than to compose open-ended statements to describe their incentive plans. This technique also simplifies the data analysis phase of the survey process and decreases the chance of errors resulting from misinterpretation of open-ended plan summaries.

Figure 5-5 provides an example of a structured questionnaire format for collecting information about the design and administration of sales incentive plans.

The bottom line in determining what information to collect regarding the design and administration of sales plans boils down to the information necessary to describe what plans look like and how they work. The elements of plan design about which information is sought typically include:

- Covered compensation elements (base salaries, bonuses, commissions, draws against commissions, sales contests, combinations, and so on)

Figure 5-5. Incentive plan design practice.

Please check the practices that apply for each of the survey positions.

	Senior Telemarketing Sales Reps	Intermediate Direct Sales Reps	First-Level Direct Sales Manager (no personal account sales)
1. Basic compensation approaches:			
Base salary only	☐	☐	☐
Salary plus bonus	☐	☐	☐
Commission only	☐	☐	☐
Salary plus commission	☐	☐	☐
Draw against commission	☐	☐	☐
Salary plus bonus plus commission	☐	☐	☐
2. Minimum eligibility criteria required for participation:			
Base salary level	☐	☐	☐
Salary grade midpoint	☐	☐	☐
Position or title	☐	☐	☐
Years in current position	☐	☐	☐
Other	☐	☐	☐

- Minimum eligibility requirements (e.g., salary level, job title, salary grade)
- Type of incentive awards (e.g., discretionary, performance vs. goals, formula driven)
- Performance results measured on quantitative, qualitative, or combined basis; based on group, individual, or combined results
- Threshold result required before incentive is earned (if any)
- Bonus pool established (or are individual awards determined?)
- Target and maximum caps established (if so, are they expressed as a percentage of midpoint, percentage of sales dollars, or flat dollar amount?)
- Limitations on incentive earnings per sale (windfall profits clause)
- Shared credit or double counting for shared or team sales
- Length of performance measurement period
- Timing of award payouts (monthly, quarterly, semiannually, annually)
- Cash or noncash payments

6

Sales Force Organization

6.1 Introduction

In the good old days, sales force organization was pretty simple. Top management decided how far away it wanted its trucks to be sent and then deployed sales reps to cover all accounts within that area. The number of customers was relatively limited and almost all were concentrated in urban areas within one or two geographic regions.

Management charged the sales reps: "Go forth and sell as much as you can to everyone in your territory who will buy. And mail in your orders at the end of each week." Quotas were, in effect, the sales figures for the prior year, perhaps with some adjustments. Sales reps were paid simply, either all commission or all salary. The boss's son or son-in-law often served as the sales manager. He hired people to fill one type of sales position after running an advertisement in the local paper and conducting thirty-minute interviews. He sent the rookies out with the pros for a week and then gave the recruits sample bags and their own territories.

Obviously, a lot has changed over the years. Market segmentation and business strategy make it less likely that a sales rep can, or should, sell to "everyone" within his territory. Computers and telecommunications have changed forever how (and how often) field sales reps and customers communicate with "the factory." Efficient and cost-effective transportation, physical distribution and warehousing, and telemarketing systems have made it unusual for a large company to serve only one or two regions of the country.

Today, sales forces have evolved to the point where management has a very difficult time answering such complex organizational questions as:

- Should we have one sales force selling all products, or several sales forces focused by product group?
- How many layers of management do we need in the field?
- What's the right ratio of control for our district manager—seven, eight, twelve reps per manager?
- Should a customer be served by one rep or a team? If a team, what players should be on the team?

- Should we have a national or a key accounts organization?
- How much teamwork and coordination do we need for our accounts?
- What type of support should we provide at headquarters and at regional and district offices?
- Do we really need all those positions and people?
- How much should our field sales force cost? How much should it produce?

Today, we see sales forces organized and deployed by:

- *Geography*.
    —It still makes sense in many markets
- *Product*.
    —Product line or group
    —Custom or off the shelf
    —With "specialists" and "generalists"
- *Market*.
    —Industry or segment
    —Channel of distribution (OEM—i.e., original equipment manufacturer, direct, dealer)
- *Customer*.
    —Customer classification (A, B, C, "key" or "national" account) based on such factors as size, current or potential profits, or sales volume
    —Type of customer (user, dealer, retailer, wholesaler, institution, government)
    —Customer decision-making process (headquarters, purchasing, general management, committee, buying group)
    —New versus old customers or accounts
    —Other customer characteristics (culture, sex, race, religious affiliation)
- *Individual account teams.*
- *Other factors.*
    —Value-added opportunity (tech service, applications, R&D, "just-in-time," custom, or off the shelf)
    —New versus old territories
    —Skill level required for the sales reps ("easy" or "difficult" territory)

Organizing Your Sales Effort

Keep the following principles in mind when determining how to organize your sales effort:

- There is no right way to structure a sales force. You can probably make any sensible structure work—if it is done right.
- Your marketplace is always changing—and so should you. Change, if managed correctly, can have a positive impact on the sales effort. In fact, a company that has not changed its sales effort in some way in the last two years may be headed for disaster.
- Whichever way you organize your sales force, roles and performance expectations must be clearly defined, communicated, and reinforced at every level.
- There is always a way to do it better. Never stop trying to improve.

6.2   Developing the Best Sales Organization

There are three key elements of the sales process that dictate the best roles and positions for your sales organization: competitive position, customers, and corporate culture (see Figure 6-1).

Competitive Position and Business Strategy

You must examine your overall business strategy from the perspective of your sales force. It is particularly important that you understand:

Figure 6-1. Three key elements of the sales process.

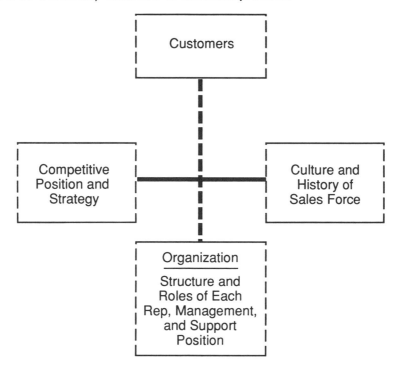

- Why your company has been successful in the past relative to your competition (e.g., product/service features, price, quality, innovation, delivery, service, technical capabilities, salespeople, and so on)
- Where your company is heading strategically (how you are investing to establish a position of advantage)
- Which objectives, when achieved, will tell you that you have arrived
- Which markets you will pursue
- What the best means are of approaching those markets (directly or via distribution, brokers, or reps, direct mail, and so on)

Most important, you must understand what role the sales force has played and will play in implementing your strategy.

Business strategy has gone through an evolution that has benefited the sales force and drawn more attention to how sales efforts are organized and managed. In the 1970s and early 1980s, top management focused on the best businesses to enter, not on how to make the most of the businesses that were already in the portfolio. (The exceptions, of course, were those businesses that were selected for investment.) In retrospect, the focus on portfolio strategy provided little help for the sales force, unless it was fortunate enough to be in a "star" business, and was actually detrimental, given the excessive short-term concern about field expense-to-sales ratios in businesses deemed "cows" or, even worse, "dogs."

More recent strategic thinking suggests that management concentrate on improving the businesses that the organization already operates. This, in turn, directs us to three variables that greatly influence the structure and operations of the sales force: *services* to the customer, *cost/profits* at the individual customer level, and *time* to respond to and service customers.

The following trends, consistent with current strategic thinking, are evident in sales organizations across many industries:

- Sales organizations are becoming flatter and much more service oriented than they have been in the recent past. This is consistent with the overall emphasis, in every industry, on time-based competition, service, and attention to the customer.
- Each sales rep/account manager tends to have fewer but larger customers than in the past. In many industries, this is true because "customers" are reducing the number of suppliers and increasing the importance of, and dependence on, the remaining "partners" that supply them, primarily on a "just-in-time" basis.
- Relationships with customers are becoming stronger and tend to involve top managements of both supplier and customer more

than in the past, particularly in those customer industries where the number of suppliers has been greatly reduced.

- The need for coordination among the various customer contact and supporting positions has complicated the jobs of most sales reps/account managers and sales managers.
- The number of management levels in the field has been reduced, placing greater responsibility, authority, and accountability on the first- and second-level management positions. In many companies, this has actually increased the number of field managers, each of whom is responsible for fewer sales reps.
- Telemarketing units have assumed the responsibility for covering medium and small accounts and have proved to be quite useful in maximizing the effectiveness of costly (and valuable) field sales resources.
- Companies pursuing "time-based" strategies are decentralizing their sales forces and giving more decision-making authority to field managers to minimize response time to customers.
- More managers are being moved to the field, along with additional supporting resources.
- Field managers are being given responsibility for "bottom-line" profits.
- Many customer product sales forces are in transition as customers—grocery, retail, and discount chains—shift decision making from the store or local department level to headquarters.
- Manufacturers are restructuring their sales forces, placing much more emphasis on the account manager position.
- Many of the tasks and responsibilities traditionally fulfilled by direct field people are being subcontracted to third parties.

Customers

Not surprisingly, customers can provide the answers to most of your important business decisions. Therefore, fundamental to organizing your selling effort is a thorough analysis of how your customers think, how they do business, how they make buying and new product decisions, how customer buying centers vary across your product line (if they do), what customers are buying from your company (product, service, value-added by sales rep, tech service, dependability, and so on), and what it costs (and with what profits) to sell and service each account.

How complex is the sale? What is required to win the order? What resources are needed to support the sales rep and serve the customer? Are your customers interested in "partnership" relationships with suppliers, or are sales of a more transactional nature? What is the potential of each account, and what, if anything, can be done to expand sales potential? Is there an attractive cost-benefit relationship associated with that expansion opportunity? Keep in mind that these practices and characteristics differ by industry, segment and, most importantly, customer.

Examine the field decision-making, coordination, and communications processes in light of what is needed to implement your business strategy. If you are to establish and maintain a strategic edge on your competition, how quickly must pricing, new product development, and project priority decisions be made to respond to and service customers and prospects? How many layers of management are needed—or can be tolerated—between the customer and your final decision makers to make those decisions? What type of coordination is needed among various levels and positions to pursue, respond to, and service your accounts? What field and headquarters costs can be tolerated to meet those time and authority requirements called for in your strategy and by your customers?

Culture

Your company's culture—its value system and the way it gets things done—has a tremendous influence on your field structure. Whether the culture is, at any point in time, as "good" as it should be is irrelevant; it will still have an influence that must be accommodated. Independence and levels of authority; the relationships between marketing, manufacturing, and financial orientation of management; short-term versus long-term focus; risk orientation; innovation and creativity; sense of urgency; customer orientation; position of sales in the professional and management career tracks, and so on, will all influence the type of people drawn to the sales organization, how responsibilities are allocated among them, and how they are deployed.

You must determine, on the basis of these factors, how people in each position should spend their time during a day or a week. The best way to do this might be to conduct a detailed activity analysis of your sales force, comparing the current tasks, call frequency and times, and call routing patterns with those that are needed to serve your customers and implement your strategy. This analysis will indicate the proper staffing levels for each position. Where you find gaps in responsibilities or coordination, you will have to create, modify, or even eliminate positions.

The number and type of field management positions and the appropriate staffing levels of field managers are functions of several variables, many of which are cultural in nature, for example:

- Management's role in each sale and its relationship with customers
- Levels of authority

- Management's need or desire to be close to customers
- The span of control
- The sales reps' skill level or experience

6.3 Who Is the Entrepreneur?

Every sales force in every industry has at least one position that is the entrepreneur, or mover and shaker—by tradition, market/strategic need, or both. This position controls sales and the relationships with the decision makers in the customers' organization. The entrepreneur may be the account manager, the district manager, or even the president. (If the role of entrepreneur varies with the individual, an organization is not under control.)

The two questions you need to ask are, In which position or positions are the entrepreneurs? In which ones should they be? The answers should be functions of the marketplace and of the fundamental strategy of the company.

In markets where there are very few customers and every one is necessary for the company's success (e.g., a one-product company with a monopoly ingredient for brewers), the vice-president of sales or even the president may be the best entrepreneur and in control of the sale, particularly for the crucial pricing negotiations. In markets where there are pockets of major accounts (e.g., hospital buying groups, which purchase on contract), the district or regional manager might be the best one to direct and control the sales relationship with each account, leaving the sales reps to service the individual accounts and ensure local compliance with the group contracts.

In a highly fragmented marketplace (e.g., hospitals, before buying groups were significant), where there is a broad product line to sell, the sales rep is probably in the best position to control all aspects of the sale as well as the overall relationship. If the account manager provides or controls the flow of technical and problem-solving skills to the customer, and that is the source of the value-added that the customer is buying, the account manager is probably the entrepreneur.

It is important to identify the entrepreneur because the organization should be structured and managed to support and reward the entrepreneur in his or her efforts to serve the customer. If it is not, the organization is not functioning as efficiently as it should. As noted above, your strategy and your marketplace—i.e., your customers—dictate which position (or positions) should be the entrepreneur(s) in your sales organization. The position that actually is the entrepreneur, however, is more than likely determined by a combination of tradition, culture, and the specific individuals in your sales organization.

This analysis of your customers, business strategy, and culture will allow you to identify the tasks and responsibilities that are needed and the emphasis you should place within the sales organization. You will determine the appropriate role and impact of the various types of sales reps, field managers, and support people. And, most important, you will understand what positions(s) *should* be entrepreneurial, as well as its (their) appropriate support systems.

In this discussion about organizational structure, we have not used one organizational chart. This is deliberate. Organizational charts tend to oversimply how organizations actually function. They focus too much on internal relationships and not enough on what the sales organization is trying to accomplish, that is, serving your customers better than your competitors do. We have tried to help you determine what types of positions and people you need to implement your sales strategy. You may draw boxes around the positions with lines connecting many of them, if you wish. But before you do, think through what's needed in a thorough, logical, and strategic way.

6.4 Alternative Sales Force Configuration: Searching for a Better Use of Sales Resources

A common but inadequate measure of sales force efficiency is dollars of sales revenue per sales representative. By dividing total sales by the number of sales reps, many managers think they have determined the contribution of their sales reps. By comparing this ratio with those of the competition and of companies in similar businesses, they gauge their company's efficiency and reduce or expand their sales forces as a result. Because it ignores the complexity of the sales task and draws comparisons that fail to highlight important differences between sales forces, this ratio is too simplistic a way to measure the efficiency of a sales force and make staffing decisions.

To improve the use of sales resources, begin with a careful analysis of the sales requirements, based on an assessment of the market and consideration of alternatives. The specific steps in this process are:

- Classifying the customer base by priority and by the requirements to be met
- Analyzing each group's selling task
- Evaluating alternative ways to perform sales tasks
- Establishing sales assignments

As previously noted, a disciplined analysis of the market provides the foundation for this process. It will help you achieve a better understanding of sales needs, so that you can effectively match sales capacity to the needs of the marketplace.

Segmenting the Customer Base

The first step is to segment the account base by type of customer, considering both the priority you give the account and the requirements to be met. Prioritize accounts by size, profitability, and growth potential. What you must provide a customer group is determined by the customer product-user requirements and the way the client company makes purchase decisions. Product- and service-user requirements include such factors as level of service, product quality levels, variety of products, and delivery and response time. To understand the purchasing decisions, you must have a good grasp of who makes and who influences the selection of vendors, the importance the customer places on price versus quality, and purchasing cycles and needs for special terms.

Analyzing the Selling Tasks

The next step is to specify the sales activities required to serve each type of account and the time that should be allocated to each activity. Determine the type and estimate the number and frequency of in-person calls for sales, reorders, relationship maintenance, and technical service; telephone contacts; correspondence; and other activities associated with each account.

The set of activities will differ for each customer group. For example, potential new accounts will require prospecting and familiarization activities, established accounts will need an emphasis on account maintenance and service, and highly competitive accounts will call for intensive coverage and a strong selling effort.

Although the program for each customer group will be different, be sure that each group sales program meets the following criteria:

- The program must reflect the mutual needs of customers and the company.
- The set of activities must effectively counter the competition.
- The nature of the activities and the time spent reflect the priority given to each customer group.
- The program provides the required level of account coverage at the lowest cost.

Evaluating Alternative Ways to Perform Sales Tasks

Developing the best program is usually a process of trial and error. For each customer group, you must consider a number of approaches. For example:

- Different levels of attention to the top accounts
- Reducing the number of, or eliminating, calls to the smaller accounts
- Using more phone contact to reduce in-person calls
- Moving from direct calls to direct mail to replace prospecting calls

Developing a sales program is not an exact science; not every contingency affecting a sales activity can be anticipated. Certainly, the program cannot be refined in the same way a time study calculates production line activities. However, if you carefully analyze and assess alternative approaches for each customer group, you will obtain useful results.

Establishing Sales Assignments

Once you have developed the sales program for each customer group, you can establish territories for the field sales reps. To determine the territory size that can be covered effectively by each sales rep, add the time needed to serve each customer and the associated travel time. A visual technique is to mark the accounts and prospects to be covered on a map, coding them by type and priority. This will show clusters of accounts and may indicate natural territories.

The process of developing efficient territory assignments also involves some trial and error. Where extensive travel time is required, such as when large geographic territories must be covered with many in-person calls, you can design alternative travel schedules and routes and calculate costs to achieve better territory structuring and sales rep placement. You may want to use some of the computer programs available for this purpose to design the deployment of very large sales forces.

Field sales costs are the major cost element in sales and marketing. To make the most of your sales resources, you need to match them with the requirements of the marketplace in a comprehensive analysis of the sales tasks the reps should perform, the time allocated to perform these tasks, and the ways they will differ among customer groups. Once you have determined these factors, you can design alternative ways to perform the sales tasks and to size and deploy the field sales force for best effect.

6.5   Segmenting the Sales Force to Improve Allocation of Sales Resources

The growing complexity of many markets and the resulting increase in the sophistication of the selling task have encouraged sales managers to consider sales force segmentation. By assigning different types of accounts to groups of specialized sales reps, you can often greatly improve the effectiveness of your sales force. Segmentation makes it possible for your salespeople to obtain product knowledge and selling expertise that a general sales force, covering all types of customers, could not develop. However, you should approach specialization cautiously to ensure that it is truly cost-effective and that the (usually higher) cost of a segmented sales force will be justified by greater sales effectiveness.

There are a number of ways to segment your field sales force, for example, by product, by large account, by industry, and by channel of distribution.

Product

Use this approach when reps must be thoroughly knowledgeable about products or services to deal successfully with a sophisticated customer. (Examples of such products include data processing hardware, pharmaceuticals, and high-tech equipment.) If you choose this approach, you will probably want to hire reps who have backgrounds in particular lines and train them to be experts in a particular product area. One problem with specialization by product is that several reps may call on a single customer, which raises the problem of account coordination. The solution is to coordinate call schedules and have the overall account relationship managed by a designated rep or by the field manager.

Large Accounts

Segmenting by large accounts means that a small group is assigned to a few large accounts. This is a commonly used approach. Large accounts, important because of their size, frequently pose special selling problems because of their organization complexities. An intricate matrix of buyers, users, and influencers may call for a special executive type of sales rep with special relationship skills. One problem with this structure is that it often creates, among the large account group, an elitist attitude that can cause friction with the rest of the sales force. But, by the same token, large account specialization can provide a desirable career path for top performers.

Industry

Specializing by industry can be an effective way to penetrate a sector. For example, computer manufacturers that sell to such industries as banking, stock brokerage firms, or utilities often find that they can most effectively address these industries with dedicated sales forces. This allows them to develop sales reps who understand the language and mentality of the customers and to penetrate the network of relationships that are so often encountered in these industries. A common pitfall of this approach is that sales managers may establish dedicated groups for industries that do not really require special treatment. In such cases, the additional cost of the group is not justified.

Distribution Channel

Specializing by distribution channel is another way to obtain specific selling expertise. Industrial companies that sell both directly and through distributors frequently divide their sales forces into groups this way. A package goods manufacturer, for example, may have one group of sales reps calling on buyers for the large regional supermarket chains and another selling to convenience stores. Again, the channels of distribution must differ sufficiently to justify this segmentation.

You can usually enhance the efficiency of your sales force by segmenting it. This may help the company increase market share. There are trade-offs, however, that must be given serious consideration before you decide to restructure. Most frequently, when you move from a general to a specialized sales force, the reps will spend more time traveling and thus will have less time available to spend with customers. Will their specialized skills offset this disadvantage? Moreover, managing a segmented sales force is a more complex task and, for the most part, a more costly one.

Travel cost increases will vary with the size of the sales force and the geographic distribution of customers. If a large general sales force with one thousand reps covering all customers is reorganized into two specialized sales forces of five hundred each, travel costs will not greatly increase. However, if a twenty-rep national sales force is divided into two groups, the travel time will greatly increase, because both units must cover national markets. Look at each situation in detail. For example, you might analyze the potential for large group segmentation and discover that all of the large accounts are in New York and Chicago, and that additional travel costs would be small. A company considering segmentation by industry might find that all customers in a proposed chemical industry group are concentrated in the New York-to-Baltimore corridor and along the Gulf Coast. In each of these situations, the increases in travel costs would be slight.

Although you can estimate the potential costs of a specialized sales force fairly accurately, estimating the benefits of segmentation is more of a judgment call. However, there is often evidence available to influence the judgment. If a competing company has recently changed to specialization, for example, you may be able to gauge the impact of the change on the competitor's market position. Or you may already have specialists within your sales force—reps whose backgrounds or training make them such. Comparing their performance with that of more typical sales reps can yield insights into the probable results of segmentation. Finally, conducting a field test—reorganizing a single territory on a segmented basis—can provide valuable information about the potential of segmentation.

Segmenting the sales force is a good idea if the products sold are complex or if several of the markets served are so different that only specialists can handle them effectively. But do not change over unless the benefits outweigh the costs of increased travel and of a more complex sales management task.

7

The Competitive Frame of Reference

7.1 Devising a Compensation Strategy

Of the various markets in which a corporation can be a player, labor resources is one of the most important. Skilled sales talent represents a rare and valuable commodity. To be a player, a company must first identify its position in the market and then develop its strategy.

It is not always true that a company's position is the same from market to market, nor that its list of direct competitors is identical.

For example:

- A company might pay above-market wages to attract and retain a highly talented financial manager, while offering only average wages, but extensive training, to entry-level sales force candidates.
- A company could choose to be a high-quality, high-value-added, and higher-priced seller in its product market. Because the product itself may well have a strong role in the purchase decision, the prominence of the sales job may be lower. As a result, the logic to pay top dollar for top sales talent becomes less compelling.

Companies frequently consider their direct and similarly positioned product market competitors to be their comparable labor market competitors as well. Ironically, it's very often not the case at all. A more strategic approach involves answering the following questions:

- What market segment are you competing in?
- What is your best strategic positioning?

To define its labor market segment, a company must first define the proper selling roles for its sales reps and the types of skills needed to be effective in those roles (see Chapters 4 and 6 for a discussion of the various selling roles). Depending on a company's product/market strategy and its degree of reliance on the sales force, the selling role can take one of several different tracks. Examples include:

- Obtaining new accounts (prospector)
- Keeping existing accounts (maintainer)
- Improving penetration (relationship manager)
- Providing technical expertise (product/vertical market specialist)
- Gathering and providing information (detailer)

Just as the labor markets for sales reps and for accountants are different, so are the labor market segments for each of the various sets of selling skills. Therefore, you should define the market for sales talent to include those companies that could also employ similar sales talent. Often, this is a broader group than simply those companies which sell similar products.

The competitive position that a company will take in its labor market depends on several other business factors. Competitive position is defined by two parameters:

1. *Average total compensation.* The sum of salary and bonus paid to the average sales rep. This often equates to average W-2 earnings for the sales force.
2. *Dispersion of pay within the sales force.* This is a measure of both the opportunity for extra pay and the downside compensation risk accepted by the sales rep.

A company's labor market strategy is defined by its market comparison curve (see Figure 7-1). Both the size (What will an average performer

Figure 7-1. Comparison of total compensation levels: company vs. market.

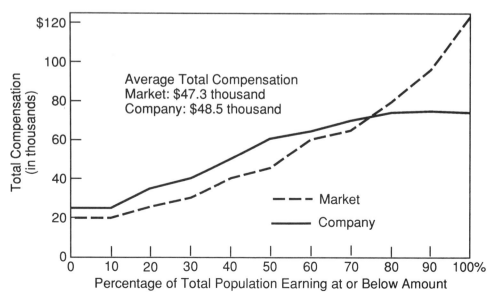

probably make?) and the shape (What is he assured of? What's his maximum opportunity?) are used to define a company's labor market strategy.

Examples of various sales force compensation strategies include:

• *High risk/high reward but a typical average budget*—a sales strategy with an emphasis on prospecting. The sales rep by his or her skills, energy, or ingenuity can make a major difference in territory results. Spending money on low performers is a lost opportunity. A more successful prospector could be mining the territory.

• *Lower risk and reward but high average pay*—characterizes a senior relationship manager whose sales cycle is long and whose territory sales volume is irregular. Stability, experience, and personal qualifications are all characteristics of the successful relationship manager. The relatively assured compensation will encourage selling for the long run, and the higher average pay can help retain qualified talent. High turnover among a company's relationship managers can be disastrous.

• *Lower-risk compensation/average pay levels*—a combination often used to attract entry-level sales personnel during their initial period of in-the-field training and maturing.

Another example of wasteful turnover occurs during the first year of employment when promising but unproven reps resign for economic reasons before they or their managers can decide on their true career potential. Recruiting and training costs can skyrocket as a result of this predicament. Territories remain underdeveloped and first-line managers are diverted from their real duties to become recruiters.

• *Lower risk and opportunity/higher pay levels*—the practice of hiring sales reps with superior qualifications, characteristic of consumer package goods companies. The intent is to move the entry-level reps through the organization as the first step to a management career in marketing, product management, or general management. In all cases, field experience is used as a training ground more than as a proving ground.

7.2 Defining What Information You Need

Gaining reliable market data is not easy. To be sure, the cocktail lounge at any airport can be a wellspring of information on what sales professionals make. But is it reliable? The information you gather depends on the time of the year and more frequently on the lateness of the hour. "Maximum potential earnings" have a way of becoming "average actual earnings." Other prolific, but often unreliable, sources include search agencies and exit interviews. How, then, does a company gain reliable intelligence?

Like most worthwhile endeavors, obtaining the information will require some work. For both of these reasons, the first step is to define what information is needed. Because you are trying to design a competitive labor market strategy, market descriptions are important. The key statistical measures include:

- *Defining those companies that are labor market competitors.* Which companies have been useful sources for some of your most successful reps? Which outfits seem to steal your best people? These may or may not be the same competitors you fight with for shelf space or for a specific contract out for bid.

- *Identifying the average total compensation for those competitive companies.* In most cases, last year's W-2 earnings can act as a surrogate for total compensation. Be careful not to get tripped up by either deferred compensation plans, 401(k) or otherwise, or by other types of delayed payment plan. Clearly define the year of actual payment and the year during which performance was measured for incentive purposes. Also, it is important to evaluate full-year data only. Therefore, you should eliminate all part-year employees from the data or correctly annualize their total compensation.

- *Calibrating the degree of variability with each company's compensation plan.* The real objective in this step is to define the pay/performance profile for each company in the labor market. Presumably, higher-paid employees are also higher performers. Accepting this premise, your ideal information would appear as in Figure 7-2. The key statistic is the ratio of actual pay to median (or average) pay for various segments of a company's sales force. To draw conclusions, you must know the total compensation for the following levels of the organization:

  — *Twenty-fifth percentile.* The level of total compensation that 25 percent of the sales force are expected to be at or below.
  — *Median.* The level of W-2 earnings that half of the sales force are expected to equal or to exceed.
  — *Seventy-fifth percentile.* The level of total compensation that 75 percent of the sales force are expected to be at or below.
  — *Highest paid.* The total compensation of the highest-paid rep in the sales force.

- *Evaluating the diversity of practice within the industry.* You still don't know whether all companies adhere to this mainstream payline or whether there are diverse approaches to this market. This last piece of information is obtained by comparing the two basic statistics, average pay levels and variability profiles, of each surveyed company against the overall survey averages and then describing how much the companies

Figure 7-2. Definition of competitive compensation: median of response.

Pay/Performance Profile	Sales Force's 19X8 Average Earnings $51,300	Mid-Range $47,200–$55,700
	Ratio to Sales Force Median	
10th	.73	.65– .80
25th	.82	.75– .90
Median	1.00	.92–1.09
75th	1.21	1.15–1.35
90th	1.37	1.30–1.40
Highest	1.65	1.50–2.30

vary either by a frequency distribution of the actual practices or by a range of results.

The flat pay/performance profile reflects the nature of the jobs (often entry-level detailers) as well as a means of preventing extraordinarily high levels of earnings that could tempt the sales rep to tarry a while in the field rather than to move into headquarters to get on with his career.

The company has to pay above-average compensation to attract highly qualified individuals, who can possibly earn more in other fields. In deciding on the overall average compensation levels it will offer, the company should consider how it stands on issues relevant to the sales rep. Some of these could include:

— Nature of automobile reimbursement or provision
— Expense account policies
— Employee benefit plans
— Training and education programs
— Prestige or desirability of the company's identity or location of territory
— Career stability and potential: as a rep, a supervisor, or in other fields

▪ *Collecting additional information to provide a context for analysis.* In addition to the data needed to calibrate the market (and your own company's position), it is often useful to have other facts for analysis. These can include the following:

— The type of plan (salary only, commission, bonus, or combinations) can help you to understand this variability and employees' perceptions of competitive practice.

— The use of draws and their degree of forgivability indicate the true compensation risk.

— Prevalence and amount of automobile plans, expense reimbursement, and employee benefits help establish a context for cash compensation numbers.

— Job turnover data can often be helpful in understanding the pay variability data, especially at the low end of performance.

— Such scope data as territory volume and number of accounts may have some usefulness in compensation analysis. However, these data are notorious for being misreported, sometimes on purpose.

7.3   Gathering Market Intelligence

As with any competitive analysis project, there is no universal or even single best source of information to tell you the amount and variability of the compensation paid by your relevant labor market competitors. Each of the various research sources has distinct benefits and limitations. To understand what role a survey has in your research, it may be useful to review each source of data.

Published Surveys

Sales managers have access to a variety of published surveys (see Section 5.6). Each survey has its own unique characteristics that may enhance or reduce its usefulness for your company's analysis. Some key questions include:

• Which companies participated in the study? Some surveys are skewed due to the nature of the publisher's normal client base. For example, several surveys are skewed toward the publishing company's clientele, the Fortune 500 companies. Another major survey has more than 80 percent of its participants below the $300 million level in sales. Does the size of the company make a difference in how much sales reps are paid to do the same job? Many times it does, and not in obvious directions. Smaller companies could have to pay more on average to attract trained reps away from larger companies that may provide extensive training but less attractive pay scales.

The sales rep position might be more prominent in a smaller company's marketing mix. In this case, more variable compensation programs could be offered. Also, some competitors may not use the same distribution channels as you do. Companies might sell only through distributors or to OEMs (original equipment manufacturers) or conduct some other practice that could affect the way the sales rep is paid. These differences don't necessarily invalidate the survey, but knowledge of them can at least help in the interpretation of results.

- What is the sample size for your relevant industry clusters? All surveys have certain industry groupings that are stronger than others. Because you intend to use the survey as a snapshot of your entire industry, there is strength in numbers—if the companies are relevant competitors. Beware of survey data that may be disproportionately affected by one or two megacompanies.

- Is the survey well documented? There are a number of widely published surveys that do not even disclose the participants making up the survey population. It is difficult to draw conclusions on blind data.

- Is compensation variability reported? There are several widely used surveys that collect data only on the average compensation of the respondents' sales forces. Be careful here. Statistics on high, low, seventy-fifth percentile, and so on, refer only to the dispersion of specific company average responses and not to the distribution of pay within a sales force. Data in the "high" column refer to the average compensation per person of the highest-paying company. You can't learn anything about how much the highest-paid rep in the entire survey is compensated from this statistic.

- How timely are the data? Some surveys are published biennially. Others have a long time lag in reporting, so that there could be a one- or two-year gap between the year in which incentives were earned and the year in which the survey is published. Unlike management surveys, a sales compensation survey must be published and evaluated annually to be useful. The labor market is too fluid and bonus levels can vary with business cycles. You have to stay on top of your data.

Because of the subtle differences in survey characteristics, you should use several different survey sources and then arrange the findings on one piece of paper to help in interpretation.

Custom Surveys

Very often, senior management will not feel comfortable with published surveys because of the age of the data or the relevance of the survey participants. In these circumstances, a custom survey may be necessary. When properly conducted, custom surveys can provide the most timely, verifiable, and accurate data on the labor market. Such accuracy is not without its costs, however, and the price a company pays is not always denominated in dollars. The most obvious nonmonetary cost is the time spent in gathering and documenting a compensation survey for both the participants and the surveyors themselves.

Because such data can be particularly sensitive, third-party consultants are usually retained to ensure objectivity, confidentiality, and accuracy. But not without cost.

Another cost is elapsed time. Even the most responsive consulting firm must depend on the cooperation of the participating human resources departments. There is usually a round of conversations between the consultant and the participants to ensure proper job matches and to clarify ambiguous data. Thus, even the most aggressive timetables will require five to eight weeks to gather the data.

A third, more subtle cost is the loss of any competitive advantage the analysis could provide. The price for your participants' cooperation is that they see the same information at the same time you do. Where's your competitive advantage?

All these costs have to be considered as partially offsetting the benefits derived from a custom survey.

Compensation Data Bases

Several consulting firms have ongoing compensation data bases in which they maintain annually updated files on the actual compensation and position scope data of management and professional positions. These firms have recently added a number of sales rep and sales manager positions to their data bases.

The appeal of the data base approach is that it can offer the focused selection of participants of a custom study combined with the speed and lower cost of a published survey. For this approach to be practical, the data base must have a number of your most relevant competitor companies already in the fold. You could then choose to run a selective data base extraction of the compensation data at those competitors. Alternatively, you might need certain companies whose data are indispensable to understanding your labor market.

This solicitation process, of course, requires much less cost and elapsed time than starting a survey from scratch. Industry clusters begin to form over time. When a data base is well represented in one segment—say, chemicals or business machines—then the remaining companies are quick to sign on.

Some companies have also found these dynamic data bases to be a cost-effective way of sponsoring an industry survey. The methodology forms, report formats, and software are already in place. The cost per company is nominal, well below $1,000. The dynamic data base approach also means that during any year one or several companies could be added or custom studies run without incurring the cost of a large project.

Data base consultants are, of course, more willing to help you in this regard.

Recruiting and Exit Interviews and Other Sources

The incentive element of sales force compensation can complicate communications. It is often very difficult to determine whether quoted compensation figures are the maximum opportunities, reasonable expectations, longer-term averages, or actual recent results. Depending on the source, your company could be depicted as being well above or well below the market. It all depends on the sources' motives in talking to you or about you.

Even specific information on a competitor's program is of limited help. Unless you know the stretch in the competitor's quota-setting process, and the size and growth potential of territories, it's often tricky to determine reliably the average compensation or the variability of the pay. Nevertheless, these sources can all help to verify and reinforce information from other sources. They have a place in your competitive analysis but not as the centerpiece.

7.4   Conducting a Custom Survey

Conducting a custom sales force compensation survey may not be the most cost-effective means of gathering market information, but there are times when you must do one to ensure the most timely input or the most precise selection of competitor companies.

A manager in charge of a sales compensation survey must strive for the best balance of costs and benefits. The primary objective, of course, is to gain the participation of certain specific competitors. Anything that inhibits participation is counterproductive. Yet questionnaires that are unduly comprehensive and lengthy are all too common. The logic seems to be as follows: "Because we're going to go to the expense of asking, we might as well get all the information we can." The result is a cumbersome questionnaire asking for superfluous information on job descriptions, job ranges, incentive plan designs, benefit programs, automobile policy details, territory volumes, commission formulas, and merit raise procedures. The size of the instructional guide or the questionnaire alone can discourage participation because of the time and effort required. Remember, for a survey document to survive, it has to move out of the compensation analyst's in-basket.

Remember also that such information is often kept in different departments—e.g., sales volume in marketing, salaries in human resources, incentive payments in finance. Even if the competitor company elects to participate in the survey, the lead time can be extended to the point where the timeless objective is compromised. Finally, keep in mind that the more information you request, the greater the chance that a competitor will refuse to participate because of concerns over confidentiality or legal issues.

The secret to a successful custom survey is to focus on the total compensation paid last year to each full-time sales rep of the competitor company. Additional information can help in understanding the context of the payments or can assure you that proper analysis has taken place at the competitor.

The objective of the custom survey is simply to understand the amount and variability of compensation within the companies participating in the survey. There is an obvious assumption that the selected group of companies is a balanced and representative cross section of your labor market for sales talent. The display of the necessary data can be equally straightforward.

You should make use of computer technology in gathering as well as in processing the raw survey data. There are several approaches you could take:

- Mail out a data collection worksheet to each participating company. You should format the workskeet as a .WK1 file, the Lotus 1-2-3 standard. Most competing spreadsheet products can be converted to this format.
- Request that the participants submit data in one of the standard relational data base formats, for example:
  —Paradox
  —d Base IV
  —SQL
  or as a flat (ASCII) file. There are utilities in most programs to make similar format conversions.
- As a last resort, request data in hard copy format.

When processing the survey data, you should also use a spreadsheet program. Although the ability to sort and interrelate data and the report generation capabilities are not as strong as relational data bases, spreadsheets are preferred. Why? They're easier to learn and use, and the number of trained operators is far greater. Many hands can speed the process. Professional survey firms may use more sophisticated programs or hardware, but consider the ubiquitous .WK1 files on a quality spreadsheet program with a reasonably powerful PC.

Figure 7-3 demonstrates the key information needed to describe the labor market fully. Processing this information is pretty straightforward if your data base is established by means of a spreadsheet program. Each record need consist of only three fields:

Figure 7-3. Data collection worksheet.

Company ————————————————

Division ————————————————

Position Code ————————————————

Effective Dates of Data

        Salary ————————————

        Incentives ———————————

Case Number	Total Compensation	Case Number	Total Compensation	Case Number	Total Compensation
1		21		41	
2		22		42	
3		23		43	
4		24		44	
5		25		45	
6		26		46	
7		27		47	
8		28		48	
9		29		49	
10		30		50	
11		31		51	
12		32		52	
13		33		53	
14		34		54	
15		35		55	
16		36		56	
17		37		57	
18		38		58	
19		39		59	
20		40		60	

Check all that apply: Incentive award is paid:

        Base salary ——————   Monthly ——————

        Commission ——————   Quarterly ——————

        Bonus ——————   Semiannually ——————

Company car or allowance ——————   Annually ——————

        Reimbursed expenses ——————   Other ——————

- Position code
- Employee case number
- Total compensation paid in most recent completed year

However, computer records could be optionally embellished in several ways:

- If you have a third party process the data, you could add a "company number" field to enable later analysis by company or by groups.
- Add separate yes/no indicators if the employee receives other economic items, such as automobile allowances, expense reimbursements, benefits eligibility, contest/promotion eligibility.
- Add the employee's actual salary, which may be of interest at times for salary plan purposes. It's not really necessary to understand the labor market, however.

To evaluate the market, you will need to sort the records. There are two basic approaches in evaluating the labor market. Each has its advantages and drawbacks. Depending on your needs, one or the other may be more appropriate.

The Total Market Approach

In this approach, your aim is to understand how much total compensation is paid to sales reps and how it is distributed among the universe of reps in the reporting companies. The end product of the analysis can be presented in graphic and tabular formats, as shown in Figure 7-4.

The graphic format clearly depicts the distribution of W-2 earnings among all the reps in the reporting companies. An arithmetic mean has been calculated and printed in the upper left-hand corner of the chart. To determine the pay at any level within the industry, simply scan across the X-axis to the desired segment—say, the eightieth percentile—and then read the Y-axis value for the line. The result is that level of W-2 earnings that equals or exceeds the pay delivered to 80 percent of the sales reps in your industry. Put another way, only one in five reps makes more than that amount.

Because most companies now classify their sales rep positions into several job titles or categories, usually from two to five, you could run separate analyses for each position. Note that extra effort is now required to be sure that the positions from different companies are grouped into comparable categories. To ensure proper matches, you should send out capsule job descriptions that will detail the years of experience required as well as the types of accounts called on, the breadth of products

Figure 7-4. Cumulative distribution of earnings: senior sales representative.

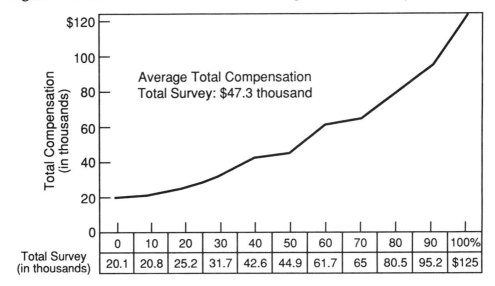

Percentage of Total Population Earning at or Below Amount

presented, and the degree of supervision the position either receives or provides to other positions.

If the data neatly separate, you might want to display your results on a single chart. Unfortunately, real world data are not usually this cooperative, so separate charts may work best.

The Market Analysis Approach

This second approach is based on the premise that the labor market is not dominated by a collection of individual sales reps but, instead, is composed of a group of companies that administer their programs to reinforce their own product/market strategies. From year to year, quotas and territories are revised and refined, and compensation policies determine the overall increase in the sales compensation budget. As with professionally published surveys, there are two statistics that are being measured by this method:

1. Overall average compensation cost per sales rep
2. The degree of difference (or dispersion) of actual W-2 earnings within the sales force

The logic of evaluating the two separate statistics is based on the following assumptions:

• The average compensation cost per sales rep is a "managed" number at most companies today. Sales managers set quotas and territories to correspond to a targeted earnings level for the "average" rep. Even when commissions are used for the incentive element, this targeting goes on. Either knowingly or not, territories or accounts are assigned and commission percentages are designed to reflect some notion of "a fair day's pay for a fair day's production."

• The degree of dispersion of actual compensation within a sales force will vary from company to company. The official (and informed) methods of assigning quotas and territories can be managed to provide equal compensation *opportunity* or equal compensation *in fact*. In either case, it can be instructive to understand how much more a well-paid (and presumably strongly performing) rep is compensated than is an average performer in the same sales force.

This two-step analysis addresses the question of whether one can advance his or her personal net worth by either moving to a higher-paying company or delivering stronger performance. The two-step process can be of significant benefit if you are planning a large survey or are in an industry with very large sales forces. Otherwise, you could exceed your computer's capacity or have a very time-consuming process. The data request to your participating companies is quite straightforward. Basically, you've asked them to rank their own sales reps by W-2 earnings. Either the entire sales force or several separate position categories can be reported. You then simply ask for the W-2 compensation for each company's:

• Median-paid rep
• Twenty-fifth percentile ranked by pay
• Seventy-fifth percentile ranked by pay
• Highest-paid rep

Once again, additonal information about automobile and expense reimbursement, benefits eligibility, and use of contests or other awards can be useful if not carried to an excess.

The computational steps you would take in your analysis are equally straightforward. In a nutshell, they are:

• Calculate the arithmetic mean of the responses to the average W-2 earnings per sales rep.
• Divide the compensation reported for other major distribution points for each company by that company's average compensation. The major points are:
　—Twenty-fifth percentile

—Seventy-fifth percentile
—Highest paid

Record this unit as a ratio (i.e., .98, 1.07, and so on).

The average unit compensation expense and the ratios for the major dispersion distribution points now define that company's compensation profile. In reporting the data, you could take one of several approaches. In order of usefulness, these are:

- Take the mean of each statistic and report the results as the overall industry practice.
- Compute the mean of the statistics and also represent key levels of how the companies varied by showing the twenty-fifth percentile, the seventy-fifth percentile, and the highest response from the list of companies.
- Assign each company a code letter (e.g., S) and then list each company's response or the ratio. This last approach, of course, requires a third-party consultant or service bureau to ensure confidentiality.

7.5 Interpreting the Raw Survey Data

To this point, you should have gathered as much market intelligence data as you could find. The next step is to interpret the raw information. To do this, recall the results you hope to achieve:

- A cumulative distribution of compensation for a representative sample of your labor market. Because this is often easier said than done, two desirable alternatives can achieve the same or better information.
- A distribution of the average pay lines, be they budget or actual expenditures, that competing companies allocate for their sales forces.
- An estimate of the degree or patterns for actual pay distribution within competing companies.

To accomplish this, your raw data must be adjusted and then interpreted. The adjustment part is easy. You should adjust each data source, whether it's a survey or a specific company's information for inflationary effect, from the period when the data were gathered to the day of the analysis. This is particularly critical with sales compensation data because the period of performance and of pay delivery will tend to be further in the past than with management compensation surveys.

A second key issue is assessing sales force compensation in the industry's business cycle. Most sales incentive payments will be higher during stronger business years. Commission plans and the natural lag in sales volume and quota forecasts will ensure this cyclical effect. When interpreting data from different years, you must include the effect of these cycles in your interpretation.

To organize your assessment, try a control sheet similar to the one shown in Figure 7-5. To avoid confusion, adjust the data for aging before entering it on this chart. As the exhibit indicates, the data collection process won't be perfect, and there will be numerous holes and inconsistencies. As a manager, you're paid to make decisions based on less than complete and perfect information, right? Here's another case:

After the data are arranged, your task will be to make a judgmental composite of both the distribution of average pay lines and the amount of dispersion in the way compensation is delivered to the various types of performers within the sales force. When making this evaluation, there are a number of factors to keep in mind. Some of these considerations follow:

- If the company or survey group is dominated by certain larger companies that provide strong training or entry-level opportunities, total compensation may be somewhat lower, on average, and dispersion less pronounced because of the entry-level personnel.

Figure 7-5. Data analysis control sheet (dollar amounts in thousands).

	Data Source	Efffective Date	Percentile Distribution				
			Low	25	50	75	High
1.	XYZ Industry Group Survey	7/1/90		$29.7	$33.0	$37.0	
2.	Company A Pay Range	7/1/90	28.0		37.5		85.0
3.	Company B Plan Document	7/1/90			43.2		
4.	Company C Actual	7/1/90					67.0
5.	TPF&C—Consumer	7/1/90	25.5	31.1	42.4	51.4	69.9
6.	TPF&C Office Equipment	7/1/90			48.2		57.0
7.	Confidential Interviews	7/1/90			32.0		40.0
8.	ECS Consumer Durable	7/1/90		45.0	51.5	58.2	
9.							
10.							
11.							
	Composite		$27.0	$35.0	$41.5	$50.0	$63.2

- Once again, a strong fear for the industry could show misleadingly high compensation levels as well as upside dispersion.
- The reliability and degree of survey documentation should affect your judgment on how much weight each data source should receive.

After you have devised the judgmental composite of the labor market compensation profile, you can define the parameters of your overall compensation strategy. The results of this exercise can tell you how much you will want to pay on an overall budgetary basis and how you want to disperse the compensation to the various performance levels within your organization.

8

The Goal-Setting Process

8.1 Why Goal Setting Is Important

Sales reps are among the most goal-oriented people. What makes a sales job so exciting is the fact that the rep is out there alone, with just the customer and a goal.

With all sales jobs, some measurement of sales performance always exists, whether it is based on a period of time (monthly, quarterly, or yearly), on volume, or on some other factor. It may be called quota, target, or expectation—but it's still a goal.

If you ask a cross section of your reps to list their goals, the responses might surprise you. Some reps will mention one or two areas without being specific. Others will be very specific. Still others will list the company's stated goals and some personal goals. Most, however, will probably cite goals whose achievement is treated by the compensation program.

Whenever a company announces a new sales compensation plan and assigns territories, reps can usually determine at once how they feel about the plan. Goals and performance help shape their response. Some plans (often bonus plans) explicitly set goals, whereas others (often commission plans) provide inherent, unstated goals that depend on the income aspirations of the sales reps.

A sales compensation program provides the means by which you can establish the goals to be driven and reinforced by the sales incentive plan. You can set goals in as simple or as complex a fashion as your sales managers, information systems, and communications systems can handle. As a general guideline, more than three or four distinct goals in a given time period will diffuse sales focus, but these goals (and their relative incentive plan weight) can vary by territory. Other goals over and above any incentive directives (e.g., teamwork, paperwork, service level) can be incorporated into the overall system if meaningfully communicated and treated as part of the overall assessment at the time of a salary review.

To be effective, however, goals must be meaningful and fair. And they must be clearly communicated. Management must strive for goal clarity, a state in which individuals know what is expected of them and how their roles fit within the company's strategy. Too often organizations ignore these guiding principles, creating confusion or discontent among the sales force. Therefore, in setting and stating goals, consider the consequences carefully.

8.2   Illustrating Explicit Quotas

Sales managers can incorporate sales quotas into a field sales compensation program in a variety of ways. These include:

- Base salary validation
- Thresholds
- Commission accelerators
- Quota "kickers"

You should base the precise form of the sales quota upon the objectives you are trying to accomplish with the sales force and, of course, the ability of your management processes and measurement systems to support the plan's design.

Base Salary Validation

Base salary validation provides the easiest method of setting sales goals. Assume that you have two sales reps whose respective base salaries are $35,000 and $30,000 per year and that you want to pay reps a 5 percent commission after the attainment of a minimal level of acceptable sales performance. If you set an equal sales goal for both reps (for example, $500,000), you might be criticized for inappropriately determining equitable performance standards, for one might assume that the sales rep with the higher base salary is more experienced and more able to carry a higher level of expected performance. By dividing their base salaries by the commission rate, you can convert their compensation to an equivalent level of sales performance, thus setting a sales goal that represents an equal relationship between expected performance and compensation. For example, the sales rep earning $30,000 would have a $600,000 quota, while the one earning $35,000 would have a $700,000 quota. (Whether you should consider such a mechanical approach to quota setting is an issue that will be discussed later in this chapter.) Note that this approach to quota setting creates a disguised commission, in that the base salary represents a more stable element of the compensation program. In some ways, it resembles a draw. Unlike a commission plan, however, the base salary would not have to be recaptured if the sales rep did not attain the required sales. Over the long run, sales management would have to weed out unacceptable performers from the sales force rather than have the commission plan eliminate those who couldn't meet the sales challenge.

Thresholds

Thresholds represent another way to set sales quotas. In some ways, thresholds parallel the base salary validation approach but without the direct link to a rep's earned compensation. For example, you might provide no incentives for the first $500,000 of sales, 10 percent on the next $500,000, 8 percent on the next $1 million, and 5 percent on all sales in excess of $2 million.

Commission Accelerators

On the other hand, commissions can accelerate with higher levels of sales performance or with the introduction of new product lines or expansion into new customer bases. Suppose that you want to encourage rapid introduction of a new product line that will require your sales force to direct more time and energy to nontraditional customers. In addition to the introduction of a new product commission schedule, you might also consider an additional commission on sales of existing product lines, once some level of new product sales is attained. For example, you might say that in addition to the commission for the new product, if you attain new product shipments of $300,000 by the first quarter (net of returns and/or allowances), you will receive an additional 5 percent commission on all other product sales for the year. If you attain $300,000 in new product sales by the second quarter, you will receive an additional 2½ percent commission on all other product sales for the year. Furthermore, there will be no additional commission for new product shipments during the last half of the year, except for the basic commission associated with the product.

Quota "Kickers"

In some industries, the need to achieve balanced line sales in each territory is paramount. Instead of merely setting individual product line quotas and related commissions and hoping for the best, the sales compensation plan can achieve this objective through a commission kicker based on quota attainment in each line. For example, assume that you are paying a graduated commission on three product lines, each representing the underlying profitability and difficulty of the sale. To reduce the inclination to sell only the product with the highest close rate, you could develop a plan that adds an additional commission at year end if aggregate quota attainment exceeds 100 percent (and each product line has at least 75 percent quota attainment). Clearly, this approach requires great confidence in your quota-setting process (if it is to be perceived as equitable) and sales reps must have confidence that they can attain some additional award. Furthermore, setting too low a quota in one product line can result in more volatility in the comparison of performance, allowing sales reps to "play off" the various plan elements to their economic advantage.

The issue of quota setting strikes at the heart of the commission-setting process. Because quotas integrate opportunity (as defined by territory characteristics) and performance (as measured by sales results), you have to be wary of performance assessments based solely on an individual's compensation. Absent specific information concerning territory characteristics (e.g., number of opportunities, concentration of customers, size, and business characteristics), you may be operating on the assumption (perhaps mistakenly) that all territories are equivalent and, therefore, a uniform commission structure will accurately represent individual performance.

On the other hand, your management task will become infinitely more complicated if you try to set individual quotas, in effect "handicapping" each member of your sales force by setting different rates to yield equivalent compensation for performance that is perceived to be "equivalent." Such as approach is time-consuming and your sales force will quickly perceive that you are managing compensation rather than performance. Unless weak performers are removed, this can have a chilling impact on motivation, as employees who are managing large territories/accounts see their compensation opportunities equivalent to those of other members of the sales force with lower performance.

Consequently, in setting commission quotas, you have to evaluate the outcome in light of the interaction of the commission rates and the nature of the territory. Sometimes the nature of the business is so long-term that the measurement of results (and hence the determination of an annual commission) can be misleading. This is especially true in circumstances where the development cycle is long, product specification is a critical task and, once accomplished, current year's sales results are more a result of the health of the customer's business than the sales rep's efforts. In these instances, the compensation plan should have a more long-term focus. For example, the sales rep's base salary range could be related to the nature of the territory volume and product mix as measured over a rolling time period. Some sales managers may view this technique as lacking, in that the retrospective focus in the compensation plan may result in a gradual erosion in performance.

8.3 Implicit Quotas

Although not all plans incorporate sales quotas explicitly in the income determination process, all plans contain implicit quotas. The implicit quota is represented by any of the countless patterns of performance results, which, if accomplished, enable the rep to outearn targeted (or comfortable) income levels. The danger inherent is quite apparent. The company has inadvertently promised to overpay (versus targets or average) under certain patterns of performance. If the sales rep can achieve that income "comfort level," while concentrating on certain aspects of the sales task to the exclusion of others, then the purpose of the plan is defeated. The sales rep can be expected to take "the path of least resistance" toward the highest possible income. The company must ensure that an unreasonably easy path cannot be selected.

8.4   The Limits of Revenue Accounting

Although it is a fact of life in business, traditional revenue accounting measures paint an incomplete and possibly misleading picture of effectiveness. Sales is a continuous process; revenue accounting recognizes only discrete twelve-month periods. Sales reps usually have their greatest influence on bookings, yet revenue accounting recognizes shipping and billing, at which point the sales rep's job may have been over for months. Furthermore, many sales rep activities affect future sales, or sales in other territories, or sales that will occur if other conditions (such as price competitiveness) are also met.

For these reasons, revenue accounting measures must usually be supplemented by measures that are closer to the control of the sales rep. For example, suppose that you have two reps and that each has landed a major account in the same industry. Both accounts need the part that you supply. Both reps have worked hard to be sure the customer has exactly what it needs: the right product specification, the necessary customizing, and so on. And both reps have great bookings to show for it.

The only trouble is that two years later, when your customers' products hit the market, one of the two products has a feature that sends sales through the roof, to the detriment of the other customer. One will now have to cancel shipments; the other will have to increase them. Except for some minor troubleshooting with regard to setting up delivery, your sales reps have both moved on to other prospects, secure in the knowledge that they have done a good job. Although both *have* done an excellent job, the revenue accounting system will show that one has terrific billings while the other is in a slump.

In fact, the key performance criterion, getting the product specified, is *not* captured in the current accounting system. The revenue accounting system becomes increasingly flawed as a measure of sales success when the product development and/or specification cycle is greater than the calendar year. In these instances, effective sales management mandates an activity-based performance system to supplement the accounting system. For example, identifying sales prospects, obtaining bid opportunities, closing the bid, and managing subsequent execution would more accurately represent the factors that should be measured to differentiate sales success.

One might conclude that in short-cycle sales processes (where there is a short time between the purchase decision and shipment) the revenue accounting system is not flawed. As is often the case, the answer is "it depends." If territory design has created balanced territories, then this indeed may be the case. On the other hand, consider the differences in performance measurement if one territory is made up of a group of customers concentrated in a small geographic area, while the other is dispersed over an area that requires four times the amount of travel to reach all customers. Clearly, the sales rep in the latter territory is going to have fewer opportunities to meet with her customers. Consequently, her sales level, as measured by the revenue accounting system, may not be as noteworthy as those of her colleague.

Notwithstanding the problems of accurately differentiating levels of sales performance, revenue accounting systems can be even more misleading if you hold the sales reps responsible for pricing and you are not able to track the gross margin of the products your sales reps are selling. If this were to occur, you could "give away the store" and not realize it. For example, if the accounting system tracks revenue, large volumes of business could be perceived as representing excellent sales performance. Unfortunately, if the outcome derives from inappropriate pricing, you may be on the road to disaster.

8.5 "Typical" Goal Setting

One of the most frustrating responsibilities for sales and marketing managers is setting equitable and realistic sales goals in relation to corporate strategies. Even as simple a tactic as distinguishing, via the incentive plan, between selling to new customers and selling to existing customers goes unused by many companies.

Part of the problem is that in pursuit of simplicity and fairness a sales manager may either divide up the regional sales quota, assigning an equal portion to each rep, or tie every rep's quota to his or her sales results from last year. These approaches may be simple, but they are rarely fair or effective.

To reflect territorial and other differences, the sales manager should assign to each rep a customized set of objectives (volume, product line, accounts, profit) along with a strategy for attaining them. This makes goal setting more complicated, but not too complicated, for the average rep to understand. Some managers worry that reps will see their increased involvement in goal setting as a chance for negotiation and will share only as much information as will strengthen their hand. These obstacles can be overcome, however, and the results are well worth the effort.

You should start with the assumption that if you pick a single number as a dollar-volume goal, that number will probably be wrong. It gives the illusion of precision but is based on a variety of assumptions and subjective judgments. You and the sales rep, however, can probably agree on a range of assumptions—regarding prices (yours and those of your competitors), production levels, interest rates—that represent the spectrum from "worst case" to "best case," with the "most likely case" equaling the dollar-volume goal. Incentive payments will usually rise steadily from the minimum (probably resulting in zero incentive payout) to the maximum.

Naturally, this combination of a top-down/bottom-up process lives or dies by the amount of information available. Given sufficient information about the market, the territory, and your corporation's plans, however, you and the sales rep can establish an equitable range of goals for each territory, thus creating effective motivation for each rep.

8.6 Top-Down Quota Allocation Approach

The goal-setting process typically involves the fragmentation of a large random number and the arbitrary allocation of a manufacturing forecast among sales territories. Let's consider the motivational implications of such an approach and evaluate the effectiveness of this method in accomplishing your principal objective: to ensure organizational success by selling customers products that generate a fair return on shareholders' investment.

Unfortunately, the planning scenario often has the following characteristics: Last year's sales represent the foundation for the planning process. A pricing decision is based on last year's sales figures and the increase in costs. This number crunching creates a financial model for the organization, but does it represent market realities?

Faced with a projection of sales volumes that, for example, have increased in aggregates of 10 percent from the prior year, the sales manager now has the challenge of allocating this "nut" to the regional and district sales managers. Furthermore, the financial model may have been predicated upon a specific product mix, which must also be distributed among the sales force if the corporation's overall goals are to be met.

So the goals come cascading down from on high. The allocation can take many forms: equal distribution by sales rep, allocation based upon last year's performance, a "push" into specific market segments, or allocation on the basis of sales reps' compensation. (Let's say the rep makes $x in base with a y percent commission; he or she will have to sell $z million to make target compensation.)

But where do the customer and your competitors enter into this equation? Because the model was manufacturing driven, you're selling what you're making; unfortunately, your competitors have redesigned their products in response to a market shift and you haven't gotten your company past the tooling stage. Or, perhaps more fortunately, you're leading your competitors into the market with a new product but you're only allocating 30 percent of production capacity to the new line. Sales demand is brisk and your sales force is forced to go on allocation, "spreading out" the supply so everyone is at least a little bit happy. This tactic, however, did not establish you as the principal supply for several dominant players.

The list of what-ifs is endless, but the message is the same. Top-down quota setting is fraught with peril, because it separates you from the most important source of information concerning your customers— i.e., your sales force. Who else spends more time in contact with the most important element in the success of your business? Who can tell you more about what the market is requiring, both now and in the future?

Unfortunately, rather than viewing the sales force as an ally, sales management often views it as an adversary. For example, management may suspect that wily sales reps "underestimate" product demand to get low quotas, or management may believe that the reps' job is limited solely to getting "this year's numbers, . . . so we'll let the marketing staff worry about two years out."

To do the job right, sales management needs information, lots of it. On the basis of customer demand and buying patterns and shifts in competitive pricing, the sales force can provide a bottom-up forecast of what can be sold, and at what price. You should then factor in this point of departure into the manufacturing plan to verify whether the company's financial goals can be met.

With this approach in hand, the sales force can strive to increase market share and profitability by selling what your customers want, rather than what you think they want. Customer-driven sales plans have a greater opportunity for success than do manufacturing-oriented programs.

8.7 Macro vs. Micro Goals

Even when the overall macro goal has been appropriately determined, the likelihood that it can be directly transferred into valid micro goals, which can adequately reflect individual sales goals, is slim. There are two principal causes for this problem. The first cause, *variability*, is based on the inevitable variability in such areas as customer requirements and buying patterns, which leads the sales rep to realize that goals do not reflect a specific target but rather a desired range of potential results that represent "satisfactory" performance.

Thus, the sales quota becomes a form of lottery in which the sales rep participates, assured of attaining some minimal level of satisfactory performance. In some years, if the rep is "lucky," performance will exceed norms; in others, he or she will "only" make quota.

The other factor, *time*, overlooks the reality that selling is an ongoing process, one that is not bound by the calendar. In fact, merely measuring the rep's performance in one year probably overlooks the single most important sales performance criterion: consistent sales over business cycles and changing market conditions.

8.8   Is a Dollar Equal to a Dollar?

Andy Salesengineer closed the year with $2 million in bookings, while Sarah Fieldsales finished with $3 million. Who had the better year and who deserves the higher pay?

Unless Andy and Sarah are selling to the same type of customer, you couldn't even begin to tell. Even if they did have similar sales roles, a single year's sales results might not be meaningful. If everything else were equal and the nature of the job made one year's sales relevant, Sarah had the better year. But these conditions occur less often than you might think.

Let's examine these points more carefully.

Figure 8-1 shows sales compensation versus volume for a fictional company with three different sales jobs. One force sells to major national accounts. A second sells to regional accounts large enough to merit direct sales coverage but not quite national in scope. A third sells to distributors (the distributor has its own sales force, marketing a wide variety of products to small accounts). To get items quickly, large accounts also buy from distributors on occasion.

The exhibit shows three distinct curves, all representing different linkages of sales dollars to compensation. The national salespeople manage a long-term account relationship. That curve starts higher, because higher levels of selling and technical knowledge are required. The curve, however, is fairly flat. Once the relationship is established, further sales are driven more by the national account's own successes. Regional sales reps don't need as much experience to undertake the job, but if they're good, they can have a dramatic influence on results through prospecting and penetration. Hence, the regional curve is steepest. The distributor sales role falls between that of national and regional roles, as does the distributor curve.

Figure 8-1. Sales volume vs. market value (regional, distributor, and national sales).

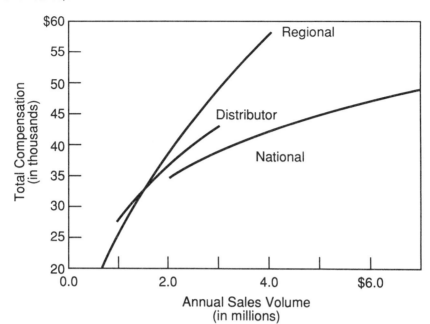

Is a dollar equal to a dollar? No. In this company's business, $3 million of sales requires selling skills commanding approximately $39,000 through national accounts, $43,000 through distributors, and $49,000 through regional accounts. Moreover, an extra dollar of sales is worth more in regional and distributor accounts and less in national accounts.

Note that these relationships vary from industry to industry. In some, the national and regional curves might be closer (or perhaps even reversed). So don't revamp your compensation systems to match these curves without first understanding the sales skills required in each role. But the basic point remains: A dollar of sales in one job isn't necessarily equal to a dollar in another.

All sales dollars aren't equal for another reason. Volume doesn't always provide the best way to measure results. For example, in the national sales job, you would find a fairly wide dispersion of pay versus sales volume, even in an organization where the best-paid salespeople are also the best performers. Why? Because selling national accounts is generally a long-term business, and the accounts most difficult to sell (and therefore requiring the highest selling skills) aren't always the largest. Other things being equal, more sales deserve more dollars, but things are equal less often in the national sales role than in most others.

Conversely, the regional role would probably have a tighter relationship of sales volume to performance, and the sales reps *within* the distributor organization would probably have the closest relationship of all.

The bottom line? Sales effectiveness can't always be measured in dollars. Some situations, per dollar of revenue, simply cost more to sell. And why not? We don't expect the ratios of R&D, advertising, or many other expenses to sales in the business world to be the same across different industries. Why should sales (which may sell related products, but to customers in different industries) be any different? Certain dollars of revenue indicate selling accomplishments better than others do.

8.9 Planning vs. Compensation Functions

One company faced the problem of dwindling sales. A corporate strategic planner offered her solution to the division general manager:

"We must spend more on marketing and improve our product quality," the planner recommended. "Furthermore," she added, "the sales force has been too complacent this year. It must sell more. With dedicated sales efforts, an improved product, and a bigger marketing budget, we must sell $100 million this year with $8 million net income. Actually, we ought to be able to sell $110 million."

"Eight million net!" exclaimed the general manager. "We did only $4 million last year."

"Nonetheless, we must strive for $110 million, or at least $100 million," said the planner. "There is no other way."

After considering the planner's advice, the divisional head decided to carry out the plan. He realized, however, that the company couldn't simply increase margins and marketing/product development expenses at the same time. Therefore, he trimmed 20 percent from the expense budget. Convinced that the sales organization really had been lax, he concluded that if he needed $100 million in sales, he'd better ask for $110 million.

The general manager called a meeting with his top sales managers to explain the situation. He concluded by telling them, "We've got to get $110 million in sales, and here are your quotas."

You know the rest of the story. The sales managers met with their sales reps, and each divided up the group's sales quota. The process continued until each dollar was allocated down the line.

Put yourself in the shoes of a rep who has managed to reach $1 million in sales the past year (an increase of 50 percent over the prior year). Her share of this year's quota is $1.5 million. Below $1.4 million she gets no incentive pay at all.

Other than increased anxiety among the field staff, what has been accomplished? A poor sales performer might be forced to work a bit harder. But does it make sense to treat the entire sales organization this way? Field sales is usually the first to know when trouble is coming. By the time the corporate "rain dance" starts, the average field organization is working as hard as it is going to.

All that has been done is to tell the field to "go sell." *They know that already.* To get them to sell more effectively, you must tell them more about what to sell and how to sell it. Let's review the process. We began with $100 million, a figure of questionable validity (some studies suggest that corporate strategic plans tend to overestimate actual results). We then took this probably optimistic figure and reduced the odds of attaining it by cutting the investments on which it was based. We next increased the $100 million by 10 percent to make sure that we'd get what we really needed. And then, worst of all, we allocated the result to the field, holding people accountable for the same narrow range of results (plus or minus 10 percent) we did at the corporate level.

Because of the law of large numbers, this last point is the coup de grace to a constructive goal-setting process. If you've got a random event with a central tendency, the more events observed, the more accurate the estimate of what's likely to occur. That's one theory behind conglomerates: When division A is down, division B will be up, and we'll all survive.

The same logic applies in reverse. If plus or minus 10 percent of $100 million is a reasonable range of performance, mere statistics suggest the range around $10 million must be greater than 10 percent, and the range around $1 million greater still.

Ironically, we've accomplished the exact opposite of our intentions. Sales reps within the performance band—a small group, because it's a narrow band—*do* have incentive to do better: They're "in the game." But those below (and with little chance of earning anything) might as well coast or look for another job. Those above might just as well coast too—or do the minimum to ensure they get the sales they know they can realize.

The goals and objectives developed for corporate planning purposes *can* serve a constructive purpose. But if blindly applied to the selling situation, these measures can actually hurt. Unlike a corporate manager who can hire additional people and add other resources, the sales rep's resources are fixed. Sales reps have about two thousand hours to work with in a year. To improve their effectiveness, they must apply those hours in a better way. If the message from corporate is "Do more," but with no guidance as to what to do, the best you can expect is no change, and the result might well be detrimental.

If you want your sales force to sell more, you have to tell them how.

8.10 Nonrevenue Goals

The revenue accounting statement cannot acknowledge any sales event, no matter how important, that does not immediately generate short-term revenue. Yet, in many sales jobs, sales impact is best reflected by nonrevenue results. One way to capture this important aspect of performance is through special or key account objectives.

Key account objectives can focus attention on accomplishing definite goals with significant accounts and prospects. Goals should be selected for their importance to profitable sales and territorial growth, through either immediate increase or laying the groundwork for future growth.

When the manager and sales rep meet to set objectives, each account and prospect should be thoroughly reviewed and analyzed. This review should address two fundamental questions for each account: What do we really want to accomplish? and How can we do it?

The answer to "What" comes from thorough analysis of the competitive sales situation. (Figure 8-2 lists some helpful questions to explore in this analysis.) The answer to "How" then becomes the specific objective.

To the extent possible, tentative objectives should be listed for every account of consequence. After each has been analyzed, the list should be reviewed and the most important opportunities (from a profit-making perspective) selected. For these, a specific objective that satisfies these criteria should be formulated:

- The objective is important: It relates to overall company strategies and is worth stating.
- It is accomplishable given what we know about the account. (If it is not, but still worth trying, what would have to happen to make this a good objective for the next period?)

Figure 8-2. Questions for account analysis.

- What new requirement does the prospect/account have that we can address?
- How can we address it?
- What are the steps we must take?
- How can we help the account sell?
- Are there any implications for marketing, product development, etc.?
- How can we increase volume?
- Who is the competition?
- What are the needs of the account?
- How can we meet these needs?
- Where are competitors weak?
- What new developments are occurring?
- What are possible matches between developing product lines and future customer requirements?
- Where can we increase profits?
- What new products or programs provide opportunities?
- Which prospects are the most attractive?

- It is clearly stated and verifiable, so the sales manager and sales rep can agree about whether it's been accomplished.
- It builds on prior objectives and can support new ones in future periods.

Setting sound objectives is difficult. Impossible objectives are self-defeating; objectives that are too easy don't accomplish anything and can demoralize top performers. It's generally best to have the sales rep select the objectives and have the manager approve and refine them. This approach also helps build commitment to attaining the objectives. Other ways to strengthen the goal-setting/performance relationship include:

- Using shorter performance periods (e.g., six months, four months, or a quarter)
- Building in a means to revise, reweight, and substitute objectives (especially when required due to changes in company priorities)
- Allowing recognition, where warranted, of "nonprogrammed" objectives (events you couldn't have known about in the past but could get credit for recognizing and exploiting)

Not all of these steps are appropriate in every circumstance, but they're worth considering in volatile sales environments.

In all situations, the key to success is using the program to establish rapport at all levels in the sales organization. Through program documentation, communication, and training (e.g., in setting objectives), make sure that the process is consistently and equitably applied.

8.11 Account Analysis Worksheet

Each account and important prospect should be analyzed to determine likely future volume. One approach is to use a worksheet filled in by the sales rep and then reviewed in a discussion between the rep and sales manager.

Figure 8-3 illustrates one possible worksheet format. The volume history columns show product sales last year, this period last year, this year to date, and the most recent period. The estimated-volume-this-period columns would be filled in jointly, after consideration of such relevant field conditions as:

- Changes in other products and services that would affect sales of this product line
- Market acceptance due to changed business conditions
- Changes in prices, advertising policies, and other elements of the marketing mix
- The competitive climate

Figure 8-3. Territory volume objective worksheet.

Account	Prior Quarter Volume	Last Year's Volume	Volume to Date	Volume This Quarter Last Year	Most Likely	Highest Possible
Territory _____	Sales Engineer _____		Account Manager _____		Year and Quarter _____	
	Volume History				*Estimated Volume This Quarter*	

Figure 8-4. Territory report of incentive earned.

Quarter _____

Territory _____   Sales Engineer _____   Account Manager _____

Volume Objective and Results:	Volume Objective Range _____ to _____	Actual Volume	Assigned Points	Points Earned
Account Objectives and Results: Key Account/Prospect			Assigned Points	

Total Points Earned _____
Times Point Value X $ _____
Incentive Earned _____

The totals of the most likely estimates and the highest possible estimates from the product volume objective worksheet then become judgment points used to establish final product volume objectives for each territory.

8.12 Worksheet for Computing Awards

A final step in the goal-setting process is to summarize the objectives established and track progress in achieving them. This can be a very powerful communication and motivational tool.

Figure 8-4 shows a form that can be used to track progress and calculate final incentive payouts. It combines both sales volume and key account objectives. The "accomplishment" part of the form would be filled out by the sales rep as the year progressed and objectives were met. The form would be reviewed from time to time by the sales rep and manager. At the end of the year (or incentive period, if shorter than a year), the results would be evaluated, points assigned, and payments made.

9

Information Needs/Support

9.1 What Is a Sales Information System?

A "sales information system" is simply a formal compilation of the collective knowledge of the sales force (and other relevant information) and a set of procedures for using it.

The sales force has specialized knowledge of current accounts, prospects, sales projects (which can run the gamut from undeveloped ideas to the number of components on regular order), customer contacts, and competitors. This information may exist partly on paper, partly on computer, and partly in people's heads. When properly applied and integrated with company strategies and objectives, this knowledge can greatly enhance the prospects of sales success.

The purpose of a sales information system is to help the sales force sell effectively—not just increase quantity, but improve quality as well and bring sales more into line with company profit and strategic goals. Therefore, a sales information system should:

- Store and generate information that the sales force needs to develop account strategies and allocate time
- Help focus sales efforts constructively
- Guide the company in supporting and coordinating sales efforts

9.2 Why Do Many Systems Fail?

A lot of sales information is kept informally: notes about a possible opportunity, remembering a buyer's wife's name, and so on. Trying to include such minutiae in a formalized system would force salespeople to spend too much time preparing input. But somehow, even companies that make a well-intentioned effort to develop a system with the right degree of structure end up attempting to collect too much information and providing too little benefit.

Sales information systems most often fail because they are designed around what the company wants to know, not what salespeople need to know. Because the focus of sales attention is the account, the system should contain information about an account that is essential to managing it well.

Systems that try to control, or solicit information from, sales reps rather than to assist them are also likely to fail. Unless the system is constructed so that the salespeople see clear benefits in using it, they won't use it. Or, if they can't ignore it, they will find some way to sabotage or avoid it.

Finally, some designers of systems erroneously equate systematization with computerization. Most of the information salespeople need to sell effectively is specific to their accounts, an inherently decentralized data base. Moreover, much of the data deals with account changes that don't always have a predictable structure. A centralized, rigidly structured, and computerized data base provides few advantages for the salesperson over paper and memory and is a lot harder to use. Fortunately, the advent of personal computers, laptops, and user-friendly and flexible software—and their successful deployment in field sales information systems—has helped make computers a more workable choice because of their ability to compile, sort, and share vast amounts of data in a systematic fashion.

9.3 Why Is Sales Information Different From Finance (or Market) Information?

When computers first entered the picture, the financial community seized on the mainframe. Ever since, information systems have centered around the finance and control functions. These are legitimate and important needs, to be sure, but the sales effort requires different information.

For example, many accounting-oriented systems report how much a customer *company* purchased last month. But the sales rep deals with individuals, not companies. Especially in industrial selling situations, there is often more than one buyer within a single company, and the sales rep must treat each buyer as an individual customer. Worse, many systems show only total sales, with no breakdown by product line. These system faults add up to a sales rep's receiving reports that tell him something about how he is doing overall, but provide no clues as to his particular strengths or weaknesses. Only with definitive information about each buyer and product line can the salesperson identify areas that need attention.

From the sales rep's point of view, what's left out of financially oriented systems is a bigger problem than what's in them. Some report only orders billed, rather than those booked. Few keep any record of prospective opportunities in the sales pipeline. Fewer still track companies (or individual buyers) that aren't currently customers but ought to be. Even those that do keep track of current versus prior sales or targets, do so in the form of abstract financial projections. Almost none support productivity analysis by constructively analyzing how salespeople spend their time. And, generally, they do not have any information on competitors' situations.

Marketing information systems also have different objectives and require different input from that useful to the sales force. Marketing data, for example, are oriented toward long-range and strategic trends, while sales data focus on specific accounts and opportunities.

Most sales information systems that are built as extensions of marketing information systems don't work for two main reasons: Such systems require the sales force to provide a lot of apparently meaningless information and don't give back data that the sales force can really use.

Clearly, financial and marketing information systems need some sales force input and should provide some useful output to the sales force. But the differences in the nature and use of information required in the two systems are so great that to try to "refine" one to meet the needs of the other is probably impossible. The key to a successful system is a design that fully meets the particular needs of its users. Input to the financial or marketing systems can be an important by-product of a sales information system, but the primary purpose must remain helping salespeople perform more effectively.

Figure 9-1 sums up a few of the key differences among sales, finance, and marketing information systems.

9.4 Components of an Effective Sales Information System

What, specifically, *should* a sales information system do? What processes should it support, and what components does it need to do so? The following are components of a sales information system:

Data Base

The sales force needs four basic kinds of data:

- *Account and prospect records*—useful facts about each customer and active prospect. The nature of the information gathered and available depends upon a number of variables, including the types of products sold, buyer characteristics, and sales objectives.
- *Company data*—information on internal items that affect the sales effort, for example: new products, application ideas, territory structure, time allocation, and the sales force itself.
- *Competitor data*—who they are, where their market is, their strengths and weaknesses.

Figure 9-1. Information system characteristics.

Characteristic	Information Systems Application		
	Sales	Finance	Marketing
Audience	• Salespeople	• Accounting/ finance	• Marketing/ strategists
Objective	• Support high	• Control reporting	• Explore/ strategize
Data Nature	• Account buying trends competition	• Billings/ receivables	• Macrotrends
Organization	• Decentralized	• Centralized	• Centralized

• *Other environmental data*—business trends, possible regulatory issues, etc.

Update Process

Sales information isn't static. All the elements of the information system must interact and be updated appropriately. The sales force itself assumes part of the responsibility for keeping data current, recording changes in customer personnel and other account-related information. The remainder of the burden falls on the company. It must communicate changes in supply situations, product and market objectives, and so on.

Sales/Marketing Analysis

The data base can be useful to sales management in making decisions about the sales effort in the following categories:

• *Organization*—Should the sales force be organized along geographic lines, industry lines, or other lines? The decision hinges on how the buying decision is made and by which *individuals*.

For example, managers sometimes conclude erroneously that even though a single company buys two types of products, having two sales reps call at the same location would be inefficient. Quite often, however, the two product lines are purchased by two different individuals within the company. That means that there are really two separate customers at one location, and two different sales reps may be necessary to keep the account. In addition, if there's little overlap in competitors for the product, specialization should be considered. Otherwise, the salespeople are at a competitive disadvantage. Your company rep would need to be familiar with two sets of competitors, whereas a specialized sales force would need to keep up with only one set of competitors. Examining account/prospect records to see who buys what and the competitor data base to test for overlap can help determine how to organize the sales force.

▪ *Deployment*—Do you need more salespeople or fewer? Where should the changes be made? There are two ways the data base can help answer these questions.

First, if the data base contains prospects, not just accounts, then it's possible to determine a sales productivity function. For example, suppose a company sells a product used by steel mills and cement manufacturers. The company knows that every million dollars of steel sales yields, on the average, a thousand dollars for itself; and a similar relationship exists in cement. From any of several sources, the company can obtain, for each territory, the number of customers and their approximate sizes. Together, these two pieces of information indicate the market potential of each territory. By comparing potential with sales realized, the company can tentatively identify areas where either the market is saturated or there is room for growth. The company would have to look a bit deeper before acting on that information, however, because sales dollars aren't always equal—for example, a large but concentrated plant might not require as much sales attention as would a small but decentralized one. But it's a place to start.

A second way to use the data base to make deployment decisions is to look at the *marginal* productivity of each account. That is, sales reps estimate the additional sales that would result from an extra call at each account. Especially with large accounts, the salespeople may be making calls out of habit. If the average call to a large account produces $1,000 in sales, but an "extra" call yields less than $100, while an extra call on a medium account generates $400, it would obviously be better to make one less call on the large account and one more on the medium one. A shortcut for the above is to examine the number of calls made at each account relative to sales (or gross profits) realized. This type of analysis is usually undertaken to help sales reps set priorities. But if it shows that two sales reps are calling on the same types of accounts, with (because of territory loading) one averaging twice as many hours per dollar of sales as the other does, that's a clue that deployment needs better balance.

▪ *Development*—Examining records of account strategies and their results can uncover developmental opportunities for individual sales reps. This aspect of the data base can also provide examples for training others.

▪ *Compensation*—The compensation system shouldn't require any information that isn't already in the sales information system or readily available. Pay should reinforce the key aspects of the sales role, and those measures should already be incorporated in the data base. If they aren't, either the sales information system design is faulty, or the compensation program is incorrectly directed. However, the costs and benefits of a direct link between compensation and sales information systems deserve some thought. Will a tie-in make people more likely to use the sales information system meaningfully, or will it create obstacles?

9.5   Designing Effective Sales Information Systems

How do you design a sales information system that works? A successful designer must begin by thoroughly understanding the selling process.

The most important design principle is to build the system around essential sales role characteristics. What does the salesperson need to know to influence a buying decision? Over what time frame will that influence take place? What will be the steps in the process and what observable events will signify that sales influence has been successfully brought to bear?

Designing the system to support the sales organization is about 60 percent of the effort. The other 40 percent lies in developing a system that's easy to use and accepted throughout the company. Like any element of the sales management process, the sales information system needs to be "sold" to the sales force on the basis of how they sell, not what or how the company wants to sell. Here are some general guidelines to make the process easier:

- *Separate wants from needs.* People want a lot more information than they'll actually use or be willing to provide. Understanding the nature of the selling process is a good basis for deciding what's really important.

- *Consider the applications as well as the data.* Look at both the information to be collected and how it will be used. What kinds of decisions do you want the data to support? How often do you make them? How precise must the information underlying them be? By answering these questions you can help determine which of several alternative information sources is the best and whether getting more accurate data is worthwhile.

- *Make sure the system is useful.* No one will provide information out of altruism for any length of time. It's better to have system inputs tied to useful reports, so that all the data providers realize a direct benefit from the information they supply.

- *Make the system as easy to use as possible.* Neat forms and user-friendly computer screens tell the sales force that you've really put thought and money into supporting them. In addition, be sure to consider how the system will be used, and where. Oversize forms, for example, don't lend themselves to being filled out in cars.

• *Reinforce the system through all organizational elements.* Allocate sufficient resources not just for developing the system but for introducing and maintaining it as well. Where data are available from another internal source, try to take advantage of it rather than asking the sales force to provide the same information more than once. Finally, make sure that your reward structure doesn't penalize people for using the system.

• *Be practical.* Rome wasn't built in a day; neither was the perfect information system. Development in stages according to a realistic schedule is the approach most likely to succeed. It is also important to consider how the transition from the old to the new system will be made. If only to create acceptance, plan for some field trials and a debugging period.

Companies with successful sales information systems almost always developed them by starting from scratch and then integrating them into existing company systems (rather than the other way around).

10

The "Menu" of Choices

10.1 Incentive Design Alternatives

Up to this point, we have examined the role of the salesperson in the marketing mix, seen how to determine the aggregate compensation requirements relative to the competitive market, and studied the concept of risk as it affects sales behavior and compensation. Now we are ready to turn to the main question that this handbook is intended to answer, namely, "What choices do you have in paying your salespeople?"

Fortunately, or unfortunately, depending upon your perspective, the sales manager has a tremendous variety of choices. The four basic components of compensation—salary, commission, bonus, and contests—can be mixed and matched in numerous ways to create a compensation approach that fits your marketing plan. Note that we are covering only *direct* compensation, i.e., cash or cash equivalents. Benefits are not generally considered to be effective in shaping the specific behavior of salespeople. Let's consider the uses, advantages, and disadvantages of these four components and some of the ways they are typically combined to form compensation plans.

10.2 Salary-Only Plans

When most managers think of sales compensation, they usually think of incentives. So why would you ever consider a straight salary approach? Because, in certain circumstances, it may be the approach that makes the most sense. Let's look at several examples, keeping in mind that straight salary is not necessarily the only alternative:

- *Engineering-oriented sales.* This term refers to any situation where the product or system being sold must be heavily tailored by a team of individuals to suit the customer's needs. Therefore, the sales rep is a technical facilitator/coordinator but does not generate volume from his or her own creativity. One example is the sale of steel to automobile manufacturers, where a complex, long-term design and trial process is required before orders are placed. The sales representative functions as both project coordinator and relationship manager, while the "sales team" consists of engineers, chemists, and manufacturing process specialists.

   ▪ *Infrequent, long–time-frame sales.* Some products are purchased only after long and careful deliberation due to their cost and the critical nature of their application. The sales rep for such products spends much of his time maintaining relationships with users and known prospective users and providing continual education and support so that he will be positioned properly when the next sales opportunity occurs. Straight salary will compensate these sales reps during their long dry periods.

   ▪ *Pull-through sales.* Some sales reps concentrate their efforts on creating demand rather than on selling directly to the end user. One example is the agricultural chemical salesperson, who spends much of his time educating farmers about agricultural chemicals generally, and his company's products specifically. This service is intended to increase demand for the products so that the company can sell more to agricultural supply distributors.

   Because it is difficult to link the salesperson's efforts directly to sales of the product in such cases, a straight salary approach may be appropriate.

   ▪ *Service selling.* Some jobs are mostly service in content but involve some minor selling. For example, consider the individuals who drive delivery trucks, "selling" bread to grocery stores. Such "salespeople" influence only shelf placement and availability and have no control over the many other factors that affect consumer buying decisions. Therefore, it may not be appropriate to link their compensation to volume. Here again, straight salary compensation seems appropriate.

   ▪ *Rapidly changing marketplace.* Some products or markets demand that sales management have the ability to change priorities on short notice, reassign territory responsibilities or restructure territories, or send one rep to another territory to help or train another. Straight salary is the best approach when management needs to retain such control, because the more compensation depends on sales results the more each rep will want to retain control over his own activities so that he can maximize results.

   ▪ *Unpredictable marketplace.* There are situations where demand cycles do not fit known patterns or are related to factors that cannot be fully known in advance (e.g., the sale of steel, copper, iron ore). This makes it difficult to set goals, establish quotas, or pay a rep based on performance. In such cases, straight salary plans can be the most effective method of compensation.

   ▪ *Training and transfers.* Straight salary can be used to compensate a new sales rep during a training period, lasting however long management thinks it takes to "get up to speed" in the job. The salary may be expressed in part as a draw or guaranteed incentive to facilitate the eventual transition to an incentive plan. This is also useful in certain transitional situations, e.g., the transfer of an experienced person to a weak territory to improve territory results. Depending upon the specifics of the situation, management may provide a straight salary or other form of guaranteed compensation until territory results improve and sales can move forward in a normal manner.

The Advantages of Straight Salary

- It is simple for reps to understand and for the company to administer.
- It encourages customer service, because getting the next sale is not uppermost in the rep's mind.
- It protects income in situations where sales results vary dramatically due to conditions beyond the rep's control.
- It facilitates team selling situations by eliminating the need to split credits.
- It reduces the potential for employee relations problems in situations requiring substantial input to the selling process by nonsales personnel.
- It gives sales managers maximum flexibility in changing sales reps' priorities on short notice.

The Disadvantages of Straight Salary

- It limits management's ability to use compensation as a tool for shaping behavior.
- It *increases* fixed selling costs because compensation costs cannot be varied directly with incremental business results.
- It lowers the rep's incentive to dramatically increase business results.
- It may attract security-oriented sales reps who will not willingly shoulder any of the risks of the business.
- It provides no attraction for successful, aggressive "stars."
- It results in "stars" subsidizing "underachievers" among the sales force.

Although the straight salary approach does have a place in sales compensation, its uses are limited.

10.3 Straight Commission Plans

The concept of a "piece of the action" distinguishes commissions from other forms of incentives—bonuses and contests. From the sales rep's perspective, the straight commission plan represents the most entrepreneurial approach. Very few companies pay straight commissions, however, because few selling jobs have the requisite combination of very high prominence and low barrier to entry that make such compensation appropriate.

The basic straight commission plan is very simple in concept. The rep receives a percentage of the sales price, typically paid once a month. Expenses may or may not be paid by the company. If they are not, the commission rate is generally somewhat higher. Commissions are usually paid from the first dollar of sales. There may be accelerated commission rates beyond a certain level of achievement.

In its most traditional form, the commission is a flat percentage of the sales price. Over the years, however, many variations have developed. These tend to fall into two basic categories:

1. The commission rate is applied to something other than the sales price, for example, the list price. This evolved in response to reps' concerns over differences in product profitability and the effects of discounts from list price.
2. Commission rates are subject to break points. In addition to establishing different rates for different products, companies may have varied rates on the same product. Rates may be reduced on volume above a certain level, either in aggregate or on an individual order (a less onerous restriction than applying a cap). Alternatively, rates may vary at different levels of performance against quota, e.g., the rate may increase once quota is attained to reflect the additional effort required to generate sales beyond that point.

A straight commission plan approach may be appropriate if:

- The sales rep's success is fully measurable in short-term results, i.e., immediate sales.
- Few factors other than the rep's personal selling skill figure in the success of the sale.
- No significant nonsales activities need be performed by the rep.
- Cyclicality or seasonality is not significant.
- The company has little investment in the rep in terms of training or company-specific experience, so that turnover is not costly.
- Ongoing customer relationships are relatively unimportant.
- Limiting earnings by, for example, capping the amount earned for an individual sale is not important.

The Advantages of Straight Commission

- It allows management to attract high-performing salespeople who are willing to share the risks of the business.

- It forces nonperformers to leave the organization.
- It makes compensation costs completely variable.
- It is easy for employees to understand and for the company to administer.
- It encourages maximum sales effort, making it very useful in penetrating new and familiar markets.
- It minimizes the need for supervision by treating the employee much like an independent contractor.

The Disadvantages of Straight Commission

- It severely limits management's flexibility to direct sales reps' efforts, require nonselling activities, modify territories, influence levels of performance, relocate reps, or promote salespeople into nonselling positions.
- It encourages a short-term orientation, possibly at the expense of longer-term, business-building activities.
- It enables sales reps to obtain a high level of income from mature territories without pursuing improvement opportunities.
- It fosters a rep's pursuit of the greatest payoff for the least effort to maximize his income. Attempting to combat this through the commission structure may be exceedingly difficult.
- It can create conflict between the rep's dependence on volume and the company's ability or willingness to fill every order.
- It generates little loyalty.

10.4   Salary/Commission Plans

This approach can be thought of as a "joint venture" between the sales rep and the company. Through commissions, the rep shares in the business that he helps to generate and, at the same time, the company pays him a salary that can be considered a fee for the experience and skills the rep brings to the relationship.

A combination of salary and commission is often appropriate if:

- Barriers to entry (see Chapter 4) require a level of guaranteed income to compete in the labor market, especially for inexperienced salespeople.
- Sales results are directly related to the activities of sales reps but are not fully controlled by them, making it appropriate for the company and reps to share the risk. In a cyclical or seasonal market, for example, a salary helps to retain sales reps when sales are down.

- Sales results are important, but management wants to retain some control over the reps' nonselling activities. A salary enables the sales manager to encourage, for example, aftersale service, customer education, market research, or paperwork.

The relative weight of salary and commission is a function of two factors: the prominence of the selling job (see Chapter 4), and the interplay between barriers to entry and the competitive total compensation level for the position. The more prominent the sales job, the larger the commission element. At the same time, highly competitive total compensation will demand a higher salary component to attract and retain highly skilled personnel.

You may pay salary and commissions together or separately. When paid together, they are most commonly paid monthly. When they are paid separately, a company's exempt personnel payroll procedures generally apply to salaries (e.g., biweekly or semimonthly), while commissions are paid monthly or quarterly. The frequency of commission payments can be influenced by a number of factors, including the size of payments, the nature of the sales cycle, and administrative (accounting and performance tracking) capabilities.

The Advantages of a Salary/Commission Plan

- It attracts sales reps who have skills beyond pure selling abilities.
- It enables a company to compete with employers offering alternative careers.
- It helps retain employees during tough times while maintaining a variable element in the cost of sales.
- It permits the sales manager legitimately to include nonsales activities in the sales job.
- It emphasizes pay for performance.

The Disadvantages of a Salary/Commission Plan

- It can become so complex that it is difficult to understand and administer.
- It can dilute emphasis on key results because of a tendency to try to control too many specific sales rep activities through either the commission or the merit increase process.

The salary/commission combination represents a very popular approach to compensating sales reps. The commission element, especially, provides great flexibility for the company and significant opportunity for the sales rep.

10.5   Salary/Bonus Plans

The salary/bonus approach resembles the salary/commission plan but is more appropriate in situations where the sales rep has less influence on the buying decision or where the job is structured with less emphasis on direct sales. Because of this, a bonus is almost never used without a base salary.

A bonus will generally prove more effective than a commission if:

- *Results cannot be measured in dollars.* Sometimes a company wants salespeople to spend time on tasks that contribute toward achieving the company's marketing objectives but do not directly generate immediate sales, e.g., conducting training sessions for a distributor's sales force, manning a booth at a trade convention.
- *Sales dollars are not a direct reflection of the quality of performance.* Some sales situations require a certain level of effort and achievement on the part of the sales rep but produce widely varying results. For example, process control systems for paper plants vary tremendously in price, depending upon the size of the installation, but the steps required to make the sale are substantially the same regardless of price.
- *Getting the account is more important than boosting volume.* The sale of services, especially data processing and telecommunications, generates a continuing revenue stream that grows and varies based upon service provided by nonsales personnel. The sales rep's job is to penetrate the account. Although initial volume is to be considered, management wants the sales rep to obtain many accounts rather than a few large ones. Thus, the company should pay for accounts rather than for revenue.

Under the salary/bonus approach, salaries are almost always paid according to procedures used for other exempt personnel. Companies typically issue bonuses quarterly or annually, although instances of semiannual and monthly payments can be found. Most monthly bonus payments occur in plans that also incorporate a commission. The time frame to use generally depends on the mix of salary and bonus (the greater the bonus as a percentage of the total, the more frequently payments are made), the nature of the performance cycle, and the administrative capabilities to handle performance planning and measurement.

The Advantages of a Salary/Bonus Plan

- It provides flexibility in balancing short- and long-term objectives and selling and nonselling objectives.

- It enables management to change territory structure and sales goals easily from year to year because the bonus feature allows for easy calibration of earnings potential, sales objectives, and earnings results.
- It provides flexibility in determining the amount of incentive to award to the sales rep.

The Disadvantages of a Salary/Bonus Plan

- It allows suspicion over goal setting, to the extent that the sales force distrusts management. This can happen because the goals for each rep vary and management's evaluation of a rep's attainment of nonquantifiable goals is necessarily subjective.
- It can create administrative difficulties because bonus plans are more complex to administer than are commission plans. Greater effort is required in performance planning on an individual basis.
- It can result in a complex array of goals and payment opportunities that dilute the importance of key objectives because of a tendency to try to cover every aspect of the job with a bonus.
- It can enable some sales reps to succeed on bonus-compensated, nonsales objectives alone while generating no sales revenue at all for the company (if the plan is not carefully structured).

Some companies have combined bonuses with commissions and salaries in fairly complex compensation plans. In principle, there is nothing wrong with this approach, but there are some practical guidelines to follow:

- Make the plan as simple as possible. Introducing a set of bonuses into a plan that already has varying commission rates can cloud the original intent of the incentives.
- Make communication a top priority. The more complex the plan is, the greater the need to communicate it clearly. This requires not only a well-run orientation session and a well-written brochure, but also monthly reports that show results clearly and quickly and offer reps tools for making effective improvements.
- Explore the results of the plan at performance extremes. Bonuses and commissions typically have different payout curves. Commissions, especially those that are uncapped, tend to offer attractive compensation opportunities, and bonus activities may be ignored in the pursuit of commissioned sales.

The salary/bonus approach is extremely flexible. It can prove especially useful if nonsales activities are important or if great flexibility in setting performance objectives is required.

10.6   Commission Plus Draw Plans

The commission plus draw plan is a variation on the straight commission plan. A company pays a draw on a regular basis, but as an advance payment of commissions. The draw is always deducted from commissions earned (if it were not, it would be a salary). A reconciliation (draw paid versus commissions earned) is typically made monthly, but can be made quarterly or even less often. A draw offers salespeople income stability without committing the company to paying a salary.

A draw may be "recoverable" or "nonrecoverable." A recoverable draw is one that must be paid back to the company out of future earnings if earnings for the period are less than the amount received as a draw. For example, if at the end of a year, the rep has earned $2,000 less in commissions than she has been paid in draw, that amount will be deducted from her commissions in the following year until the company has been paid back. In the case of a nonrecoverable draw, the company "forgives" the $2,000 and the rep starts off the new year with a clean slate. A nonrecoverable draw is very much like a salary; in fact, it can be thought of as the equivalent of a salary coupled to a commission plan with a high threshold, or the "validated salary" approach described in the next chapter.

You may use a draw in the same selling situations as you would a straight commission, but it is especially applicable if:

- Sales are seasonal or cyclical, resulting in periods of low earnings that are not within the rep's power to change.
- A new rep needs time to begin generating sales due to a learning curve related to the territory or the company's products.
- A new territory takes time to become productive.

An expense allowance usually accompanies a draw, against which actual and reasonable expenses are reconciled on a monthly basis.

The draw plus commission approach has essentially the same advantages and disadvantages characteristic of the straight commission approach.

10.7   Sales Contests

Although contests can be used in conjunction with all of the compensation plans described above, they should not be an ongoing or a significant part of the total compensation package. Rather, contests should serve to focus efforts on a specific short-term result. Contests are most often used to:

- Increase total volume
- Obtain new accounts
- Introduce a new product or increase sales of an existing product

Contests may provide awards in the form of cash, prizes, travel, or other forms of recognition (e.g., plaques presented at formal ceremonies).

A well-designed contest can create excitement and generate positive results immediately. A poorly designed contest can result in negative feelings on the part of the losers that outweigh the positive feelings of the winners, or can even cause behavior that is at odds with company objectives. To illustrate, there's the story of the bank that offered a prize to the teller who opened the most Christmas club accounts for $25 or more. A manager was dismayed to observe one teller open twenty separate accounts for a customer who wanted to start a $500 club.

The Advantages of Contests

- They create enthusiasm, resulting in extra effort (and hopefully extra performance) over a short period of time.
- They give winners a psychological boost that often lasts beyond the end of the contest.
- They renew the competitive spirit, which is part of the fun of the job.
- They are inexpensive relative to the return the company gets in boosted sales.

The Disadvantages of Contests

- They can become addictive. But if you have one going all the time, you will lose the surge of excitement that a contest is designed to generate.
- They compete with the rest of the compensation plan for the sales rep's attention. And if the plan is already complex, contests can further weaken points of emphasis.
- They create more losers than winners and have reps competing against one another rather than against competitors. Where territory potential varies, losers may believe that the cards were stacked against them. This can jeopardize the credibility of your goal-setting processes.
- They may tempt a rep to load up his customers' inventories. This may be good for the company's short-term results, but it can leave customers with bad feelings.
- They are frequently designed by product managers (or suppliers) who want the sales force to focus attention on their products. It is important to ensure that this doesn't upset the balance that has been built into the existing incentive plan. At the extreme, the

contest can encourage sales behavior *in conflict with* the company's strategic priorities.

Contests can be good for the company and exciting for the sales force. Nevertheless, the sales compensation manager should carefully consider the advantages and disadvantages in light of the company's business needs and the potential results.

11

The Mystique of Packaging

11.1 The Concept of Compensation Risk

The amount of incentive that a particular sales compensation program contains is related to the amount of *risk* that has been built into the program. Risk is the probability that an expected compensation result will not be attained; as such, it is the inverse of opportunity. Generally, expected compensation approximates the competitive compensation level for similar positions.

Although it is obvious that the different compensation approaches described in the previous chapter vary with respect to risk, it would be wrong to assume that each approach carries a specific and unvarying amount of risk. With the exception of straight salary, plan types can vary considerably in risk, depending on how they are designed. This gives the designer tremendous flexibility in influencing the behavior of the sales representative. Let's explore the use of risk, both high and low, in incentive plans.

11.2 The Strange Case of Salary/Commission Plans

The ever-popular salary/commission approach has an interesting characteristic: It is effective in both low- and high-prominence situations, but is less effective in between, at middle levels of prominence. Think about this for a second. We look toward straight salaries in low-prominence situations, and toward straight commission in very high prominence situations. What is it about the two that makes for an effective approach? The answer is that we can make a salary/commission plan look, from an operational perspective, very much like a straight salary plan or like a straight commission plan. However, we cannot make it look like a salary/bonus plan, which is what works best for sales situations in the middle of the prominence scale. Specific examples of how this can be done are included later in this chapter.

11.3 Low-Risk Plans

A low-risk plan is one in which the sales representative is highly likely to make close to the expected level of income, regardless of the form in which it is paid. The level of performance required to hit the targeted level of earnings is the critical element here, rather than whether payment is in the form of salary, bonus, or commission. Management "backs into" a commission rate or bonus schedule based upon the targeted earnings level for the position and expected sales results in the territory. Frequently, the commission rate is tailored to the territory, resulting in the apparently illogical result that a sale in one territory is worth more or less than the same sale in another territory.

Where sales results are very stable over time, this approach is easy to implement. Where they are not, various rules are constructed to ensure that the sales rep's income stays within acceptable boundaries. The most common example is the use of a cap on incentive earnings, or a windfall clause enabling management to reduce or eliminate credit for sales that do not meet certain parameters (generally loosely defined).

Let's construct a simple example to see how this might be done. Assume that territory volume is expected to be $1.5 million and earnings are targeted at $60,000. Further assume that, based on current prices, territory volume has never been less than $1.2 million or more than $1.8 million. We could pay the rep a salary of $45,000 and a commission of one percent of sales (which would be $15,000 on $1.5 million). Based on territory history, the range of earnings is likely to be $57,000 to $63,000. That is not much variation. If we wanted to ensure results within this range, we might cap incentive earnings at $20,000 or $25,000. We have created a low-risk incentive plan.

Why bother with incentive plans that have low risk? There are several reasons:

- To make the sales rep feel like a contributor to the business. There is no greater source of alienation in business than the feeling that our existence does not matter to the company. Even a small amount of variation in pay based on results will help to maintain a focus on the results.
- Low prominence does not mean no prominence. Focusing the rep's attention on job performance will probably generate some additional results.
- There may be a philosophical reason to use incentives. If the company has other, higher-prominence sales forces or makes substantial use of incentives outside of the sales area, it would be an anomaly to have a salaried sales force.

11.4 High-Risk Plans

We frequently think of commissions as high-risk plans, although we just looked at one that carried low risk due to the nature of the territory.

When a "stretch" level of performance is required to generate incentive earnings and the base salary alone is insufficient to enable the representative to live comfortably, we have a high-risk plan. Carried far enough, it becomes the equivalent of a straight commission plan.

Let's go back to the example that we used before, but change the incentive element. Instead of paying one percent on all sales, we pay no incentive below 90 percent of expected sales of $1.5 million. Thus, at $1.35 million, we begin paying an incentive of 10 percent of marginal sales. At the expected sales level, we still pay $15,000 in commissions (i.e., the difference between the $1.5 million target and the $1.35 million threshold). But we do not pay any commissions in part of the range of expected performance (between $1.2 million and $1.35 million). At the top end of the historical performance range, $1.8 million, we will pay $30,000 in commissions (10 percent of $300,000) for a far different top end of $75,000 total cash. We have just expanded the compensation range to between $45,000 and $75,000 from between $57,000 and $63,000, thus introducing significantly higher risk into the situation. Whether this is appropriate is a separate issue and depends on the sales rep's ability to influence the actual results within that range.

Why not just use a straight commission in this situation? Because high barriers to entry may require a substantial level of fixed compensation to attract personnel with appropriate skills or to hold them in place during short-term slack periods. Further, security-oriented companies may find it culturally unacceptable to use straight commission plans.

11.5 Percent Incentive/Salary Alternatives

The mix of compensation, that is, the relative levels of salary and incentive in the package, can be misleading as an indicator of the level of risk. The two examples provided above illustrate this point. Both packages had a salary/incentive mix of 75 percent/25 percent ($45,000 in salary and $15,000 in incentive at the targeted total earnings level). Yet the second package had substantially higher risk than did the first, due to the introduction of a high threshold.

Following through on this concept, we can construct a wide variety of mixes, all having approximately the same degree of risk. Conversely, we can introduce varying degrees of risk into plans using the same mix at the targeted level of earnings. Where risk (downside earnings potential) varies, opportunity (upside earnings potential) must also vary. To impose risk without providing opportunity is irresponsible from a plan design perspective. In the second of the above examples, we increased opportunity in direct proportion to the risk we introduced.

If the competitive pay level for a sales job is $50,000 and we pay a salary of $40,000 and target incentive earnings at $10,000, we have an

80/20 mix. This sort of mix is commonly found in industrial selling situations. If, in a stable growth market in an established territory, we require a 25 percent growth in sales to earn that $10,000, we have probably created a high-risk plan. Presumably, we provide very high earnings leverage above that performance level to compensate for the risk. We can shift that mix to 60/40 by paying a salary of $30,000 and targeting incentive earnings at $20,000. If we structure the plan so that the salesperson can earn the $20,000 with an 8 percent increase in sales, we have created a lower-risk plan, even though the mix is weighted more toward the incentive element.

11.6   Disguised Salary Approaches

In certain industrial selling situations where the sales job is fairly low in prominence, salary/commission plans approximate the income consequences of straight salary. In these situations, sales results vary little from predicted results. Product usage can be predicted for each account, and the supplier has an exclusive franchise or buying patterns are such that one supplier is unlikely to exclude another from an account. The greatest potential for variation in projected volume arises if an account leaves the territory or another one comes in during the year. As in the example in section 11.3, the range of performance across which the incentive is likely to be paid is narrow, resulting in a narrow range of total compensation results. The range of performance shown in that example (plus or minus 20 percent of projected) is actually quite broad compared to many situations. Many companies can project territory volume within 10 percent of actual on a consistent basis. Under such circumstances, any incentive plan targeted to pay a given level of compensation at the projected sales level is little different, in terms of pay result, from a straight salary.

11.7   Validated Salary Approaches

In some industrial and many high-technology sales situations, sales jobs have barriers to entry *and* high prominence. This suggests both high fixed pay and a high level of incentive compensation. Fortunately, we are not necessarily forced to pay huge amounts of money by stacking one form of compensation on top of the other. There are ways of having a bit of the cake and eating it too. One of these is the validated salary approach, that is, providing a high base salary, but requiring the sales rep to pay it back before he earns any additional compensation.

Let's construct another simple example. The competitive marketplace for a high-technology salesperson says total compensation must average $80,000. We find that a base salary of $60,000 is necessary to attract the kind of person we need. Further, we expect a sales volume of $2.0 million out of the territory this year. Dividing total compensation of $80,000 by the expected volume of $2.0 million gives us a 4 percent commission rate. At 4 percent, it takes sales of $1.2 million to "justify" or validate a $60,000 salary. We can proceed in either of two ways. One is to establish a threshold of $1.2 million, below which the rep earns no incentive. The other is to calculate a commission from the first dollar, but subtract salary payments from earnings, writing the rep a check for only the excess. The latter is a draw approach; the former is a validation approach. The advantage of validation is that the rep may perceive that the salary recognizes education, professional achievement, and other factors that are more technically oriented than sales oriented. This may be important to a person with this type of background.

12

Establishing a Working Hypothesis

12.1 Incentive or Not?

The most effective way to develop a sales compensation plan is to test the outline of a hypothetical plan against key characteristics of the market, the sales force, and the company's resources. Tests for reasonableness of the incentive compensation plan represent a key step in the development process. Such tests should examine the role of the sales position and its impact. The tests should identify the behaviors and attitudes variable pay is designed to influence and should determine the features essential for a successful incentive plan. Specifically, the tests should answer the following questions:

- Are there specific *sales behaviors* and results that should be highlighted and linked directly to compensation?
- Does the sales position have discrete individual *accountability* for one or more critical end results?
- Is there significant *self-supervision* in the choice and pursuit of some sales goals, methods, and activities?
- Does the sales position exercise meaningful *control* over expected end results?
- Is it common *industry practice* for the position to receive incentive compensation?

Answering these questions affirmatively builds a case for incentive compensation. Because incentive compensation should relate to sales results, and not operate or be perceived to operate as a base salary, results must vary largely due to the efforts and ingenuity of sales employees.

Two other questions are also relevant:

1. Can you *track the results* that incentives will pay for?
2. Can you afford the *fixed costs* associated with ensuring all income through a base salary?

If required results can be tracked accurately and promptly, an otherwise sound incentive program will probably work. Frequently, however, constraints on tracking shorten the list of available compensation design alternatives. In the most extreme instances, a sales position responsible for significant revenue retention and revenue growth may not be paid an incentive for revenue because accounting systems cannot track booked or invoiced dollars to a specific salesperson. Problems of this type often occur in service businesses with multiple billing or service locations.

With respect to the second question, even if initial analysis does not yield strong support for incentive compensation—or shows that tracking will be a major challenge—you should give incentives careful consideration. Businesses that are strapped for cash or need to minimize fixed costs are usually reluctant to utilize only a base salary. Instead, these businesses must hold their break-even costs as low as possible by minimizing fixed costs and keeping the slope of the variable cost curve as flat as possible.

In many smaller businesses, the cost of direct selling can be a significant percentage of total cost. These businesses are likely, therefore, to minimize fixed compensation as much as possible. Although such financial constraints can be very real, you should make every effort to confirm that the proposed *form* and *level* of variable compensation (incentive) make good sense for the sales effort as well as the cost structure of the company.

To demonstrate how our list of questions can provide a framework for deciding whether to implement a sales incentive plan, consider the following situation. A newly formed distributor of light industrial and commercial air-conditioning equipment is actively recruiting dealer sales reps and sales engineers.

Dealer sales reps will be responsible for identifying, recruiting, developing, and supporting authorized dealers who will, in turn, market the distributor's products to developers, architects, mechanical contractors, and end users. Dealer sales reps will have a revenue goal and a territory, but they will not directly take orders from their dealers.

Sales engineers will call on consultants and mechanical contractors who are retained by developers to design and configure a building or facility, including its air-conditioning systems. Although sales engineers will not take orders from consultants or contractors, they will be responsible for stimulating "upstream" demand for their product, i.e., getting that product specified by each decision maker so that the ultimate order, placed with a dealer or mechanical contractor, is an order for that product. Because almost all orders for major installations of the type are tracked by the distributor directly, a quota for engineered sales can be established for each sales engineer's territory.

Should the sales engineer receive incentive compensation? Not necessarily, but if three conditions exist, a strong case can be made. First, there is clear accountability and a relatively high degree of self-supervision. Second, the sales engineer's control over the ultimate end result, orders placed with dealers and contractors, is strong in some cases and weak in others. Third, key sales results can be identified that could be reinforced by an incentive plan, for example:

- Formal specification of the company's products by consultants
- Revenue
- Gross profit
- Average gross margin on volume from consultants and contractors

You should note that industry practice varies, with some distributors offering straight base salaries and others offering incentives ranging from discretionary bonuses to commissions.

In this example, there is good support for incentive compensation. Individual accountability has been defined, objective measures of key sales results exist, the sales engineer can exercise moderate control over these results, and there is significant day-to-day self-supervision in the field.

Industry practice varies, with most sales engineers compensated with a base salary only. The subtleties of tracking these results accurately and developing credible performance norms require careful handling.

12.2   Key Results

You must establish the relationship between achievement and compensation and then construct an incentive program around key results for the participant(s) to achieve. Many variable compensation programs, such as informal "on the spot" bonuses and totally unstructured discretionary awards, are not explicitly constructed around key results. Therefore, they do not really represent incentive programs because the employee does not know in advance what must be done to earn an award. Uncertain returns on the unknown achievement of blind objectives can provide an incentive for the desired employee results only if other cues in the work environment provide effective substitutes for defined payouts and goals.

The key results suitable for use in sales compensation design are generally those that most prominently require sales skills to achieve an important business objective. This is an important point. It means that many readily available yardsticks of overall business performance may not be suitable yardsticks of sales performance. It also means that measurable selling activities and results with weak or indirect links to important business objectives may be unsatisfactory as well.

Rarely will you see return on shareholders' equity, earnings per share, operating income, or net income used as measures of sales performance—primarily because the *accountability* and *control tests* defined in Section 12.1 cannot be satisfied. Similarly, you will seldom find yardsticks of sales performance that capture only effort or activity, such as the number of calls completed, forms filled out, or proposals drafted, primarily because none of these activities leads directly to the required business result.

With respect to the air-conditioning distributor, which key results are likely to surface? And what are acceptable measures of selling skill and contribution? In a distribution business—where pricing, freight recovery, installation cost, advertising support, and volume are critical success factors—companies usually employ some combination of bookings, shipments, gross margin, and gross profit (or contribution margin and contribution profit). These results stand midway between compensating the sales force with a finder's fee for every sale, at one extreme, and compensating with annual profit sharing only, at the other.

Suppose that our hypothesis for a sound incentive compensation program for the sales engineer position worked, in broad outline, as follows:

- Every engineered order yields a minimum bonus to the sales engineer of x.
- Every order that is twice last year's average size yields a bonus of $3x$.
- No order with a gross margin of less than m percent will receive sales credit.

What would you expect the sales engineer to do when compensation is measured in this manner? Because *orders* are compensated rather than revenue or profit, one would expect the widespread "unbundling" of traditional orders into orders for each element of a system, except in cases where a larger order would earn the larger bonus. One would also expect some disruption at the consultant and contractor level as sales engineers attempt to repackage one traditional order as two or more. You should not expect the sales engineer to focus on the consumer's purchase of all the options and add-ons available. Nor would you expect steady requests for reduced pricing from sales engineers. The minimum margin stipulation should have little effect if set low, except when senior management decides to "buy" some select business with aggressive pricing.

These expectations show that our hypothesis for a sound incentive plan could significantly harm the business because part of the sales force would have been inadvertently encouraged to ignore revenue, total profit, and overall profitability from the assigned territories. Clearly, another approach is required.

12.3 Commission or Bonus?

A commission, as defined earlier, is a specific rate of pay for a discrete unit of results. The measure of results can range from revenue, to profit, to items sold. A commission can be designed as a constant or variable rate. A bonus is any incentive that is not expressed in a one-to-one relationship with volume or profit. Companies frequently design bonuses around goals, with continuous and lump sum payouts available along the way and at specific performance levels, such as threshold, quota, and multiples of quota.

Should the incentive element of the compensation program be a commission, a bonus, or a combination? The answer lies in an examination of the *nature* of sales force influence on key results. The following rules can help guide this critical step in the development of an overall compensation package:

- If the volume, revenue, or profit from the sale can vary and (1) the salesperson can materially influence one or more of these factors, and (2) it is desirable to increase the volume, revenue, or profit from a sale, you should increase incentive pay as volume, revenue, or profit increases.
- If sales results are directly attributable to a sales position—and these results can be objectively measured—you should rely on deterministic versus subjective payout mechanisms.
- If a unique one-time sales achievement warrants recognition, and the *fact* of the achievement rather than its *size* is key, you should use a lump sum award versus an award that varies with size.

Generally, the more influence a sales position has on the variability of a business result, the more appropriate a commission-type incentive plan is. Furthermore, the more control management can and should exercise over a sales position, the more appropriate a bonus-type incentive plan is (with goals). As your ability to measure sales results objectively declines, more subjective bonus arrangements tend to work better. And, finally, if the business result is discrete (for example, a new account) or nonrecurring (for example, achieving 100 percent of quota), then a bonus is usually more effective than a commission because a bonus directly matches an "all or nothing" pay event with a unique sales event.

If you have established a hypothesis for key sales results and the basic form of an incentive plan, that is, a commission or a bonus plan, you still need to specify the exact form of a plan before the hypothesis is complete. A commission plan can take one of eight basic forms, when the following four design parameters are combined either with or without an expense allowance:

- Flat rate
- Progressive rate
- Regressive rate
- Differential rate

For example, a flat rate/no allowance plan best suits a start-up venture with few cash resources, significant business potential, and minimal salesperson setup costs. A progressive rate plan works best in an environment where more volume beyond a given level is known to be tougher and where an incentive to keep selling is an important tool to offset potential "sandbagging." A regressive rate plan is rare and almost exclusively used to encourage sales to more accounts and/or to smaller accounts by limiting earnings on revenues or volumes from larger accounts. A differential rate plan varies the commission rate by sales category so that special emphasis can be given to newer, strategically important, higher-profit, or other products requiring additional support.

If you choose a bonus plan, there are essentially four forms to choose from:

- Lump sum bonus—defined payout for defined achievement
- Lump sum bonus—discretionary payout for defined achievement
- Lump sum bonus—discretionary payout for general achievement
- Continuous, defined payout for a continuous defined achievement

In combination with one of these basic forms, you could add such specialized design devices as thresholds and accelerators to arrive at a finalized bonus program. The most common type of lump sum bonus delivers a defined payout for a defined achievement. This is usually easy to administer and an effective motivator when the required achievement can also be defined easily. Companies often employ a discretionary payout if the interplay of performance factors is too complex to rely on a simple bonus formula or award value or if there is no reliable way to measure an individual's performance. In the latter case, a bonus pool may be created by the unit sales results, with discretionary distributions then made from the fund. A continuous defined payout formula is almost always anchored to the attainment of a goal, where the salesperson's incentive income increases as the percentage of goal attained increases. This form of bonus program occurs frequently, especially in organizations that choose to compensate goal attainment as well as sales production.

12.4   The Hypothesis

On the basis of the issues considered in Sections 12.1–12.3, you could develop a hypothetical incentive plan for the position of sales engineer as follows:

- The core of the incentive plan should permit income to increase as revenue and gross margin increase because more of each from each side is desirable.
- A minimum average gross margin (percentage) should be established (1) to ensure that margin is uppermost in the mind of the sales engineer and (2) to permit senior management to insist on some very low-margin (but strategically important) sales that will only slightly lower an engineer's *average margin*.
- Given the moderate control of each engineer over total sales in the assigned territory, using a bonus formula that ties every dollar of incentive to the percentage of goal attained will not be effective. Given the importance of goal attainment, however, you should offer a lump sum bonus for goal attainment as a pure add-on earnings opportunity—while making the bonus large enough to motivate.
- A progressive commission schedule should be established that pays an increasing percentage of revenue or gross profit as *both* revenue or profit *and* average gross margin increase, an approach that encourages extended performance as the next increment of performance becomes more difficult to produce.
- A multiplier is needed that will increase core commission earnings as the number and quality of consultant specifications of the distributor's products increase.

This hypothetical plan, which emerges from an analysis of the role and impact of the sales job, can now be tested and revised through computer simulation, or "scenario analysis," and discussions with selected salespeople.

13

Base Salary Design/ Administration

13.1   The Role of Base Salary and Other Assured Income

To understand the role played by base salary and other forms of assured income, consider what happens when incentive compensation is the only available source of income. Incentive compensation will vary as every factor that affects sales opportunity, sales success, and sales event tracking varies. To the degree that the sales rep can control the frequency, extent, and timing of these factors, and where it is possible for the rep to quickly establish a territory that produces a sustaining level of sales on a regular basis, incentive compensation should reflect the rep's "prominence."

High prominence, by itself, is not a sufficient reason for relying solely on incentive compensation. You must also establish that there are few barriers to entry into the job, because such barriers represent experiences and skills that can often command a minimum assured level of income (base salary) in the labor market.

Candidates for a sales job that requires specific experiences and skills can usually bargain for some assured income. They may also understand that these selection criteria command a base salary in non-sales positions that require the same attributes. On the other hand, if the selection criteria for a sales job stress only general attributes (e.g., attitude and willingness to work) and not specialized attributes (e.g., experience and training), you will need to provide few, if any, income assurances. General attributes are labor market "givens" and seldom carry a price that the employer must "ante up" before recruiting. The mere possession of these attributes rarely gives a candidate any leverage in seeking income assurances.

Once a company stipulates that specialized experience or training is required, however, it will usually have to provide the rep with some type of assured income. Furthermore, if a rep must build a territory from scratch, if the sales cycle is long, or if orders are volatile, some type of assured income—such as a draw—is usually necessary to meet the rep's *cash flow* needs. This can be true even when the barriers to entry into the job are very low.

Base salary and other income assurances, therefore, play two primary roles:

1. To compensate an incumbent for the minimum "going value" of the experiences and skills required by the job
2. To provide a cash flow "floor" for the rep when there is a risk that routine personal needs cannot be met with incentive income

Whether these assurances are delivered to the rep in the form of a base salary, a draw against future incentive income, or a guaranteed level of incentive income earned on a "book of business" in an established territory is critical. The choice that is made will have a profound impact on the overall design of any compensation plan.

Your decision should begin with the barriers to entry into the sales job. If the barriers to entry are high, you can expect the talent pool to be small. In this case, significant base salary is probably appropriate because the value of scarce talent will be "bid up" in the marketplace. The rep, presumably, has employment alternatives, some of which include income assurances. An experienced sales rep will usually find assured income decisive in making his employment decision.

What does base salary purchase? Because a base salary is payable independent of immediate sales performance, it provides income assurance that may be valued by the rep. If it is, a base salary may purchase some degree of rep commitment to the job. An employer, on the other hand, may expect significantly more than this for its investment of base salary and associated benefits. Some sales managers speak of basic sales activities (as distinguished from end results) as being "paid for by the base." Other managers see base salary as evidence of the rep's long-term success in fulfilling the enduring accountabilities of the job. Still other managers regard base salary as simply an unavoidable fixed cost that ensures the retention of the sales force and should be neither over-interpreted nor overmanaged.

The answer to the question, "What does base salary purchase?" depends on the practices and objectives of the employer. If company A pays the same base salary to all its salespeople and feels free to change this amount with little explanation, base salary may meet only the minimum cash flow expectations of the sales force. In this case, base salary is a passive cost that purchases only nominal commitment to the company.

If, on the other hand, company B pays different base salaries that fall within a base salary range and uses a formal performance planning and appraisal process to determine whether each rep merits an increase in base, base salary is probably performing some work for the company. What salespeople are doing, how they do it, and their attitude toward their work may be influenced by a base salary administration program that makes distinctions between the performance and value of each player.

In theory, higher base salaries are effective in purchasing rep commitment and management control over rep activities. In reality, higher base salaries may purchase only passive commitment (i.e., not looking for another job) rather than active commitment (i.e., performing the current job with skill and energy). This proves especially true in industries where sales reps are accustomed to high-incentive opportunity, if their high base has been offered at the expense of such opportunity. Furthermore, even though the base may be high, management may experience little increase in control over field activities because it doesn't know how to make the base perform work for the company.

This is a common challenge for sales and human resources managers as they sort through the complex interplay of two key factors:

1. Competitive labor costs—and the latest market trends for those costs
2. The budget and criteria for merit increases to base salary

Especially difficult is the merit increase. Many companies use an informal, smoke-filled-room method for determining merit increases for each sales rep. In effect, these organizations *stack rank* all reps, from first to last, and apportion increases from a predetermined budget according to the ranking.

Although this method is superior to treating all reps equally, which amounts to not using the idea of individual merit in determining base salary, it suffers the major weakness of being opaque to the sales force. This doesn't always create a problem at first. Over time, however, enough suspicion about the process can compromise the efforts of management to recognize sustained performance.

The performance appraisal process is a particularly difficult tool for sales managers to master in their effort to separate the performance that justifies base salary from the performance that triggers incentive payments.

Base salary's role is to deliver the assured compensation needed to attract and retain the skills and experiences required by the sales job. And it does this in a decisive way: The base is virtually guaranteed as long as the rep is an employee in good standing in the job. This role can be enhanced by linking any increases in base salary to the achievement of identified objectives.

If the barriers to entry are low, you will need to provide little (if any) base salary, which guarantees some level of pay to which any incentive earnings are added. Any income assurances that are still indicated—to meet the rep's cash flow needs—can be provided by a draw, i.e., a minimum income level below which the rep's income cannot fall but against which all incentive earnings are netted before any additional income is payable to the rep.

For example, consider a rep with a weekly draw of $500. If sales are $6,000 during one week and the commission rate is 10 percent, commission earnings will be $600 and the net payable to the rep at the end of the week, $100—or the difference between the amount drawn at the beginning of the week ($500) and the amount earned during the week ($600).

A draw is cash that is advanced against future income, that is, a loan. A *recoverable* draw is a loan that can be settled against all future income, whereas a *nonrecoverable* draw is advanced against current income only. Consider the following example of a recoverable draw: Suppose a rep receives a $500 draw at the beginning of each week and that commission earnings are $400 in week A and $650 in week B. The rep is short $100 in week A. If the draw for week A is recoverable, this leads to a commission in week B that is reduced from $150 to $50 (i.e., $650 commission earnings in week B minus $500 regular draw minus $100 owed from week A). A recoverable draw, therefore, recovers unearned cash advances by carrying the "debt" forward to the next incentive period, indefinitely, until the debt has been paid. A nonrecoverable draw does not carry a balance forward into the next incentive period. If the draw is not covered by incentives earned in the current incentive period, the employer forgives the shortfall and absorbs it as a loss. This is the only type of draw that offers true income assurance to a rep.

The difference between base salary and a draw is that base salary represents a direct payment by the company for something; a draw, on the other hand, is a loan rather than a payment—a loan that is secured by the expectation that future sales performance will generate incentive earnings that are sufficient to service or "cover" the debt.

13.2   The Interplay of Mix, Base, and Disguised Base

To administer base salaries for salespeople, you must clearly differentiate between base salary and assured income. A base salary is a fixed and regular payment that is provided by a formal part of the sales compensation program. Assured income, on the other hand, represents the total of all formal and informal payments on which the rep can rely, although some flexibility in the estimate of a rep's assured income (to account for such factors as changing quotas and economic climate) is possible.

The level of assured income can often exceed the base salary. For example, many organizations offer reps who have been asked to build an entirely new territory a draw (for a limited time) in addition to a base salary. This draw gives the rep additional income assurances during a period of weak sales volume. Also, many incentive plans for established territories deliver incentive income from the first dollar of sales. Because it is extremely unlikely that every dollar from that territory is literally reearned each performance period and that some revenue would reappear *on its own* for a while, some incentive pay is virtually guaranteed.

When the mix of base salary (fixed) and incentive (variable) compensation is established, you must be sure that either *the incentive plan* produces truly variable compensation or the base salary is set somewhat lower to allow for the additional assured income built into the incentive plan.

This additional assured income, which has been referred to as "disguised base salary" in recent publications, is the most commonly overlooked feature of a sales compensation program. Yet it can be decisive in determining sales force response to the incentive plan and the base salary merit increase program. Obviously, the greater the level of disguised base salary, the less the other features of a pay plan will matter.

The actual mix of assured and variable compensation is, therefore, often different from the actual mix of base and incentive.

13.3 Factors Affecting Base Salary

Think of the factors that affect base salary on two levels:

1. Factors that affect market rates
2. Factors that affect an individual's personal base salary rate

Consider first the factors affecting market rates. Here, you should further distinguish two general classes of industry: type A industries, which rely heavily on proven sales talent drawn from other companies *within the industry,* and type B industries, which recruit broadly or train their own sales talent.

In type A industries, companies must respect base salary market rates. A pattern of prevailing base salaries as well as incentive levels emerges within the industry. The active exchange of reps and sales managers among the industry's players leads to a clear sense of accepted opening bid levels. Type A industries, therefore, represent internal markets for their sales talent, with each company's compensation practices governed more by external supply, demand, and traditional industry practice than by its own preferences for program design.

In type B industries, base salary market rates reflect prevailing practice more than prevailing necessity. At the extreme, in industries where companies almost never recruit from each other, the collective sales compensation practices of the industry are almost meaningless to someone trying to establish adequate base salary levels for a specific company. Far more important are market rates in the other areas where sales talent is actually acquired.

More commonly, companies in type B industries tend to recruit entry-level sales reps and train them internally. At the time they are hired, these employees may have had no prior sales experience, or none within the industry. Such companies rely on internal development and promotion and rarely "go outside" for senior sales talent, including management talent, so that employee loyalty can be forged.

This equilibrium in the industry works as long as all the players practice the same internal development philosophy and there are few new entrants into the industry. New companies, however, usually "buy" their sales forces, especially their management teams, from other companies within the industry. When this occurs, hiring and compensation practices are destabilized. A type B company now needs to think about market rates in two areas:

1. Its sources for entry-level recruits
2. Its own industry, where local competitors try to lure away its investment in proven talent

Most type B companies consequently need to pay attention to competitive market rates for base salary, incentive, and total cash compensation in their respective industries, especially at the senior levels of their sales structure.

The general factors that affect market rates include industry growth, prominence of the sales force, supply of sales talent, availability of internal training resources, and any statutory requirements that may govern payments to sales reps. In addition, there appears to be an effective minimum annual income that even unskilled salespeople in low-prominence positions can expect in today's marketplace. This effective minimum, which is usually defined by the income of certain inside sales and inbound telemarketing positions, is governed more by social forces and quality-of-life issues than by any market forces specific to sales talent. This minimum may vary significantly between urban centers and smaller cities and between professionally administered compensation programs and the ad hoc practices of small businesses.

The factors that affect an individual's base salary are more easily characterized. Usually, a sales rep's base reflects performance over time, tenure in the job, tenure with the company, the specific practices of the company, and promotions to higher positions. It can also reflect the pattern and frequency of changes in employer, especially if these changes are in response to changes in the industry.

In industries experiencing a shortage of seasoned sales talent, the price of that talent is usually bid up until price and supply reach some equilibrium. Higher prices (that is, compensation) will attract sales reps from other segments of the same industry and even other industries and will also encourage salespeople in the host industry, particularly those with alternatives, to consider a change. In a rising compensation market, this can be the quickest way to raise personal income. It also represents a competitive climate where pay plan provisions and revisions will be critical to attracting and retaining talent.

13.4 Influence of Customer Characteristics on Base Salary

Sales rep attributes should only partly determine a company's hierarchy of base salaries. Customer characteristics should also play a role. If all sales reps serve the same types of customers, it often makes sense to provide a higher base to those reps with greater experience, success, and tenure, simply to avoid losing more experienced salespeople. Here, base salary should act as a retention mechanism.

Indeed, many industries commonly identify three or four sales rep levels that represent little more than a *maturity ladder*, i.e., a compensation scale that ascends with increases in relevant sales experience. Compensation surveys in these industries typically match pay levels to generic job descriptions and years of experience. They reveal that years of experience largely determine the way data are reported and jobs classified.

Some of these surveys also allude to increasing job content and to responsibility for larger territories and customers as accompanying advances in job title. And, indeed, many companies do match a larger title and greater pay with greater job content. Not all do, however. Some rely almost exclusively on experience as the determinant in income level for both base salary and incentive. These varying practices make the interpretation of much of the available survey data difficult, ensuring that the market-pricing exercise will always remain as much an art as a science.

Ideally, the hierarchy of base salaries should reflect the following key considerations:

- Customer characteristics (e.g., buying cycle, size, local versus national scope of customer operations, and number of decision makers involved)
- Organizational characteristics (e.g., the need to recruit the best salespeople from established territories to national account manager positions with little or different revenue responsibilities and the need to lay out a "promotional footpath" for salespeople that permits increases in base to match increases in job content)
- Individual characteristics (e.g., experience, tenure, and current performance against qualitative and longer-term goals established for the position held)

When all of these factors are considered, the target mix, the level of compensation, and the recruiting criteria will vary with the sales job. And each rep's experience and performance (as ranked within a salary range that is appropriate for his or her position) will determine the level of base salary.

13.5   Administering Base Salaries

There are five general approaches to administering base salaries to salespeople. Each can be appropriate in a given context. The approaches are usually characterized as:

1. Single rate
2. Experience or tenure
3. Stack ranking
4. Merit
5. Discretionary

With the exception of the single-rate approach, these methodologies do not strictly conform to their theoretical descriptions. For example, most longevity programs simply give more weight to tenure or experience than to the results of a performance appraisal. Similarly, most programs based on an evaluation of the rep give more weight to the appraisal process than to tenure or experience.

13.6   The Single-Rate Approach

In those relatively rare situations where the sales force is unionized, labor negotiators will often argue for the single-rate approach. Unions generally try to ensure a contractual rate at which all members will work free from management's discretion, and have the freedom to suspend or modify any compensation arrangements on which the sales force may have relied.

The single-rate approach can also prove useful in maintaining a sense of internal pay equity among salespeople when the incentive earning opportunities are significant and the control of the sales force over personal performance and income is great. In these situations, sales reps may interpret significant differences in base salary as arbitrary and unfair, because the means and the opportunity to have more income through personal sales performance are clear and available to everyone.

Furthermore, in new sales organizations, where the management practices that are needed to support a formal performance appraisal process seldom exist, it may simply be necessary to use either a single-rate or an experience/tenure approach to setting base salaries. Often, a rep joins the organization at a lower starting rate and, after successfully completing an orientation period of selling, quickly moves up the control-rate, base salary level. You should remember, however, that single-rate approaches are best suited to high-prominence sales jobs with a clear and immediate opportunity to earn incentive income based on individual achievement.

Where prominence is low, sales results come more slowly, or other indicators of achievement are equally valid, the base salary will tend to represent a greater percentage of pay. Where it does, there must be some flexibility in its administration, that is, some range of base salaries, to reflect real differences in performance from one sales rep to the next. A single-rate base/low-incentive arrangement offers few opportunities to differentiate performance through pay. As such, it offers entitlements for the rep and correspondingly modest leverage for management.

13.7 The Experience/Tenure Approach

The experience (maturity ladder) or tenure (longevity) approach delivers more base for more experience or tenure. In its simplest form, a maturity ladder system raises the base as years of relevant sales experience increase, *no matter where that experience was acquired.* Literally, as a rep matures, his compensation—base and incentive—"ladder up." Similarly, a longevity approach increases base as years of *internal experience* increase. The relationship between years of experience/tenure and base salary can be well defined or loose. Most companies prefer to avoid a strict relationship, whereby a qualifying number of years would *automatically* assure each rep a higher base.

On the face of it, neither of these seems acceptable as a stand-alone practice because neither is directly related to performance. Yet each *is* usually related indirectly to performance, because increasing experience or tenure is normally difficult to acquire when one is not performing. The ultimate appraisal system is always at work, that is, the one that reaffirms periodically that the rep continues to meet the minimum standards for the job.

Indeed, where the rep must consistently meet explicit minimum selling levels as a condition for continued employment, the wheat is sorted from the chaff, and a longevity approach to base salary can work. In those cases where it does, the tenured rep is simply "promoted" from a sales rep I position to a sales rep II position, and so on up to a III or IV level. For a rep II, III, or IV, the base usually increases either to a single rate for that level or to a rate within a very narrow range for that job. This technique recognizes the rep's service and competence over time— and, therefore, merit—without getting involved in direct one-on-one management assessments of each rep's performance against an array of goals and standards.

A modified longevity approach also relies on an informal management assessment of a rep's entire performance. This serves as the basis for a simple or stack-ranked recommendation for a base salary increase. Here, you weigh the rep's tenure, his results in all areas for the year, and the increase he can work with, such as "an increase of 3–7 percent."

13.8   The Stack-Ranking Approach

The stack-ranking approach to base salary administration has two basic elements:

1. A high-to-low rank ordering of each rep's annual performance in a given job
2. A budget or "pot" set aside for base salary increases for eligible employees in that job category

Once the pot has been established and each employee's annual performance has been graded, the highest-ranking individual receives the largest increase—either in percentage terms or in dollars, depending on the system in use—followed by the second-ranking individual, and so on. In essence, this method tells the sales force that the reps with the highest grades will receive the greatest rewards.

With respect to the experience/tenure approach, stack ranking focuses on what the sales rep has accomplished rather than how long he or she has been working at it. Stack ranking differs from the merit approach in its informal way of arriving at the actual size of the increase received by the rep. The only constraint on the size of the increase in a pure stack-ranking system is the overall increase budget. (Some modified stack-ranking programs also stipulate a maximum and a minimum increase in an effort to maintain some level of internal equity.) In a merit program, fairly strict rules determine a rep's percentage increase based on his or her appraisal rating, position in the salary range and, in some programs, tenure.

13.9   The Merit Approach

Human resources managers overwhelmingly prefer the merit approach to base salary administration for sales personnel. Enthusiasm for this method, however, is not as pervasive among sales managers. The merit approach combines at least the first two of the following administrative elements:

1. A formal performance appraisal form and process
2. A budget for merit increases to base salaries
3. A salary increase guide that links increases to the position of the rep's current salary in the salary range for the job

A plain vanilla merit program establishes a budget for base salary increases that can be spent by the company as a whole, the exempt population as a whole, a functional area as a whole, or a department. It also creates a link between the budget and the performance evaluation received by a rep. To standardize this linkage, the evaluations are usually expressed by an overall numerical score (e.g., 3.00 out of a possible 5.00). A specific score translates into a specific percentage increase to the rep's base salary, or an increase range within which the manager may choose a specific percentage for the rep.

A more elaborate merit program links the merit budget, the performance evaluation, and the rep's current position in the base salary range to the increase percentage that is awarded. Under this approach, those with the highest evaluation and the lowest salary would receive the largest percentage increase because, relative to their performance, they are the most deserving.

The most basic performance appraisal form/process for salespeople requires the manager to evaluate the rep's performance throughout the year against stated objectives, standards, and key job responsibilities. Objectives can include traditional production quotas (e.g., revenue or gross profit goals) as well as special objectives for selected accounts, products, and marketing programs. Standards usually include considerations of professional conduct and competence, minimums for call frequency and production, and demonstrations of initiative, creativity, and teamwork where appropriate. Key job responsibilities outline the basic steps and end results expected of any satisfactory performer in the job.

More elaborate performance appraisal systems include a skills inventory, which usually comprises standard indicators of sales skill, customized indicators that apply to the industry, and standard nonsales indicators. In this way, the sales manager explicitly states *how well* the rep delivered, not just *how much* the rep delivered.

The most common concerns that sales managers express about the use of the merit approach fall into five categories:

1. Too structured, not intuitive enough.
2. Not enough differentiation between the performers and the non-performers. Under the merit program approach, you have to give everyone receiving an increase a raise of 3–8 percent. With a less formal system, you could show greater differences.
3. Too time-consuming. The paperwork and face-to-face performance reviews are draining and yield questionable improvements.

4. The tendency to double-dip, that is, to count the percentage of quota attained twice—once in the incentive plan and once in the base salary program—giving a rep a large increase in base when his incentive earnings for the year are also very good. This results in an increased fixed cost (i.e., the higher base), which is especially painful when yesterday's high flier is today's glider pilot. Such a problem would be less likely with a single-rate approach or even a maturity ladder/longevity approach.

5. The sales force gets less than its fair share of budgeted base salary dollars (because other functions complain that sales is already treated too well, with its cash incentives and travel awards). A single-rate or longevity approach might not produce the same reaction.

All of these concerns are legitimate because a merit program can be improperly designed or administered in each of these ways. A merit program, however, provides an easy target because it makes the effort to adopt explicit policy—policy that is pledged to linking pay equitably to performance. Single-rate, longevity, and discretionary approaches to base salary administration do not make this pledge. Pure varieties of the single-rate and longevity approaches use uniform rules for assigning base salaries, but that isn't the same thing as following equitable policy. A uniformly applied rule can be uniformly unfair.

The merit approach will prove more effective than the other widely used techniques if the following conditions exist or are anticipated:

- Sales management accepts the value of a more "obective" method.
- The performance appraisal form and process are tailored to sales measures, objectives, standards, and skills.
- Sales managers are trained and supervised in the development of evaluation scores and the delivery of written and verbal feedback to their direct reports.
- The performance appraisal restricts, by design, the opportunity and the temptation to double-dip.
- Merit budgets are adequate to do the job, and senior management understands the importance of maintaining the intended ratio of base salary to incentive income in the program.
- Salary increase guidelines are provided, which link appraisal score, position in the salary range, and the recommended increase in base.
- The salary ranges for sales positions are wide enough for meaningful increases to be given the better performers yet not so wide that the company's exposure to extensive double-dipping is great.

When these conditions exist, merit programs usually work well and yield results that are superior to the traditional alternatives. When two or more of these conditions don't exist, however, the danger is that everyone will go through the motions without the commitment. This outcome can be truly counterproductive. Simpler alternatives, such as the single-rate approach, can often work if matched correctly to the setting. In general, sales managers need a renewed understanding of the potential power and appropriateness of these alternatives.

13.10   The Discretionary Approach

The discretionary approach to base salary administration is less a stand-alone method than a technique to modify three of the other approaches, namely, the experience/tenure, the stack-ranking, and the merit systems. The discretionary approach refers to the practice of using discretion rather than a formula or a published guideline to determine the size of the base salary increase received by an individual rep.

To show how the other approaches can be modified in this way, consider the following illustration:

Some sales organizations are strongly committed to acknowledging a sales rep's experience, tenure, and title, especially in a growth business where new reps expect to be promoted once or twice within their first two or three years of employment.

In these companies, significant relevant sales experience qualifies the new hire for either a higher-than-normal base for a starting rep or entry at the intermediate or senior sales rep levels. In addition, successful tenure inside the company converts to promotability and an increase in base salary at the time of promotion. This pattern of experience, promotion, and increases in base may not seem to leave room for discretion in determining the level of base salary. On the contrary, however, discretion plays a role in the administration of most of these programs.

First, the timing of a rep's promotion is almost never automatic. The sales manager usually must agree that the rep is ready to move up. So, indirectly, the rep's base salary level is controlled through the timing of a rep's promotion. More important, the amount of promotional increase received by the rep may also be influenced by the sales manager. Within some framework, managers frequently exercise influence over the size of a promotional increase, largely on the basis of personal opinions concerning how much of an increase is deserved.

This is especially true in informal settings. There, the process for arriving at the size of an increase may be essentially discretionary, within broad parameters. This practice has the natural appeal of being simple to administer, flexible, and theoretically comprehensive in its inclusion of all the relevant performance factors. It also delegates authority to sales management that is usually shared with the human resources function in settings that are closely governed by stated compensation policies.

This type of discretionary modification to a pure longevity or stack-ranking approach is very common. Indeed, it remains the most widespread approach to base salary management for sales people. Why? Because companies seldom prefer to lose all control over a major source of employee income, a loss that comes with use of a pure rule-driven method for setting salary levels, just to achieve some administrative simplicity.

The power and appeal of discretionary practices are, however, balanced by some potential drawbacks. These practices can be seen as arbitrary and are easily corrupted by bias and carelessness in arriving at a conclusion for each employee. To minimize the inherent weaknesses of a discretionary approach, a company can require one or more stages of management review before signatures are affixed to each rep's new base salary rate.

14

Incentive Plan Design

14.1 Introduction

A medium-size industrial company that was struggling with the design of an incentive plan hired a vice-president of sales. After only two weeks on the job, the vice-president offered his proposal for the new plan.

The plan was the same as the one that had worked well at his two previous employers. It was a salary-plus-commission arrangement based solely on volume. The vice-president argued that the plan would succeed and would require only limited fine-tuning. And, in fact, the plan appeared to work for about six months before it went sour.

Under the new incentive plan, sales reps began to focus solely on high-volume accounts and to ignore lower-volume but highly profitable accounts. After a year, the company had experienced moderate sales growth, significantly lower profits, and record high payouts to the sales force. Needless to say, the company changed the plan abruptly the next year to include a variable commission rate based on gross margin. Because this resulted in reduced commission payouts, the sales force viewed it as unfair. Sales reps believed that the company was "changing the rules" because it didn't want them to earn large commissions.

Many of the company's top performers left the organization over the next twelve months. Volume slipped, margins remained about the same, and the vice-president of sales departed to "pursue other business interests."

This story demonstrates the potential pitfalls of installing a new incentive plan without a sufficient understanding of all the relevant factors and plan determinants. Simply copying another company's incentive plan can lead to disaster. An incentive plan will succeed only if it reflects the organizational dynamics of the particular company.

Designing an incentive plan is a relatively straightforward process once you have clearly defined such factors as the plan's objectives and performance measures, competitive practices, customer characteristics, barrier to entry to the sales position, and prominence of the sales force in the selling process.

14.2   Compensation Mix

To determine the appropriate proportion of incentive to total cash compensation, you must consider the following factors:

- Barrier to entry
- Prominence
- Competitive industry/relevant labor market practices

Barrier to Entry

The barrier to entry determines the amount of low-risk compensation (e.g., base pay or virtually guaranteed incentive payout) needed to obtain a certain set of skills in the competitive marketplace. The higher the barrier to entry, the higher the level of low-risk compensation. Used car sales represent a low barrier-to-entry field in which little, if any, low-risk compensation is required to attract qualified personnel. Mainframe computer sales jobs, on the other hand, exemplify high barrier-to-entry positions in which companies must typically offer significant amounts of low-risk compensation.

Prominence

The influence or prominence of the sales rep in the overall marketing mix of an organization plays a significant role in determining the proper combination of fixed and variable compensation. Generally speaking, high-prominence selling jobs have significantly leveraged compensation packages with a large amount of pay "at risk."

Competitive Industry/Relevant Labor Market Practices

To compete effectively for selling skills, organizations must offer competitive rates of pay. As previously indicated, competitive salary survey information, which is very helpful in defining competitive levels of total cash compensation, can cause significant problems if used blindly to determine the mix of compensation. Although industry-specific data serve, initially, as reference points in developing a sense of an appropriate compensation mix, such information can be misleading.

For example, a few well-known companies dominate the personal computer industry. These companies enjoy significant brand-name recognition, large advertising budgets, and well-developed channels of distribution. At the other end of the spectrum are companies struggling to survive with low recognition, small advertising budgets, and poorly developed distribution channels. The prominence of each company's sales force probably varies dramatically, as does the amount of incentive opportunity. In short, competitive market data tell part of the story, but not the whole story.

Figure 14-1 shows various combinations of barrier to entry and prominence. A high entry barrier tends to raise the low-risk or guaranteed portion of a compensation package. This is not to say, however, that a high entry barrier influences the maximum compensation opportunity a sales rep can expect. That depends on the prominence of the sales job in the marketing mix and on competitive standards.

Figure 14-2 presents a variety of combinations of base salary and

Figure 14-1. Relationship between barrier to entry and prominence in marketing mix.

High

Barrier to Entry

High Barrier/Low Prominence

A technically trained representative is responsible for selling a highly complex piece of machinery to engineers, where the need for the machine is readily recognized, and there are few suppliers (perhaps only one).

High Barrier/High Prominence

The sales representative must have extensive experience and/or technical expertise; the product, process, or service must be sold both in terms of its need and in terms of the given company as the supplier. Creative, unique applications of the product or the process must be developed and integrated with the customer's production process in a manner that will increase the customer's profitability.

Low Barrier/Low Prominence

The sales representative has a maintenance position requiring minimal training and/or product expertise and circulates among a largely established customer familiarity with company products and applications.

Low Barrier/High Prominence

The sales representative is required to find and/or "qualify" prospects and successfully persuade them of their need for a particular product, process, or service even though a tangible need, for the company product cannot be documented objectively.

Low

Prominence in Marketing Mix

Figure 14-2. Range and characteristics of base salary and incentive combinations.

Incentive	Base Salary	Typical Emphasis on Compensation Security	Typical Prominence	Typical Barrier to Entry	Typical Context
75%	25%	Little or none	Very high	Very low	• Start-up company • Door-to-door sales • Strong selling orientation encouraged • Commission orientation • Few opportunities for management control
50%	50%	Modest	High	Low to moderate	• Sales force relied on heavily for generating sales • Modest management control • Service sales (e.g., insurance company, computer services)
25%	75%	Significant	Significant	Varies (typically modest to high)	• Mature company • Sales force equal in prevalence to other elements in marketing mix • Significant management control • Industrial sales (e.g., chemicals, instruments)
10%	90%	Heavy	Low	Varies (typically low)	• Sales force has limited influence in marketing mix • Sales trainee position • Tight management control • "Paying for talent" orientation • Selling process is probably team oriented • Nondurable consumer sales (e.g., food, candy, tobacco)

incentive. It is intended to show the range of alternatives that exist as well as to describe the likely characteristics of each scenario.

After you have determined the compensation mix for a particular sales job, can you assume that the mix will be appropriate indefinitely? Probably not. In general, the compensation mix for each sales job should be reviewed every three to four years—and sooner if any of the following factors change significantly:

- Marketing strategy
- Reorganization of sales force(s)
- Redesign of sales jobs or addition of sales support positions
- Additions/reductions to sales force
- Competitive market practice

14.3   Salary Differences: Amplify or Neutralize?

After you have determined the compensation mix for a specific sales job, you need to decide whether the incentive element should "amplify" or "neutralize" differences in base pay (assuming there are differences).

A large newspaper company in the Midwest set base salaries for employees in a particular sales position using a traditional point factor job evaluation plan. The salary grade for the job had a midpoint of $40,000. The minimum for the salary grade was $32,000 and the maximum, $48,000. The company reviewed sales rep performance annually (as it did with other exempt employees) and gave merit increases based on its performance appraisal guidelines.

The company established the target cash compensation for the job at $46,000. Because it had a large number of veteran employees, the company found itself with many sales reps at the top of the salary range. In fact, some reps were making more in base pay than the total cash target. To tack a 15 percent incentive opportunity onto a base salary already above targeted total cash was out of the question. Cutting base salary, however, was not considered a viable alternative. To solve the problem, the company decided to make the incentive a function of the midpoint and assigned each rep a target bonus opportunity of $6,000.

14.4   Incentive Payout Timing and Recognition of Results

When designing any new incentive plan, you need to consider two basic questions regarding incentive payout timing and the recognition of results:

1. When should performance be recognized?
2. How often should incentives be paid?

The correct approach depends on company-specific variables and the nature of the selling situation. In other words, there are no right or wrong answers. There are only general guidelines.

When Should Performance Be Recognized?

Most companies recognize results when an order is billed or delivered. Some companies credit a sales rep for a sale at the time an order is booked, others credit the sale at collection. Some give partial credit at one event and give the balance of the credit at another event.

To maximize the motivational impact of an incentive program, it makes sense to recognize a sale at the time an order is booked. This ensures a rapid response to a desired behavior and the rep is not penalized for events beyond his control (e.g., production delays, delivery problems). But what if there is a significant lag from the time an order is booked until it is paid? Or what if a company feels that a sales rep should be at least partially responsible for ensuring the bills are collected in a timely manner?

Without question, concerns about cash flow and sales reps submitting marginal orders are valid. You can address the cash flow issue by delaying the time at which an order is recognized for incentive purposes. For example, crediting sales reps when orders are invoiced is a reasonable way to cut the time between payment and collection. If, however, there is a significant amount of time between entering the order and invoicing it (e.g., more than six months), some of the motivational impact of the incentive plan will be lost.

Waiting until an invoice is paid resolves the marginal order concern and encourages a rep to follow up on delinquent accounts. But again, the longer the period between behavior and recognition, the more likely the motivational impact of the plan will diminish.

Many companies give partial credit at two or more discrete events to address the issues raised above and to preserve the motivational impact of the plan. A common approach in a situation where there is a long period between order placement and shipping is to credit a large portion of the incentive when the order is booked and the balance when payment is received from the customer.

How Often Should Incentives Be Paid?

In general, incentive payments should be made often enough to motivate a sales rep but far enough apart to conform to a company's sales cycle and to ensure that individual goals can actually be accomplished in the time allowed. The frequency of incentive payments should also reflect the compensation mix. These objectives often conflict, and an appropriate balance needs to be struck if a plan is going to be effective. Finally, the greater the portion of incentive to total cash, the more frequently incentive payouts should be made.

Sales reps in high-prominence selling jobs frequently receive more than 50 percent of their annual cash income in incentive payments. For these highly leveraged jobs, incentives are paid at least quarterly and sometimes monthly. This is especially true for low barrier-to-entry jobs, which typically pay low base salaries. In these cases, the rep often cannot maintain a modest standard of living with base salary alone.

Compensation theory suggests that timely feedback is critical to ensuring that incentive plans are motivational. Except for plans that assign a very small portion of compensation to incentive pay, annual payouts make little sense in terms of maximizing motivation or sales management effectiveness.

But what if a company has a particularly long selling cycle, where it often takes months and sometimes years before a sale is consummated? Should a company be expected to make incentive payments before the sales force has made the sale? Surprisingly, many companies answer yes. Some incentive plans are designed to recognize the accomplishment of "milestones" toward a sale (e.g., getting a product specified). These plans reward the rep for doing the right things to make a sale likely as well as for closing the sale. Quarterly payouts are made based on how well the rep has done in relation to the milestones or account objectives, and commissions on sales are paid when the company recognizes the sale (for example, at invoicing or payment).

Many companies use draws to eliminate some of the financial hardship many low-barrier/high-prominence reps face. Some companies vary the size of the draw based on such criteria as seniority, past performance, or anticipated performance.

A common problem arises when a company conducts an inordinate amount of its business in the first quarter or in the first half of the year. What assurances do such companies have that they will not overpay reps or lose them after the first quarter?

Many companies address this problem by holding back a portion of a rep's incentive pay until year end. This encourages the rep to remain with the company and protects the company from systematically overpaying its reps for disproportionate first-quarter sales.

Holdback schedules work in the following manner: Assume an incentive plan calls for payouts based on cumulative quarterly results. To ensure that reps are not overpaid in relation to their annual goals, the plan pays only 50 percent of incentive in the first quarter, 65 percent in the second, 80 percent in the third, and 100 percent at year end. Figure 14-3 shows how such a plan might work for a rep who had three quarters of above-average performance but who failed to earn an incentive in the final fiscal quarter.

Figure 14-3. Sample holdback schedule.

Quarter	Cumulative Incentives Accrued	Quarterly Incentive Payout	Actual Quarterly Incentive	Total Year-to-Date Payouts
1st	$ 6,000	50%	$3,000	$3,000
2nd	9,000	65	2,850	5,850
3rd	10,000	80	2,150	8,000
4th	10,000	100	2,000	10,000

14.5   Maximum Payout

When any sales compensation plan is designed or modified, the inevitable question arises: Should there be a cap? Ask the top sales executive or any sales rep and you will be told, "No, of course not—caps are 'demotivators.'" Pose the same question to your CFO, and you will most likely hear, "Absolutely, why not? Caps protect the company against windfall payouts."

Generally, the higher the prominence of the sales rep in the marketing mix, the less appropriate a cap will be. For example, in selling insurance and mutual funds and in door-to-door sales, the sales rep is almost solely responsible for acquiring customers and generating volume. In these fields, it is usually impossible for a rep to bring in too many new customers or to generate too much volume. Obviously, a cap for these types of selling situations makes little sense.

On the other hand, in such low-prominence selling as industrial sales, sales volume and new and repeat business are usually a function of other elements of a company's marketing mix (for example, advertising, product reliability, brand loyalty, and price) and are not attributable to the prominence of the sales rep. Because the selling role is more "sales facilitation" than "sales generation," limiting a sales rep's incentive opportunity is often a wise step to take.

Having covered the extremes of the prominence spectrum, where the answer to the cap question is straightforward, let's consider selling situations that fall in between.

Many organizations like the appeal of an open-ended incentive opportunity but worry about windfall payouts. Philosophically, they believe that caps are demotivators and that it is difficult to determine where to draw the line for maximum payout opportunity. If the maximum is set too low, a sales rep may "shut down" after he reaches the maximum. If the cap is set so high that no one can come close to reaching it, the cap might also demotivate.

You do not have to think of caps in all-or-nothing terms. In some selling situations, it makes entirely good sense to cap part of a sales rep's incentive opportunity and leave other parts open-ended. One manufacturer, for example, pays a straight commission for sales in a particular product line but limits the payout from any sale to $5,000. This strategy encourages sales reps to develop new customers and discourages them from focusing on only a handful of large accounts.

Another company limits commission payouts by product within a product line. Presumably, this encourages a sales rep with product line responsibility not to focus solely on one or two products but to sell all the offerings in the product line.

As with most sales compensation questions, there is no clear-cut answer to whether a sales incentive plan should be capped. You must decide for yourself by analyzing the prominence of the sales job and considering cultural values, competitive practices, and the behaviors that will ultimately be reinforced by the plan.

14.6   Types of Incentive Rates

Incentive rates can be categorized as follows:

- Constant
- Progressive (accelerating)
- Regressive (decelerating)
- Combination

Choosing the right rate is critical to the successful implementation of a compensation plan and to the sales force's acceptance of it. There are two basic approaches to establishing incentive rates. The first involves identifying the desired profit margin of a given product or territory and basing the commission rate on an appropriate percentage of it. The second focuses on providing competitive levels of compensation to the sales force by "backing into" a commission rate to produce the desired total cash compensation opportunity. Figure 14-4 provides simple examples of each of these approaches.

Constant Incentive Rates

Most companies employ constant incentive rate schemes. Examples include:

- 3 percent of total territory sales volume
- 10 percent of gross margin dollars
- 1 percent of base salary for each $50,000 of sales volume

Figure 14-4. Desired profit margin approach and competitive earnings approach.

Desired Profit Margin Approach

(1)	(2)	(3)	(2) − (3)
	Desired	Desired	
Expected	Margin	Margin	
Territory	Before	After	Commission
Volume	Commissions	Commissions	Rate
$2,000,000	13%	10%	3%

Competitive Earnings Approach

(1)	(2)	(3)	(3) / (2)
	Expected	Desired	
Territory	Territory	Incentive	Commission
Performance	Volume	Award	Rate
Exceptional	$4,000,000	$80,000	2%
Above Standard	3,000,000	60,000	2
Standard	2,000,000	40,000	2
Below Standard	1,000,000	20,000	2
Poor	500,000	10,000	2

Constant incentive rates are appropriate when performance cannot be predicted with a great deal of accuracy. Volatile markets, start-up companies, and lack of management ability to define meaningful quotas or goals are all good reasons to use constant incentive rates.

Progressive (Accelerating) Incentive Rates

The use of accelerating or progressive incentive rates after a certain level of performance is achieved is also common. Examples include:

- 4 percent of sales volume up to 80 percent of annual quota, plus 5 percent of volume in excess of that threshold
- 3 percent of gross margin between $0 and $100,000, 5 percent of gross margin between $100,000 and $200,000, and 7.5 percent of gross margin over $200,000
- $2,000 for achieving one of three goals, $5,000 for achieving two of three goals, and $15,000 for achieving three of three goals

Accelerated incentive rates are predicated on the principle that the last dollar of volume is the most difficult to attain and, consequently, should be rewarded at a higher rate than the first dollar is. This is especially true in situations where a company has fixed costs in relation to variable selling costs.

Accelerated incentive rates also encourage sales reps to maximize performance during a given period. Rewarding performance at progressively higher rates after a certain threshold is satisfied motivates a rep to book a sale promptly rather than wait for the next performance period.

Accelerated incentive rates can also help in attracting qualified sales reps to a company. Provided targets are set fairly and target earnings are competitive, companies can more easily recruit sales reps from companies offering constant or decelerating incentive schemes.

Accelerated incentive rates put a great deal of pressure on goal-setting and quota determination processes. Disastrous results can occur if the acceleration point is not applied consistently and judiciously. For example, if a plan accelerates incentive rates at a sales level equal to the previous year's performance, it is, in effect, punishing last year's top-performing sales reps by decreasing their compensation opportunity in relation to that of other sales reps.

If quotas are inaccurate in a commission arrangement, the acceleration feature can prove to be quite costly. The company will be paying a premium for performance it would have realized without the accelerator.

In short, be cautious when deciding whether to accelerate incentive rates beyond a certain level of performance. Although the accelerator offers significant motivational pull, it can backfire if quotas and thresholds are inaccurate or if the business environment is volatile.

Regressive (Decelerating) Incentive Rates

Decelerating or regressive incentive rates are the least popular of incentive rate designs. Rates can be reduced as levels of volume are attained and can also be structured so that incentives are eliminated entirely after a certain level is achieved. Examples of decelerating incentive rates include:

- 5 percent commission on the first $1 million of sales, 3 percent for the next $500,000, and 1 percent for all additional sales
- 6 percent commission on all volume from new accounts, 3 percent on all "repeat business"
- 10 percent commission on all quarterly sales with total commissions limited to 30 percent of quarterly base pay
- 6 percent commission on all volume with a maximum payout from any order limited to $5,000

Decelerating or regressive incentive rates contradict the principle that additional incentive performance is relatively more difficult to attain and should therefore be rewarded at progressively higher rates. There are, however, appropriate contexts in which it makes sense to decelerate incentives.

Decelerating rates frequently apply to situations in which a sales rep plays a very prominent role in securing an order but has no significant role in influencing volume or profitability. In such cases, it makes sense to set a maximum commission for each order.

Decelerating incentive rates are also appropriate for those companies that choose a "disguised salary plan" to ensure competitive levels of compensation. A typical approach here would be to limit the amount of earnings in a specific incentive period.

Another context for decelerating rates is one in which sales force prominence differs in new and repeat selling. It is entirely appropriate to decrease incentive rates for repeat business if a sales rep plays a significantly less prominent role in securing business from established customers.

Although there are a few contexts in which it makes good business sense to decelerate incentive opportunity, there are many examples of the misuse of decelerating rates.

Probably the most common misuses of decelerating incentive rates are to protect against a sales rep receiving windfall compensation or to establish control over a sales rep's earnings potential. These two situations are good examples of treating symptoms rather than the disease. Decelerating rates in these cases are typically add-ons to a plan suffering from either symptom or both symptoms. We can all think of examples where a company changed a plan because a sales rep had "too good a year" or because a plan just let income fall into the laps of sales reps. In such cases, the problems are not related so much to incentive rates as to the core design of the plan and the appropriateness of the incentive element itself.

Like accelerating incentive rates, decelerating rates can also place inordinate pressure on goal- and quota-setting processes. Specifying the exact point at which an incentive rate will decline or be cut off altogether assumes goals and quotas are well defined. If there are shortcomings in any part of the goal- or quota-setting process, a plan with decelerating incentive rates becomes susceptible to failure.

Decelerating incentive rates function as powerful communicators. If you feel your quota- or goal-setting processes are woefully inadequate, don't use them. If you are thinking of modifying your plan to include a deceleration feature, be sure you are treating the disease and not putting a bandage on a flawed design. Finally, if you decide to modify a plan to include a deceleration feature, be sure the reasons for the change are fully understood by the sales force. This type of change is almost always resented and requires effective communication.

Combination Plan/Leverage Rates

A combination rate plan is one that uses two or more incentive rates to compensate sales reps. Some plans "leverage" incentive rates. That is, the incentive rate on one element of performance depends on performance on another element or elements. For example, a combination rate plan might offer the following commission rates: 3 percent on product A, 4 percent on product B, and 5 percent on product C. A leveraged rate plan might entail a 4 percent commission rate on product A, if the quota on product B is met; or 3 percent on product A, if the quota on product B is not met.

If certain products within a product line have significantly different profit margins and if a company prefers a sales rep to focus on the product with the highest margin, it makes good business sense to have the incentive plan reflect this. When all of the products a rep has to sell are equally difficult to sell, he or she will concentrate on selling the product that yields the most income.

Such an arrangement will accomplish exactly what it is expected to do: encourage the rep to focus on selling the highest-margin product. The downside, of course, is that the plan might implicitly (or not so implicitly) tell the rep to focus on the highest-margin product at the expense of other offerings in the product line.

Profit margins are not the only factor influencing a company to vary incentive rates. Some products are inherently more difficult to sell than others are. Other things being equal, sales reps will focus on products that are the least difficult to sell. By varying incentive rates (e.g., offering higher rates on difficult products), companies can ensure that reps do not focus solely on the "easy sale." Although this sounds easy in theory, determining the differential sufficient to shift (or at least balance) a sales rep's attention is difficult.

After introducing a new product, companies often have to modify their incentive plans to encourage reps to sell it without neglecting the traditional product offerings. In this case, leveraging the incentive rates is advisable. For example, assume the commission rate on an established product is 4 percent and the company feels 4 percent is also appropriate for its new product. To encourage sales of the new product, the commission rate for the established product could be designed to vary, based on performance on the new product. The plan might include an additional 10 percent of commission payout on the established product if a certain level of performance is attained on the new product.

A potential drawback of this approach would be sales force reluctance, for one or a variety of reasons, to sell the new product. Consider the following example. A small commercial furniture distributor that sold furniture to Fortune 500 companies wanted to expand its range of services and to increase sales. Consequently, it began to offer relocation management to its customers. The service was simple enough—the company could help its clients not only with their furniture needs, but also with their relocation needs. Sales reps were skeptical of the idea, however, and many felt uncomfortable selling an unproven service. Some even feared that a poorly handled relocation could jeopardize client relationships.

The first option for modifying the plan took a traditional approach. Each sales rep would be given a modest "relocation management" goal, and commission rates on commercial furniture would be increased by 10 percent if the move management goal was met. Sales managers argued that this approach would fail because the sales force was so suspicious of managing relocations. They believed that most reps would ignore the opportunity to receive a premium and would continue to focus on selling furniture. Top management decided to combine a little stick with the carrot. The 10 percent premium for attaining the move management goal was left intact but a new feature was added: If the relocation management goal was not met, commissions from selling furniture would be reduced by 10 percent.

15

Noncash Incentives

15.1 Contests

A winery rarely used sales force incentives. But slow sales of a recently acquired line of red wines prompted management to create a contest in which all salespersons who sold a specified number of cases of red wine would participate. The prize was a trip to the America's Cup race. Only one winner would be chosen, although this fact was poorly communicated to the salespeople.

The six-week contest was a big hit; sales during the period increased dramatically. More than 60 percent of the sales force of twenty-one people reached the case count target. But only one person went to Australia, a salesman whose territory had a history of high red wine sales. Despite greatly increased company revenues, twenty other salespeople who tried diligently for the prize did not go. Morale plummeted, and it was the winery's last attempt at a sales contest.

This case study illustrates the pros and cons of contests, which are common incentive tools in American sales forces today. Such events entail short-term effort on the part of a sales force to maximize results for a particular nonrecurring purpose. The company offers cash, merchandise, travel, or recognition to the salespersons who achieve the highest sales volume (or other measure) within a given period of time.

Sales contests serve a useful purpose in the right arena. But they should not be viewed as a standard element in a company's sales incentive compensation program.

In their most common form, contests are designed to produce a single winner who qualifies for the prize over a short period, usually six months or less. (The contest duration could be as short as a week.) In some contests, there may be several winners: the leading salesperson in each of several sales districts, for example. And there are contests in which all sales employees can participate, with some winning more valuable prizes than others do.

Although contests serve many useful functions, they should never be viewed as a substitute for incentive pay or as a remedy for inadequate or incomplete compensation programs. Contest earnings differ from other forms of incentive compensation because there are usually only one or a few winners. Further, contests focus competition internally toward other members of the sales force rather than externally toward the competition.

Companies must offer an adequate combination of base salary and incentive compensation (in whatever form) to recruit and retain high-quality sales talent. Contest winnings are inconsistent, and the random nature of contests does not provide enough incremental compensation to offset uncompetitive earnings levels. Direct compensation affects the behavior and motivation of the sales force. Sales contests, as peripheral elements of the value system, can be powerful enhancements if used correctly, beneficial for both the company and the salespersons because they:

- Recognize the efforts of the better-performing sales personnel.
- Can improve morale and team effort toward the achievement of a common goal.
- Focus attention on specific near-term tactical sales events that might otherwise garner insufficient attention. Without a contest to fill the last fifty berths on a cruise liner, for example, the ship might sail with some or all of the berths unfilled.

A sales contest is also a relatively inexpensive way to create greater sales effort. Because the prize values are usually small, they constitute only a small percentage of an individual's annual total cash compensation. And, given the relatively small number of winners, the aggregate costs are small compared to the incremental volume a contest can generate.

Before implementing sales contests at your company, remember that they have the following distinct dangers:

- They displace sales volume from one time period to another. Aggregate sales volume might not increase; instead, sales volume normally captured in one time period will be displaced into another period. (In essence, the salespersons are manipulating orders to maximize performance during the contest period.) Such behavior has negative implications for production planning and revenue forecasting. Production may be strained in the attempt to reach desired product flows during the contest period. Further, it is difficult to estimate future revenue when volume is cannibalized from future periods.

- Contests are often designed to focus attention on a specific product or product line. This may be dysfunctional from a strategic perspective. A short-term emphasis may undermine ongoing sales management processes (and the attention of the sales force), which focus on products of greater strategic interest to the company over the long term. (There are many examples of contest winners who fail to achieve their annual volume or product-line volume goals because their attention was diverted in midyear.)

- Certain sales reps will have natural advantage because of the composition of their territories.

- Invariably, the top-performing salesperson will win the contests time after time. This will have a negative effect on the attitudes of recurring nonwinners or those who have only a marginal probability of winning.

15.2 Recognition Programs

Reaching into her mailbox, the wife of one of the company's fifteen sales reps retrieved a brightly colored envelope addressed to her. "Tahiti— First Class, the Only Way to Go" read the text on the back. The envelope didn't contain the standard advertisement for the local travel agent; instead, it contained the first of many mailings targeted specifically at spouses of the computer company's sales force. Each subsequent note would provide an update on the planned trips. But not every salesperson could go to Tahiti—only those who achieved established annual sales targets. Of course, management assumed that the spouses would provide moral support to encourage the sales reps to attain the highly desirable trip.

Interviews with the sales force revealed that the Tahiti trip was on everyone's mind and had been for months. Sales management had aggressively promoted the two-week trip and its first-class amenities. Because of this unrelenting advertising, the recognition program had become a cause célèbre among the salespersons and their spouses. Nothing could stop those who had a chance to reach the threshold for attendance. Clearly, management had gotten the attention of the sales force, whose members were working hard to join the elite "performance club."

Meanwhile, the management of a large regional bank was looking for a tool to increase its tellers' morale and commitment. Management wanted to recognize the quality of service the tellers provided, but it also wanted the tellers to remember a tactical sales objective—increasing the number of Visa credit card holders.

To achieve these ends, the bank's branch supervisors selected a four-inch tall clear Plexiglas pyramid; embedded in the center was a small gold token indicating that the teller was an award recipient. Management also created and published objective criteria for winning the "teller of the quarter" award.

This recognition tool has turned out to be one of the most popular in the bank's history. Why? Winners were permitted to display the unusual award at the front of their teller cages. Customers would invariably inquire about its origin. This gave the winning tellers many opportunities during the workday to discuss their achievement, which provided constant reinforcement.

These examples illustrate the value of corporate sales recognition programs. In many companies (including both the computer company and the bank), such programs have a greater impact on morale and motivation than do cash incentive programs.

The principal objective of recognition programs is to affirm that the company values the efforts of its better personnel. This is usually accomplished by highlighting the achievements of these employees before peers, management, or perhaps customers. Such programs can be a powerful inducement to continuing high performance.

In general, recognition programs entail defined criteria that, when met, entitle the salesperson (and possibly the sales manager and others related to the selling function) to a trip, participation in a select group, or some form of material recognition. To attain maximum value, management promotes the program strenuously and publicizes the names of those whose performance warrants recognition.

At the heart of such programs is the need to instill a sense of pride. For a relatively modest cost, a company can use a recognition program to let employees know they are doing a good job. Even when the awards are financial, many managers feel that the real value is symbolic: Status, pride, and a sense of value can have more impact than regular compensation does.

All employees presumably have an equal chance to earn recognition. This is a key issue, but building fairness and equity into recognition programs can be difficult. Some measures that work perfectly for one part of the sales force (like market share) may not work for another (market share usually favors small territories). To avoid any perception of inequity, management should consider having several winners.

For example, a company might use a common recognition measure across several sales territories, with a "winner" in each. Another technique is to use a range of measures that gives several salespersons in a given territory the opportunity to qualify—salespeople with more than 15 percent sales growth over the previous period, for example.

Most companies use recognition programs to highlight above-average sales performance. But some companies directly recognize less successful employees for their weak performances. Posting the results of all sales reps' efforts is usually enough to highlight the less-than-stellar performers. More direct recognition, such as "crying towel" awards, can be humiliating and may create anger. These forms of negative recognition should be avoided.

Recognition programs can also be used to acknowledge longevity through some material award, such as the ubiquitous watch. Today jeweled pins, rings, plaques, or merchandise are more common awards. Longevity recognition programs are typically used for all employees and are not restricted to the sales force.

Whatever their purpose, most recognition awards are nonmonetary, although cash awards can be used. In fact, many new employees and those at the lower end of the organizational ladder tend to prefer cash. But experience suggests that a combination of some form of cash incentive and nonmonetary recognition can be the most effective motivator.

As is the case with contests, managers should be wary of using recognition awards incorrectly; they can have some very negative ramifications. Here are some points to consider:

- Employees may feel that favoritism is a criterion for selection. Management must take special care to develop and fully communicate the criteria or goals to be achieved to earn recognition.
- All employees must believe that they can win; otherwise, marginal performers will not try.
- Awards must be promoted internally if employees are to be fully recognized by their peers.

15.3 Forms of Recognition

Recognition can take a wide variety of forms and can be either short- or long-term. A key factor in determining the form of recognition and the relative degree of emphasis is the selling situation.

Short-term recognition programs acknowledge an employee's achievement, but the award itself may not have lasting value. Common examples include:

- Group activities (such as lunches or small parties) to recognize the achievement of team goals.
- Small, on-the-spot cash bonuses for exemplary achievements
- Plaques, pins, and certificates of achievement
- Personal encouragement from a direct supervisor or senior management
- Letters and telephone calls of commendation from senior or sales management
- Honorary job titles

An incentive travel award program for the top-performing sales reps is a highly successful short-term tool. As illustrated in the "Tahiti trip" case study, these trips can be powerful motivators. In a typical travel award program, a portion of the sales force will become eligible to participate in the annual "club," with the achievement celebrated in an exotic resort locale. Eligibility is usually based on meeting a specified sales target or attaining a specified percentage of quota. Although these trips include some minor training and business meetings, their principal purpose is recreational.

It is becoming common for a salesperson's spouse or "significant other" to attend as well. This prevents the inevitable concerns about the lone spouse's activity. But there is a more serious benefit: creation of a "home cheerleader" to encourage more selling effort. Further, aside from their obvious value in recognizing performance, these annual gatherings allow the best and the brightest of the sales force to learn from one another and to build mutually beneficial alliances.

There are some interesting variations on the "club" concept to consider. In some companies, the very top-performing salesperson receives extra recognition during the club event, flying first class while the other participants fly coach, for example. Other extras may include a rental car, an upgraded room, special side trips, or extra time. Of course, allowing extra time away from the territory has its obvious opportunity costs.

Another interesting variation involves special consideration for those salespeople who have attended the club for several years. One company provides increasingly larger and more prestigious awards for each subsequent year of attendance. If a year is missed, the award sequence begins again. As an example, in this way, continuous performance over the years receives special attention.

Many companies are now expanding eligibility for the incentive travel recognition program to sales support. As an example, in some forward-thinking high-technology companies, top applications engineers and service people are also eligible to attend; these positions have daily interaction with the salespersons' accounts to ensure that purchased equipment meets the customer's needs and continues to operate efficiently. Although these support persons participate in many of the same recreational activities as do the sales reps, special recognition events can be scheduled to highlight their achievements among their peers. Attendance by support personnel encourages teamwork in the selling process while recognizing the importance of individual achievement.

Some recognition programs can have longer-term implications for sales and support personnel, including:

- Advancement to a new position, perhaps with different, unusual, or special responsibilities
- Special education or training opportunities to improve present skills or build new ones
- The opportunity to serve in a specialized training capacity for the

benefit of other (not necessarily more junior) salespersons
- Special work assignments where new techniques, selling methods, or tools can be developed and tested

These and similar efforts have significant longer-range benefits for the employee who develops faster, learns new skills, and transfers knowledge to other less skilled sales personnel. Obviously the company benefits as well.

Not all recognition programs will work effectively in all sales forces. The selling situation can greatly affect the success of the program.

The role of commission salespersons and their high level of influence on the sale is discussed in detail in Chapters 4 and 10. For purposes of this discussion, it is sufficient to recall that these salespeople are essentially self-directing and have little or no actual involvement with field management. They set their own day-to-day schedules and have minimal interaction with other company employees (including their supervisors) during the work week. Because of this isolation, high-prominence (commission) salespeople have different recognition needs. They lack the close supervisory environment in which frequent face-to-face encouragement is possible. Thus, recognition programs take on greater importance.

Peer recognition among such sales reps becomes highly symbolic and reflects the company's sense of the salespersons' value. Recognition programs for these employees are usually quite frequent, and travel incentive clubs focus on individual recognition. Clubs and sales meetings present opportunities to gather the salespeople at one location and recognize achievement.

Conversely, recognition programs for salaried salespersons (with lower prominence than that of commission salespersons) tend to focus on face-to-face acknowledgment, commendations, and other forms of direct encouragement. Large-scale programs may take on less importance, because the lower-prominence salespersons have more opportunity for daily interaction with their supervisors.

15.4 Dependence of Expense Reimbursement on the Sales Process

A leading producer and marketer of premium wine encourages its salespeople to entertain customers in top restaurants. A dinner for four at New York's Four Seasons or Michael's in Los Angeles will cost the winery well over $5000. Of course, only the best wines, including some from competitors, will be consumed. Is the expenditure worth it? The winery thinks so. Aside from introducing its products to the sales rep's invited guests, the expenditure further cements the relationship with the restaurant owner, who has the winery's products on the wine list.

So the restaurateur, the salesperson, and the invited guests all benefit.

By way of contrast, the perennially top-performing salesperson with a major insurance company, who has total cash earnings well into six figures, is not reimbursed for his business expenses: He is responsible for paying travel, automobile, and entertainment costs. Does this make sense? Both the insurance company and probably the salesperson will say it does.

In both cases, the company's expense reimbursement policy has taken into consideration the selling environment, the influence (or prominence) of the salesperson, and the corporate tax situation. Because the selling environment and the influence of the salesperson differ greatly from one company to another, it is not surprising that expense reimbursement policies also differ.

In fact, expense reimbursement practices run the gamut from full to no payment. In some cases, companies partially reimburse specified categories of expenses; in others, companies impose an upper limit on business-related expenditures.

The principal factor that determines the extent of reimbursement is the nature of the selling job. To state it a different way, the prominence of the sales personnel in the company's marketing mix should dictate the extent to which expenses are reimbursed.

Expenses should not be reimbursed when a sales rep's job entails significant self-direction and the probability of failure is high. Here, "failure" means that sales to most customers will not be consummated on the first try; several visits will be necessary. Furthermore, most potential customers will not buy, so the salesperson must do a lot of prospecting. In such situations, a small percentage of the total sales force develops a large portion of the sales volume. These salespeople are normally paid strictly on commission (as in the insurance case example); travel and entertainment expenses, company cars, and automobile allowances are not usually provided. Such an apparently stringent policy makes sense for several reasons:

- The company will not subsidize weak performers. By paying expenses, the company incurs overhead to maintain a marginally productive salesperson in the field. By not paying expenses, the company can redeploy its limited dollars into incentives for the stellar performers.
- The company minimizes its fixed costs. Because the cost of maintaining the selling effort is borne by the salesperson, the company avoids costs that may not be offset by revenues.
- By reimbursing expenses and automobile costs, the company provides a sense of comfort that may encourage weak sales reps to remain in its employ. By contrast, the stringent policy will encourage turnover among the less desirable sales staff.

- Outstanding performers can readily afford their own automobiles and expenses. In fact, commission rates are often set to provide a special cushion of dollars to fund such expenditures; thus, the company does not incur these costs unless actual sales are made. Furthermore, the most successful salespersons will be able to buy more desirable automobiles than those normally offered to the sales force.

In selling situations other than the one just described, companies usually use the same expense policy for salespeople as for other employees. This is particularly important where the size of the territory requires considerable travel and related expenses. A company that does not reimburse sales reps for their costs runs the risk of discouraging selling activity, because salespeople will be reluctant to spend their own money to maximize the number of calls or to take the extra trip.

Many companies pursue a middle ground between the two expense reimbursement extremes. Some aerospace companies, for example, partially offset expenses by paying a flat allowance (say $500 per month) or by providing a per-diem, a flat number of expense dollars for each day of travel. In both cases, employees are able to spend as they wish, but the company's financial exposure is limited.

It is also common for companies to fully reimburse some but not all expenses. For example, salespeople with very large territories will be eligible for airfare and overnight lodging reimbursement, but salespersons in very small territories that can be covered by automobile will not.

15.5 Forms of Expense Reimbursement

A sales rep may need to spend money on a wide variety of services and products in pursuit of sales. A typical corporate expense reimbursement policy might cover as many as thirty expense categories, which can be broadly grouped into seven classifications:

1. Travel
2. Entertainment
3. Promotion
4. Automobile
5. Telephone and communications
6. Office
7. Miscellaneous

These classifications encompass diverse selling expenses that may or may not be reimbursed depending on company culture and policy, the selling situation, and federal tax law. Figure 15-1 subdivides each of the seven classifications to illustrate the breadth of service and product expenses that might be reimbursed.

Figure 15-1. Checklist of reimbursable selling expenses.

Classification	Expense Item
Travel	• Airfare • Ground transportation • Lodging • Meals • Automobile rental • Parking and tolls • Incidentals (e.g., dry cleaning)
Entertainment	• Meals • Refreshments • Theater and sporting events
Promotion	• Advertising • Trade show expenses • Samples • Audiovisual equipment • Meeting rooms
Automobile	• Auto club expenses • Fuel • Maintenance • Insurance • License tag
Telephone and Communications	• Usage and line charges • Cellular service fees and per call charges • Equipment rental/lease • Answering service
Office	• Space lease costs • Clerical staff • Personal computers • Equipment • Supplies
Miscellaneous	• Credit card fees • Personal insurance

The most commonly reimbursed selling expenses relate to travel and entertainment. Most companies offset fares for commercial airlines, ground transportation (including some form of automobile expenses), lodging, meals, and customer entertainment.

As noted earlier, the selling environment and the associated compensation plan are key determinants of whether particular expense categories are reimbursed. Commission sales forces (high-prominence salespeople) are eligible for some reimbursement of a few expense categories, where salaried salespeople typically receive a more comprehensive reimbursement.

Automobile policies vary greatly. Recent changes in the corporate tax law have escalated a trend toward eliminating company-owned automobiles for salespersons. Although many senior executives still receive automobiles as perquisites, companies are encouraging salespeople to use their own cars and accept some form of reimbursement for relevant expenses, typically paid as a predetermined allowance, a payment for each mile driven, or a combination of the two. The typical per-mile payment is 24 cents, the current limit set by the Internal Revenue Service. In some cases, the company will pay all relevant operating expenses, including fuel, maintenance, and insurance.

Less common, but becoming more prevalent, is reimbursement of sales expenditures associated with the home office. The high cost of office locations, highway congestion, and lengthening travel time are encouraging many companies to reimburse home office costs. These might include equipment rental, lease, or purchase (such as facsimile or copier machines); telephone and supplies; and furniture. In some industry segments, such as insurance sales, the company may establish small remote offices and reimburse the salesperson for some (but not all) associated expenses, such as clerical services and equipment. These remote offices might be found in the salesperson's home or in a nearby office complex.

15.6 Benefits

A specialty drill manufacturer's salespeople make frequent helicopter trips to offshore oil rigs. Company products are used primarily to drill for natural gas pockets located deep in the sea bed, dangerous work because of the possibility of ignition of the flammable gas. It is common for sales reps to work directly with the roughnecks who attach drill tips to the thirty-foot pipe sections, and to stay overnight at the platforms.

Because of the dangers associated with the on-site work and the possibility of helicopter accidents, all company salespeople are provided with special life and medical insurance coverage—specifically, higher dollar limits on life insurance policies and broader and more valuable disability coverage than that provided to other company employees.

This illustrates the use of specialized benefit programs designed to reflect the nature of the selling task, business strategy, and the overall role and influence of the sales force. Aside from direct compensation (base salary and some form of incentive) and expense reimbursement, the total compensation package commonly includes various forms of indirect compensation. Indirect compensation is designed to protect

sales reps and their families and to build financial security for the future.
Benefit programs might include some or all of the following coverages:

- Comprehensive health insurance, which may include hospital and
  related services, outpatient psychiatric care, vision, and dental
  coverages
- Disability insurance, including both short- and long-term cover-
  age, and accidental death and dismemberment benefits
- Survivor benefits such as group life insurance and surviving
  spouse's coverage
- Retirement income programs
- Profit-sharing or productivity gain-sharing programs
- Capital accumulation programs, such as 401(k) plans
- Stock grants or stock purchase plans (although this is somewhat
  rare)

In principle, sales personnel should receive the same benefit coverages as do their peers in other company functions, i.e., those employees
of stature approximately equal to their own. Thus, benefit coverages for
salespersons at a certain total cash compensation level (salary plus
incentives) should match those provided to other employees with similar
compensation.

In reality, there will probably be some variation, particularly in
establishing survivor and retirement coverages. The key issue is the
earnings base for calculating coverages. For example, the amount of life
insurance available under the company's group policy is usually expressed as a percentage of annual compensation. For salaried sales
personnel and other employees, this calculation is straightforward. But
it becomes more complex for salespeople whose compensation comprises
both salary and variable compensation that can change significantly from
year to year. This issue may be addressed by:

- Excluding all incentive earnings and determining benefit coverages
  on the basis of salary only
- Using total earnings in the most recent full year as the earnings
  base
- Calculating coverage on current salary plus a moving average of
  several recent years' incentive payments

The first option (excluding incentives) is viable only if incentive
awards do not constitute a large part of total earnings, say 20 percent of
salary at most. It is unduly discriminatory to ignore the incentive
earnings of those salespersons who depend on variable compensation as
their principal source of income.

The second option (using most recent total earnings) may also create inequities. Benefit coverages could be reduced if incentive payments decline because of changing market conditions (outside the salesperson's control) or a one-time slump in personal performance.

Given these caveats, the third option, using a moving average to calculate benefit coverages, is an appropriate compromise.

A sales rep's role in the marketing mix is the principal determinant of benefit coverage, assuming basic benefits are generally comparable to those given to other employees. The situation is analogous to the reimbursement of selling expenses: Representatives in high-prominence selling roles, where high turnover is likely, are not generally provided with the more costly benefit coverages. (You will recall that most high-prominence sales personnel are paid on totally variable compensation, usually commissions.)

Finally, by minimizing benefits (and possibly reimbursed expenses), a company will not run the risk of encouraging marginal performers to stay with the company. Generous benefit and payment programs provide extra "comfort" to weak salespeople who need the security.

16

Managing Transition and Change

16.1 Introduction

As a communication medium, a sales incentive system can have a major impact on the behavior of sales personnel. Therefore, before changing (or introducing) a sales compensation program, you should carefully prepare a strategy to manage the communication of the change and its effects.

16.2 Selling a Plan Change to the Sales Force

The success of the transition from an old sales incentive plan to a new one will largely depend on your ability to convince sales reps that the new system can provide a "better deal." In this regard, communicating the change means "selling" the plan to eligible participants.

There are a number of ways to demonstrate that the plan offers reps a better program without implying that it will just pay more money. For example, the following additional measures can be implemented:

- *Sales rep input.* In the course of developing a new sales incentive plan, companies can solicit sales reps' opinions of the current plan. This can be accomplished through normal sales meeting discussions, a sales force advisory council, a total sales force attitude survey, or personal interviews.

Later, when communicating the new sales incentive plan, you will indicate that sales force input was used in analyzing the old plan and in considering alternative incentive plans. In this way, the new plan offers a potentially better deal in that it reflects the sales force's perceptions and comments.

- *Strategic rationale.* Sales reps often feel that their sales compensation plan was developed in a haphazard way. Communicating to reps that the new plan is based on the company's business and marketing strategies improves the chances that they will view the plan as a realistic reinforcement of those strategies.

You must take care, however, when disseminating business and marketing information, not to release confidential data. Consider a general approach, for example, "Here's where the company is going, how we intend to get there, and how the new compensation plan supports this direction."

- *Pretested design.* Companies generally model and test a new plan's design as part of the development process. This testing may utilize a few business scenarios to evaluate compensation payouts in relation to sales and marketing results. For example, the new plan can be tested using last year's actual results to indicate, in total and by individual, the incentive payments relative to actual payouts. With the increased use of personal computers, this work should not be too difficult.

Communicating to the sales force that this step was taken adds a strong measure of credibility that the new plan affords reasonable opportunities and that flaws have been removed during test runs.

- *Management commitment.* Sales reps often complain that the company changes the pay plan every year for no apparent reason. If experience indicates that management has no real commitment to any incentive plan, sales reps will find it difficult to believe that the latest plan is truly an improvement.

Although no plan can be expected to last forever, management should assure the sales force that it does not intend to make significant changes each year.

16.3 Sales Force Reactions

Whenever a new sales incentive system is introduced, you can expect the following reactions:

- The sales reps experience anxiety over the new plan.
- Depending on their individual responses to key issues, reps will feel either great relief or deep frustration.

The issues most sales reps focus on first include:

- How much can I earn?
- Who is eligible?
- What is the individual quota or commission rate? How was it established?
- Are any provisions from the old plan being grandfathered?
- Will the cash payment terms of the new plan cause any temporary

cash flow problems? If so, does the plan provide a transition or bridge from the old to the new?

A recent example will clarify this point. Under the old plan, a company's sales reps were paid a modest draw and monthly commissions. The draw accounted for approximately 50 percent of the expected total cash compensation on an annual basis. In recognizing the change in its marketplace and its own marketing strategy, the company determined that its sales positions should be paid a base salary and quarterly incentive earnings for results against a quota. Recognizing the cash flow aspects of this change, the company decided to create a temporary bridge between the old and new plans by making a monthly advance of 70 percent of each quarter's targeted incentive earnings opportunity. The bridge was discontinued after the first year of the new plan.

This leads to the following questions:

- Will adjustments to quotas, rates, and so on, be made during the year?
- How will transfers and promotions be handled?
- How often will actual results be seen?
- Will the new plan offer a capped or uncapped earnings opportunity?
- Does the new sales incentive compensation system affect a person's current base salary or draw? If so, how?
- How will the company handle special situations, for example, terminations?
- Are contests or other special recognition programs affected by the new plan?
- How does the new plan affect benefit programs?
- Who will answer questions about the new plan?

Recognizing that these are the issues that sales reps will focus on, a company would be well advised to provide sufficient time before finalizing the plan to consider its approach and to prepare written policies covering these issues. Aside from providing a logical answer to each of these key questions, however, the company can or should do nothing else to ensure the reps' personal satisfaction with the answers.

16.4 Timing of Plan Introduction

When a new or significantly revised sales incentive compensation system is implemented, one question always arises: "Should we introduce the program all at once, phase it in over time, or introduce it on a trial basis to secure participant acceptance?"

The answer is "It depends on a number of external and internal factors affecting each company's situation." Some of the major factors are shown in Figure 16-1.

Immediate Introduction

Introducing a new sales incentive program all at once could be appropriate if one or more of these internal conditions exist:

- The changes to the current incentive plan are not major. In essence, the incentive plan is being "trimmed," "fine-tuned," or "tailored" slightly to better reflect today's sales and marketing situation.
- The culture of the company is such that changes are always fully announced and quickly implemented, with the sales force able to accommodate all that this may entail.
- The systems needed to measure, track, record, and communicate performance against the new sales incentive program are already in place.
- Management wants either to shift the sales force's behavior to a new marketing and sales orientation or to begin to lower a perceived high-cost-of-sales position by focusing attention on achieving additional sales volume.

With regard to external factors, the immediate introduction of a new sales incentive plan can be undertaken:

- If the industry in which the company competes is not highly cyclical. Picking the wrong part of the cycle for introduction could demoralize the sales force.
- If a company is not dominant in its primary markets and the

Figure 16-1. Factors affecting implementation timing.

External Factors	Internal Factors
• Industry characteristics • Your company's competitive position • Competitors' response level	• Degree of change from past • Company culture • Sales force culture • Level of support systems for new incentive program • Cost to implement • Clarity and direction of marketing and sales plans • Cost of sales position

response level of competitors to its sales strategy change is not immediate. Given these conditions, introducing the entire plan at once can help build marketing position while competitors are not paying attention.

Recently, a company that had just undergone a leveraged buyout (LBO) from its parent introduced a new incentive program. The management of the LBO was interested in immediately redirecting the efforts of the sales force to stress certain high-margin, hard-to-sell product lines. Considering its internal and external situation, the company felt very comfortable in introducing the new incentive program all at once.

Phasing in a New Plan

If your industry is evolving due to such factors as deregulation, foreign competition, or domestic consolidation, you should probably introduce a new sales incentive plan gradually. With respect to internal factors, a phase-in approach should be considered if:

- The anticipated plan changes and behavior modifications are considerable and significant.
- The company's culture is to proceed slowly and cautiously and with periodic reviews of new programs or systems.
- The sales force is not normally accustomed to undergoing quick, major changes or is slowly making the transition to a new organizational structure.
- Needed support systems will not be fully in place for an indefinite period (possibly due to cost considerations).

The deregulation of the telephone companies represents a situation requiring a phase-in approach. The industry was undergoing massive changes vis-à-vis the marketplace. Telephone companies faced a Brave New World full of opportunities but also full of major transitions, new sales, and marketing programs, all within a culture that valued caution and technical excellence. Full-scale, total implementation of new sales incentive programs would have been unwise.

Trial Introduction

Testing a new sales incentive compensation system to secure participants' acceptance is not frequently done. It does, however, merit serious consideration under the following circumstances: If the industry is seasonal, or the company is the dominant market leader, or competitors are very quick to respond to your moves, you should consider testing any new sales incentive program that has a number of major design changes.

Why? The downside risks of immediate implementation may be too costly from a market share perspective if every aspect of implementation does not proceed well.

In considering internal factors, testing should be undertaken when the company's culture or that of the sales force is one of thoroughly testing new programs. In addition, where the new plan may require either a major reeducation of sales management (e.g., how to set and use quotas) or considerable additional resources, testing may provide the time and proof required for all affected parties to feel comfortable with these changes.

The correct approach for any company depends on a thorough analysis of both external and internal factors. Moving too slowly in implementation may be just as damaging as moving too quickly.

16.5   Changing From No Plan to a New Plan

As a company's business goals, objectives, and marketing strategy evolve over time, management may consider shifting sales force compensation from a base-salary-only plan to a salary-plus-incentive plan. In such instances, the incentive program should signal cultural change.

Let's examine three situations where a base-salary-only plan normally applies:

1. *A competitive labor market characterized by a strong emphasis on salary.* In such a market, differences in the earnings distribution of salespeople throughout the industry should be relatively small. In addition, the particular sales job and selling process involved in this marketplace may not dictate an incentive program.

2. *Transient field sales positions.* Companies often choose to rotate upwardly mobile sales reps through the sales force as part of the career development process. In such cases, where transfers into and out of sales from other functions are common, straight salary has frequently been the approach of choice.

Today, many companies that are experiencing stagnant growth believe that they have an oversupply of qualified middle-management talent. Consequently, career paths through an organization have slowed down considerably. As a signal to the sales group that jumping quickly into and out of the sales function is no longer possible and that outstanding performance as a long-term sales rep will be properly recognized and rewarded, companies are replacing the base-salary-only plan with a salary-plus-incentive plan.

3. *The absence of a strong incentive culture.* In some companies, bonuses, even at the senior executive level, do not represent a major

component of the pay package. Generally, a professional or technical (rather than a marketing) orientation underlies the company's value system. Sales reps more likely see themselves as engineers, a belief that is reinforced by customers who require a good deal of technical information or education from them.

In some instances, this need for technical information decreases over time as the company's customer group becomes more knowledgeable. If this happens, the company may want to signal a more marketing-oriented approach in its selling. To support this change, sales management should change the base-salary-only plan to a salary-plus-incentive compensation system.

To ensure that the message of cultural change implicit in the change from a salary-only system to an incentive program is clearly understood, make sure that the change has immediate behavioral impact.

16.6   Considerations in Implementing New Plans

In introducing a new sales incentive compensation system, a company should anticipate problems concerning design and administrative issues and establish its approach before communicating the system to the field. Examples of such issues are listed below.

Issue	*Discussion*
Payout period	If the new program has a different payout period, you may need a transition policy to avoid creating cash flow problems for reps.
Definitions for new performance measures	Including a new performance measure for incentive purposes is not uncommon. Make sure that you define the measure clearly (e.g., new account volume. What qualifies as a new account?).
Quota-setting procedures and processes	When an incentive plan includes the first-time use of quotas, it is critical that the whole process and all procedures be spelled out for the sales force. Doing so helps the sales force commit to the new program and perceive it as straightforward.
Crediting orders	Generally, orders can be credited when: ▪ The order is secured ▪ The order is shipped ▪ The invoice is submitted ▪ Payment is received

With respect to incentive plans whose design accelerates incentive earnings after a quota is fully attained, defining the exact point at which orders are credited can be very important to sales performance, motivation, and company cost.

Handling house accounts	In most instances, house accounts are managed, serviced, and "sold" by management rather than by the field sales force. In some companies, however, house accounts may be transferred back to individual sales reps, possibly with an accompanying increase in incentive earnings potential. You must carefully describe how such a transfer will be handled for incentive purposes.
Splitting credits	Companies often split credits when a customer places an order in one location for shipment in another. Generally, companies use a fifty-fifty split between the two sales reps involved. In some selling situations, however, a more detailed approach may be required. For example, in the sale of building products (e.g., air-conditioning units), one sales rep may be involved with the architect, another with the owner-developer, and another with the contractor at the building location.
Employee benefits	Addressing the question of how the sales force's benefit plans may be affected by the incentive plan is very important. The prime concern is how the earnings base for benefit purposes will be computed.
New hires and sales trainees	When a new hire will be eligible for participation in the incentive plan, and whether a sales trainee will participate at all, are important questions. In most cases, sales trainees are not included in incentive programs until they are promoted from trainee status.
Reviewing and modifying the incentive program	Companies should clearly define who will have authority to review and modify the incentive plan and who will adjudicate windfall and shortfall situations (in which

broad economic factors rather than the sales rep create sales). In some companies, a committee of three (marketing, sales, and human resources) is used to convey a sense of fairness and balance in these situations.

The treatment of such issues may suggest a constantly changing incentive plan. Nevertheless, management should assure sales reps that although emphasis points (e.g., measurement weightings) may change to support the company's marketing strategy, the fundamental program remains constant.

16.7   Transition Approaches

Although a new plan can be phased in gradually, sales managers frequently have to make immediate behavioral changes. In our culture, however, it is very difficult to reduce base salaries. How, then, can you accomplish the transition? More important, how long can you (and your boss) wait for the necessary changes to occur? The most extreme situation you are likely to face is one in which your sales force is compensated on a straight salary basis.

In these circumstances, you are asking sales reps to adopt a new mindset, one that contains more risk than they had previously encountered in their job. Keep in mind, though, that there was risk in that all-salary position. Depending on the time frame and management process, an individual's entire compensation could be lost if he or she failed to deliver the performance level expected. However, few individuals view that consequence with the same immediacy as they would a compensation program that cut their base salaries 15 percent (even if the program gave them the opportunity to earn more through incentives).

One way to ease the transition is to assure sales reps that if they attain quota they will earn no less than they would have under the prior compensation scheme. Instead of instilling confidence in the appropriateness of the new compensation plan, however, this approach may leave the sales force questioning your confidence in the plan's design. Another solution is to permit a draw against incentive payments equal to some portion of the difference between the new base salaries and the prior compensation levels. You then have the problem of recapturing the draw if performance doesn't meet expectations. Moreover, if the individual's compensation is not differentiated in the periodic pay distributions, you are foregoing an important motivational opportunity.

The key to this dilemma is to maintain the individual's cash flow over the immediate short term, with a phasing in of the variable component of the incentive plan performance criteria, and the associated influence on an individual's total compensation. You can accomplish this by verifying that your payroll systems can handle a change in reporting compensation, either through a separate line entry on the pay stub or through a separate pay check.

Your objective is to start to align the sales force's perceptions of their compensation with the eventual configuration of the compensation program, for example, base and incentive payment. At the same time, you should assure them that over the near term, their cash flow won't suffer if they attain the desired performance criteria. With this objective in mind, and assuming that you will attain your desired incentive/base salary relationship in three years (admittedly a long time, but cited for simplicity's sake), Figures 16-2, 16-3, and 16-4 illustrate the approach you could take. Simply put, instead of cutting base salary and then putting in the full incentive opportunity, you should phase in the incentive opportunity while reducing the base salary until the desired mix of base and incentive is attained.

Assume that the accounting system won't provide enough information to determine the actual incentive award until after the performance period has ended. In this situation, you should offer a "makeup" bonus to maintain cash flow during the transition period, with the actual incentive payment being made in the period following the actual performance. The makeup bonus remains constant during the phase-in, while the actual incentive payments reflect the sales rep's performance.

Figure 16-2 assumes that an individual attains the sales targets, thus substantiating his or her incentive award at the desired level.

Figure 16-3 assumes that an individual exceeds the sales targets, thus doubling his or her incentive award from the desired norm.

Figure 16-4 assumes that an individual fails to attain the sales targets, thus yielding no incentive award.

Because the remaining cash flows reflect individual performance, the first bonus payment represents the real "cost" of this type of phase-in. On the other hand, there are significant benefits to be gained, principally that the sales reps' motivation is maintained because their

Figure 16-2. Calculation of makeup bonus (sales targets attained).

Year	Base	Incentive	Makeup Bonus	Total	Incentive Leverage
1	$28,600	$ 0	$1,400	$30,000	5%
2	27,200	1,400	1,400	30,000	10
3	25,800	2,800	1,400	30,000	15
4	25,800	4,100	0	30,000	15

Figure 16-3. Calculation of makeup bonus (sales targets exceeded).

Year	Base	Incentive	Makeup Bonus	Total
1	$28,600	$ 0	$1,400	$30,000
2	27,200	2,800	1,400	31,400
3	25,800	5,600	1,400	32,800
4	25,800	8,200	0	34,000

Figure 16-4. Calculation of makeup bonus (sales targets not attained).

Year	Base	Incentive	Makeup Bonus	Total
1	$28,600	$0	$1,400	$30,000
2	27,200	0	1,400	28,600
3	25,800	0	1,400	27,200
4	25,800	0	0	25,800

standard of living will not be disturbed (assuming the reps attain targeted performance). More important, the phase-in approach increases the motivational impact of the plan by demonstrating to those who fear they may be unable to cope with an incentive environment that they can improve their economic standard with enhanced performance. Finally, by slowly lowering compensation for those who cannot meet performance expectations, the plan encourages them to seek other employment opportunities.

If an organization has not used incentives in the past, its goal-setting process is not likely to be as strong as it would have been if compensation depended on performance against established goals. Therefore, the phase-in helps reduce the impact of weak goal setting (in an absolute sense) upon compensation levels.

Of course, you may discover that your current compensation levels are competitive with the base salaries of other competitors who employ incentive compensation plans. In this instance, if the adoption of a competitive total compensation level would create your desired mix between base and incentives, then you merely have to add the incentive to your present compensation program.

Finally, if competitive norms indicate a relatively low level of incentive opportunity, you may consider freezing base salaries and transferring the base salary increase into an incentive opportunity. In a sense, this is the reverse of the salary reduction approach described above.

16.8   Adding Participants

Companies sometimes expand incentive eligibility to incorporate groups not previously included in the program. Such a decision usually relates to changes in the sales and marketing strategies and the realization that other members of the sales organization can influence sales success. The adoption of an "at risk" element in the compensation of nonsales employees can be an important recognition of this fact but must be done carefully to meet both the company's and the participants' expectations.

Before deciding to increase participation, you should consider whether you will be able to verify the impact of the new group on some aspect of the sales process. This assessment will not only ensure that an expansion is appropriate, but also indicate the performance measures that you should consider in the new incentive plan.

Changes in marketing strategy can often mandate the inclusion of additional participants in a sales compensation plan, especially when one objective of such an action is to change the participants' behavior and attitudes. For example, a company with a well-established customer service operation wants to increase the time available to the field sales force for prospecting. One way to accomplish this objective is to reduce sales force involvement in fulfilling routine orders and tracking delivery problems. At the present time, however, the customer service group is not organized along customer lines, nor does it view itself as anything more than an order expediter. Nevertheless, this group represents the staff resources for freeing field sales force time.

Clearly, much has to be done if this strategy is to prove effective. At the very least, a portion of compensation should be put at risk for individuals who have not had a specific customer orientation and have not been evaluated against sales-specific performance expectations. For such an approach to be successful, you must train the customer service personnel in their new role, and they have to develop the skills and orientation necessary to align their activities with their customers.

Incentive compensation can provide an important reinforcement to this change, but such a step, by itself, is unlikely to represent the catalyst for change in the overall organization. Although the change may mandate a reevaluation of the position's worth, you may find that the addition of an incentive element may be enough to reflect the increased responsibilities and accountabilities of the revised role. If this is the case, then the transition will be relatively easy. On the other hand, you will have a different challenge if you find that current base salaries are competitive with total compensation levels and you want to add an incentive element. Cutting back base salaries is the only alternative and this, as we have seen, must be done carefully.

Adding participants to an existing program can be dangerous if the available funds are diluted or if standards applicable to the existing group are not readily transferable to the new participants. The following checklist highlights the considerations to be addressed from the perspective of plan design, organizational design, information management, compensation and benefits design, and individual expectations:

Plan Design

- What are the key performance factors for the existing sales compensation plan?
- Are they appropriate for the new sales compensation plan participants? For a particular group of customers or territory? Over a different time period?
- Are there subordinate measures that would more accurately align the sales compensation plan with participants' responsibilities?

Organizational Design

- Do the present incumbents possess the skills necessary to accomplish their new role? If not, can they be trained?
- Do present recruitment/career paths represent an appropriate source for future hiring needs?
- Are you trying to create a career hierarchy within the position, or will someone's career naturally take him or her out of the department to a position ineligible for incentive compensation? If this is the case, will your plans be thwarted because the compensation plan (in concert with base salary) is presently providing earnings that are equivalent to the higher position?
- Is there a union contract in place that will require negotiation of the incentive formula?
- Do your supervisors possess the skills required to administer an incentive compensation program?
- Is the nature of the sales environment such that the plan will work only if it is team oriented?
- Can you differentiate among levels of individual contribution within the team environment?
- Will employees accept such a differentiation?

Information Management

- Will the new program base incentives on individual or team performance?
- Can you link customers with the responsible employees in the information system?

- Will employees have access to customer information so that they can assess the impact of their actions?
- How will the organization control the inflow of new customers and allocate opportunities across the group of employees?
- Are there customer characteristics (e.g., central purchasing but dispersed distribution) that require a service team?
- Will the participants control pricing within an allowable range, and should profitability be a factor in the incentive compensation plan?
- Are the participants responsible for allocating product resources throughout the customer base? If so, there may be a need to resolve potential conflict between sales reps.

Compensation/Benefits Design

- Do you employ a percentage-of-sales criterion for the total sales compensation costs that will limit your ability to add participants?
- Will the participants remain in the salary administration program, or will all of their increases be incentive driven?
- Will there be a single salary rate for the position?
- If an employee is promoted to a nonincentive position, will his or her salary and increase be determined from his or her current salary (influenced by the existence of the incentive plan), or will the total compensation form the basis for the salary associated with the promotion?
- Are benefits determined from an employee's base salary? If so, does the existence of an incentive plan create a situation in which the employee's benefit plan participation is adversely affected? Do W-2 earnings make more sense?
- Is volatility in earnings from year to year so high that some type of averaging must be employed for determining the compensation base for benefit purposes?

You can add participants to a plan in a number of ways, depending on their role, impact on the sales function, and compensation.

Clearly, the easiest transition is one in which the new participants have a direct impact on a specific segment of the organization's sales and their current base salary levels do not require reduction. In this circumstance, you merely add the incentive opportunity to the base salary, communicating the performance expectations, measuring the eventual outcomes, and calculating the incentive payments.

The most difficult situation may be one in which current base salaries are above competitive norms, and some type of reduction must be effected if you are to accomplish your objective without increasing compensation costs.

Depending on the particular details, you can align base compensation with competitive norms by:

- Cutting base salaries, either immediately or in steps, while increasing the incentive elements
- Decreasing base salaries for new hires, while treating the "excess" salary paid to incumbents as a guaranteed advance against incentive payments

The techniques for making the transition from an all-base salary to a base-plus-incentive mix are important. More important, however, is the communication of the transition, so that plan participants understand:

- What activities relate to sales success.
- What the economic benefits (risks) are under the new approach.
- What new career steps are possible.
- Why employees are being included in the incentive plan, how they should modify their interactions with customers, and how they can maximize their incentive opportunity (assuming, for instance, that the new plan participants have an indirect sales support role, for example, customer service).
- What type of training or experience an employee must acquire to become eligible for promotion. Is there a greater degree of career risk, and are quantitative and qualitative performance standards now in place?

Consider the following case involving the realignment of a customer service group. In the past, this group responded to questions from the field or from customers concerning product availability, back-order status, pricing, and so on. The sales force handled all sales responsibilities but, in many instances, acted as an "information broker" between the customers and customer service. Sales rep utilization was lower than it should have been because a significant part of the reps' time was spent "taking care of the orders."

Management recognized that the customer service group could assume more responsibility. Therefore it assigned senior members to a large corporate account and gave them the responsibility for coordinating product shipments, order execution, and so on, with the sales force. Concurrent with a customer segmentation strategy, the company set up a telemarketing unit to act as the principal contact with the company's lower-volume customers. In view of these changes, management decided that the base salary approach might not be the most effective way to reinforce the new sales strategy. By creating a modest at-risk element in the compensation plan, it sought to develop a proactive customer service group. Furthermore, a higher at-risk portion would motivate the telemarketing unit to stay in touch with its customers and increase sales volume.

Although the compensation program was the smallest element of this strategy, it was perceived as the glue that would bind the program elements together. Unless participants saw the plan's introduction as a dramatic departure from past practices, they might not develop the desired combination of energy and new vision.

Management understood that it was more important to create heroes than it was to identify poor performers, and that the short-term cost of overpaying was far less significant than the potential of long-term erosion in share and continued erosion in margin that could be attributed to the old system. So, with a clear vision of its objectives and acceptance of the phase-in approach, the company developed an implementation strategy that had broad performance spectrums with an award scale that rapidly accelerated (or decelerated) only at the extremes of the performance spectrum. Thus, in the beginning, most participants felt that they were meeting objectives.

16.9 Termination of Plan Participation

When an individual ceases to be a participant in the sales incentive compensation plan, a company's approach should reflect sound business judgment. The nature of the termination of plan participation will dictate the appropriate approach, as shown in Figure 16-5.

The approaches suggested in this section are guidelines that should be perceived as fair and equitable in most situations. But there are always exceptions. A company can use whatever approach seems to make good sense in context; the most important thing is to be sure that the rules are spelled out in advance and understood by all plan participants. In general, a company should make the rules as tough as possible without reason. For example, it is reasonable to deny incentive pay to those who terminate before the end of the measuring period. If, in a given case, the company wishes to be more generous (for example, if a sales rep is accepting a position with a major customer), it is much easier to liberalize the rule interpretation than it would be to do the reverse.

16.10 Considerations for Handling Employees in Transition

Promoted Employees

- Is it reasonable to continue some forms of sales incentive in the new position? If not, are other variable compensation techniques viable, for example, stock options, corporate incentive plans (short- or long-term)?

Figure 16-5. Payment of incentive upon termination of employment.

Reason for Termination of Plan Participation	Appropriate Approach to Determining Incentive Earned	
	Incentive Period Completed	*Incentive Period Not Completed*
Voluntary termination of employment	• Paid as soon as practicable.	• Forfeited; completion of incentive period should be condition of earning award.
Involuntary termination of employment	• Paid as soon as practicable.	• Forfeited as above; amount accrued could be paid as part of (or in addition to) severance benefits.
Promotion or transfer to a position not eligible for any incentive compensation	• Paid. If a long-term sales cycle, employee could continue to receive awards for period of time (e.g., six months to two years).	• At least the amount earned to date of transfer should be paid. Participant would continue to end of current period (even longer if a long-term sales cycle) to facilitate transfer.
Promotion to a position eligible for a different bonus plan (e.g., executive incentive plan)	• Paid for incentive period completed. Participant then terminates.	• Same as above, except that awards from sales plan (if any) following transfer date could be deducted from executive incentive award earned for that period.
Retirement (normal or early)	• Paid as soon as possible.	• Pro rata accrual share paid as soon as practicable.
Death	• Paid to estate as soon as practicable.	• Pro rata accrued share paid to estate as soon as practicable.
Long-term disability	• Paid as soon as practicable.	• Pro rata share paid as soon as practicable.

- If no incentive compensation is viable, where should the employee's salary be placed in the new salary range?
    - —Equal to his prior year's W-2?
    - —At some percentage of her former total compensation, for example, 80 percent?
    - —At the level that would be generated if she met quota (performance objectives)?
    - —At some average of the past several years?
- If the sales process has a long time frame for completion, will the employee receive all, or a portion, of the sales incentives for sales that close after her transfer?
- If the sales rep has had access to a company car, will you provide a one-time bonus to purchase the vehicle? Should the promoted rep retain the vehicle?
- Is there a net gain to the employee that should be factored into the termination discussions? For example, if the definition of earnings is base salary, and not W-2 income, will moving to a higher salary significantly enhance the former sales rep's total compensation?
- Does the transfer represent a desired change in life-style, for example, no travel or a different career path, which should not be considered in the termination process?
- If an entire group of employees is being removed from plan participation, do their base salaries require adjustment to realign their no-risk compensation with other comparable jobs in the organization?

Retiring Employees

- What will be the "residual," if any, paid for sales that close after the individual's retirement date?
- How long should residuals be paid?
- Is there any benefit in having the retiring employee involved in introducing the new sales rep to the customer base?
- Should the retiring sales rep receive a portion of the new sales rep's incentives if he is responsible for influencing a smooth transition?

Terminated Employees

- Does the employee receive payments for sales that close/ship after the termination date?
- If the employee has a deficit in his draw, will any severance payments be reduced by the amount of the deficit?
- If incentives have been earned but are unpaid, will payment be deferred pending compliance with any noncompete clauses?
- Will payments be withheld until the terminated employee returns

company sales literature, keys to the company car, company computer, and so on?

- Will the treatment vary if the termination is for poor performance or for violation of a company policy?

Employees Still in the Sales Force—Plan Terminated

- If an employee is doing the same job, will his base salary represent the average of prior years' total compensation?
- For how many years will performance be used to calculate the average?
- Will the payment be based on each individual's past performance or the average earnings for individuals in the same job?
- Will there be any other form of incentive that will influence the calculation described above?
- Will benefit participation be enhanced because the employee has a higher base salary?
- Are compensation levels such that no increase in current base salaries is warranted?
- If past compensation levels are such that the employee's compensation is above the new base salary range, will you:
  —Reduce salary to the range maximum? Red-circle salary and allow increases only when salary falls into the range sometime in the future?
  —Continue to allow salary increases but only at a percentage of range movement?

16.11   Selling the Plan

The success of a sales compensation plan depends on how well you sell plan features to the sales force. Above all, the sales incentive compensation plan should function as a medium of organizational communication. Comprehensibility, therefore, becomes paramount. Too often, management neglects to do what is necessary to *demonstrate* that the plan (or the revisions) represents a good deal for the sales force, one that strengthens an already attractive compensation package.

To obtain the behavioral changes you seek, you must win employee acceptance of the plan. Face-to-face meetings with the sales reps and members of management or, if more feasible, group meetings with management representation, live or on video, are well worth the time and effort involved. And if the new plan requires (as it frequently will) a strengthening of the goal-setting process, you should conduct training sessions, in advance of plan introduction, for those field sales managers who will be using the sales incentive plan.

The best approach to communicating change is the one that fits the business context and management style of the sales organization. The more dramatic the change, of course, the more elaborate the communication effort should be. If plan change is a signal of a fundamental change in business philosophy (e.g., introducing a "theme" of greater customer awareness), then the communication of the sales compensation program could involve group meetings, videotape presentations by senior management, sales manager workshops in final setting and evaluation, management training in account analysis and classification, and continuing reminders (for example, periodic statements of incentive earnings). If the plan changes are minor, a memo clearly explaining changes (and the underlying rationale) may suffice as the communications medium. In all cases, however, the company should aim at sending the field force the following messages:

- We have an excellent, competitive, equitable pay system.
- We have listened to your concerns and addressed them.
- We have made the plan *even better*, so that you can make *even more* income based on your own productivity. Here, in detail, is how the new plan will work.

16.12 Educating Managers

Effective sales compensation plans integrate rewards into the sales management process. Field managers must understand the rationale behind the plan design and their role in its administration. A properly designed sales compensation program will recognize differences in sales rep performance and in the managerial skills of the sales management team. The worst possible situation is one in which sales managers sit in the audience with their subordinates and learn of the changes at the same time that the subordinates do. This situation leaves the managers ill-prepared for the inevitable questions they must answer and suggests that they are, in fact, not managers but merely higher-level sales reps who happen to have sales staff reporting to them. Instead, sales managers should be in a position to enthusiastically introduce the new program to their subordinates and outline how each individual can improve his or her performance and compensation under the plan.

How can you gain acceptance of the critical first communication to the sales force? The degree of difficulty will vary with the magnitude of the change in the sales compensation plan. The recalibration of plan formulas lies at one end of the spectrum of change, while the development of a completely new plan in response to changing strategy lies at the other. In both cases, you are asking sales managers to think differently about the relationship between sales performance and the compensation of their subordinates.

Experience suggests that sales managers, like other managers, feel uncomfortable about the effects of plan changes on individual compensation. Many try to avoid dealing with a situation requiring the reduction of their subordinates' pay. From the sales reps' perspective, unless they understand the underlying reasons for the changes in the compensation program, they may conclude that management is merely trying to control pay levels. Assuming that the compensation plan was properly designed in the first place and that the high compensation levels were the result of performance and not windfalls, the principal risk that companies face is that the most talented sales resources will seek other employment opportunities where their contributions will be properly remunerated. Therefore, sales managers represent the single most important link between management and the field, and they must be prepared to carry forward willingly the change in the compensation program.

Involving the sales management team at an early stage in the revision of the compensation program can prove decisive in building their eventual acceptance and support of the plan. In the final analysis, however, revisions to a sales compensation program should be viewed in the same light as is any new product introduction. Although every product moves from product design to marketing research and field testing, to product revision, test marketing, and final rollout, the relatively small size of the sales force may prevent you from applying these same steps.

Nevertheless, sales managers can be a critical resource in the revision of the plan, and they should not be ignored. As the management resource closest to the field, they can recognize areas where the plan may need strengthening, as well as the "hot buttons" that should be considered in communicating the plan to the field. In most instances, sales management rose from the field organization, and while their orientation is toward management, they may still feel some personal allegiance to the sales force. Therefore, sales managers should be armed with as many facts as possible, so they can answer the questions that are a part of any compensation plan change. Specifically, they should be prepared to answer such questions as:

- Why are we considering change?
    - —New strategy, competitive changes, new product introductions, lack of sales force productivity, reorganization, and so on?
- How will the study be conducted?
    - —Task force, field management?
    - —Timetable for completion?
    - —Review process?
- What will be our role?
    - —Develop plan within broad design parameters?

    —Give input, but final decision to be made by senior sales management?
    —Only communicate changes?
    —Field testing and/or simulation?
- Who will be interviewed (and how will they be chosen)?
    —Sales force and sales management?
    —Customers?
    —Suppliers?
- Is the sales manager's compensation plan being evaluated as well?
    —How will the plan link with that of the field sales force?
    —On what factors will the plan be based?
    —Will the program be rolled out before its announcement to the sales team?
- What are the features of the new plan?
- How will the compensation levels be affected?
- What communications approach will be employed?
- What will the sales force have to do differently to maintain their current level of compensation?
- Will there be a transition period between the plans?

In most instances, there is insufficient information at the outset of the task to answer these questions. As the project progresses, however, periodic updates should be presented to the sales management team; in this manner, a sense of participation is imparted, and the support of the field management team for plan changes can be secured.

As with other management initiatives, most sales compensation reviews have at their core a fundamental issue that must be addressed. There is more to be gained than lost by communicating this issue to sales managers (and even the sales force) at the beginning of the study. Some of the issues that are commonly addressed include the following:

- Have customers changed the way they are purchasing?
- Has the company changed its objectives or the way it wishes to interact with its customer base?
- Are sales costs out of line?
- Have new product introductions lacked sufficient support?
- Is there a lack of congruence between compensation and your perception of the high performers in the sales force?
- Are you losing your best people to competitors?
- Do high performers believe that they have to get out of sales to succeed in the company?
- Are you overlooking opportunities by focusing too much activity on existing customers?
- Have you reorganized internal support groups to provide the sales force with more opportunity to prospect?

Telling the sales management team the underlying reasons lets them know why changes are in the offing and how they have to adapt their management style to maximize their subordinates' performance. More important, as the interim findings are disclosed and the new program begins to take shape, the sales management group will be able to provide advice and counsel to ensure that the best possible design is implemented.

As the study nears its completion, the management team needs to be fully informed about impending changes and the impact they will have on the sales team. At the very least, management team members need to see copies of the introductory material that will be sent to the sales force. If they are going to be responsible for introducing the plan changes, they need to know the details of the plan and the design rationale so they can answer questions. Last but not least, they need to know the impact on their people so they can plan for the one-on-one communications that are so important in any plan revision.

Although specific communication strategies are described in the next section, it should be obvious that communication is an integral part of any successful plan revision. If through your actions the sales management team is forced to guess senior management's intent by analyzing the plan, team members may read the signs incorrectly. Keeping communication lines open throughout the plan design process will help ensure managers' support.

16.13 Announcing Changes

As in all other aspects of sales management, planning provides the foundation for success. Planning involves assessing your company's working style and developing a communication plan that reflects its values. Nevertheless, selling the sales compensation plan, or particular changes in it, is the single most important key to the plan's success. No matter how well designed and administered a plan may be, you cannot expect it to sell itself; it must be marketed. If members of the sales force fail to grasp the advantages of the new plan or react negatively to it, the entire plan is jeopardized.

When designing the communications program, you should prepare answers to the questions sales reps are most likely to ask concerning organizational performance:

- How is the company doing?
- What are its goals?
- How can the sales force help meet these goals?
- How am I doing?
- What can I do to meet sales goals?

- Why this new plan?
- What will it mean to my compensation?
- What will it mean to the way I manage my sales activities?
- What will it mean to the way I will be evaluated?
- Will I need different skills to be successful?
- How will I get them?

The Communication Process

At the very least, you should provide the field force with a printed summary of the new plan and its mechanics. This is only a start, however, to the communication process.

In the likely event that the situation calls for more than a simple memo or letter, you may plan meetings and/or audiovisual presentations to publicize plan changes. If the sales force is spread out over a wide area and you cannot attend each meeting, a videotaped introduction of the reasons behind the changes may prove helpful. However, you should carefully assess your comfort with this medium. If you appear ill at ease because of your inexperience with video, the audience may infer that your discomfort stems from the plan changes you are communicating.

Meeting Strategies

Any change to someone's compensation is significant, and the last thing you should do is announce it through a letter or memorandum. Personal involvement is necessary, by either the sales manager or the sales manager's direct subordinates. The compensation plan is one "product" that you as sales manager have to sell to your customers, the sales employees you supervise. You should be able to employ the same sales skills that make you successful in the other aspects of your job. Let's consider the advantages and disadvantages of various types of meetings.

The Advantages of a National Meeting

- All sales force members hear the same message at the same time; the grapevine is eliminated.
- It is possible to build a high degree of enthusiasm.
- Questions can be answered quickly.
- The meeting can be linked with other regularly scheduled meetings.

The Disadvantages of a National Meeting

- Bringing the entire field force together at one time can be expensive.
- Disgruntled sales members may spread unrest if questions/objections are not properly answered.

- Because of its size, a national meeting may not permit the personal interaction necessary to answer individual questions.
- Unless national meetings have been used in the past, a special meeting may create suspicion.

The Advantages of a Regional/District Meeting

- It can reinforce the sales manager's role in the eyes of the sales force.
- It is cost-effective if it is made part of the normal sales force meeting schedule.
- It can permit discussion of the plan within the context of specific market/customer characteristics.

The Disadvantages of a Regional/District Meeting

- The excitement associated with a large meeting is often missing.
- Without the proper tools or training, managers may convey inconsistent messages.
- Questions relating to policy may not be answerable quickly.

The Advantages of a One-on-One Meeting

- Communication is focused directly on each individual.
- Questions of a personal nature can be answered quickly.
- You can focus on specific customer/territory configuration.
- Lost sales time is minimized.

The Disadvantages of a One-on-One Meeting

- Such meetings are least likely to build enthusiasm.
- This type of meeting is very time-consuming for the sales manager.
- Inconsistent messages are likely to be sent.
- The grapevine can influence your message.
- It takes a long time to answer unanticipated questions.

A strategy that sales managers have found very effective for introducing new plans involves making a general presentation to a full gathering (for example, the entire sales force, the regional sales force) followed by a meeting with the next level of sales management conducting the discussion. Between meetings, sales rep questions can be answered and the individualized communication materials distributed. During the breakout sessions, sales managers can collect questions that were asked and repeat answers of a general nature when the group reconvenes.

Other Communication Methods

You should take the same care in communicating the sales compensation plan to your sales reps as you would any product to your customers. You do not have to go to the expense of a three-color print job; today desktop publishing software and laser printers provide a relatively inexpensive means of preparing high-quality printed materials.

More important, personal computers and spreadsheet software permit you to model the outcome of the revised plan and project each sales rep's compensation under various performance scenarios. With such support, you can go a long way toward reducing the uncertainty associated with the introduction of a new plan and garner support by indicating that you have anticipated the impact upon each individual and planned accordingly.

If personal computers are readily available to the sales reps, you might consider providing each with a diskette containing the model of the sales compensation plan. The reps could use this not only to expand upon management's planned performance scenarios and related compensation impact, but also to project their actual compensation, during the plan year, based upon current personal performance.

In many ways, a revised sales compensation program is the most significant new product you will roll out. Treat it as such.

16.14 Following Through

If properly designed, your sales compensation plan will communicate sales priorities to the field. More likely than not, however, some confusion over plan elements will remain. Therefore, you should provide ongoing, sustained communication to ensure understanding and, hopefully, to bring about the desired behavioral change.

Here are some follow-up techniques that you can employ.

Postintroduction Audit

After the initial plan communication, determine if your messages were understood and if any areas of uncertainty exist. The field management team can prove invaluable in this regard, especially if they were instrumental in the plan's introduction. To assess the need for further communications, gather information concerning the types of questions asked either during or after the meeting held to introduce the plan. Perhaps some technical issues that remain unclear can be clarified in writing.

Consider the attitude of the sales force. Are they charged up as a result of the new plan? Or are they so filled with fear or anger that they are not selling? If the latter is the case, you have a serious problem. On the other hand, if the sales environment has changed substantially and you need a sales force with a different risk profile, the sales compensation program can complement other management programs designed to transform the characteristics of the sales team.

Because of the qualitative nature of sales force attitudes, don't hesitate to discuss the plan with a spectrum of sales employees. Don't introduce bias into your information by talking only with the high performers; you need to consider the attitudes of the good performers and those who are not meeting expectations.

With the results of this work in hand, you should plan the activities necessary to ensure the success of the program. These could include informational and/or skills training, more coaching on the part of sales management, and enhanced communications to share sales strategies and successes. Alternatively, you may conclude that further action above and beyond the normal sales management process is unnecessary. Although consistency in leadership direction is necessary to instill confidence on the part of your subordinates, don't be doctrinaire in your planning. If new information indicates that changes have to be made, communicate this fact as quickly as possible, along with the changes you seek.

Midyear Audit

If plan changes are significant, you should assess the impact on sales force performance after a reasonable period of time. Because most sales goals are set on a yearly basis, a midyear review will allow you to use the information as part of the goal-setting process that typically begins during the third quarter. What elements should you consider in this audit?

First, you should determine whether there is any cyclicality in the sales process and whether you can project annual sales performance from year-to-date (YTD) results. Or, it might be better to contrast performance to the prior year's YTD results.

After making this decision, assess the plan's impact on your sales force. Have the desired behavioral changes occurred (either activities and/or actual sales results)? Has the desired impact on compensation been achieved? Have you lost any of your key people to competitors? Has the plan design encouraged less productive sales-force members to seek other nonsales careers? Is the targeted level of compensation being achieved? Is the distribution between the highest-paid and the lowest-paid employee appropriate? Are the outcomes influenced by any windfalls or any unanticipated broad-based changes? Are you attaining your desired cost-of-sales targets? Are the right customers receiving appropriate attention? Are the right products receiving enough emphasis?

Finally, given the fact that not enough time may have passed for a sound quantitative analysis to be made, how do you feel about the changes? Is your intuition saying that your decision was correct, or are you beginning to second-guess the plan design?

Based on the information you develop, you should consider some communication to the sales force on the status of the plan and your anticipated approach for the coming year.

17

Paying the Sales Manager

17.1   Introduction

The sales manager, by the very nature of his or her job, has a direct influence on the success or failure of the field sales compensation program. Strangely enough, many companies ignore this crucial link when developing their sales managers' compensation plans. Some organizations even give their sales managers compensation goals that are in conflict with those of the sales reps. For example, while reps are in hot pursuit of volume, sales managers may be paid to chase down gross margin percentages that are adversely affected by high-volume, low-margin accounts. Other companies include sales managers in an incentive plan that covers various nonsales departments and levels of management. Generally, such plans hold managers accountable for corporate or divisional goals. These are inappropriate for the sales manager, whose influence and focus are confined to a specific district or region.

In short, sales managers are often the victims of compensation programs that have ambiguous or even counterproductive objectives and uninspiring incentives. Most companies would benefit by developing a plan based on the role these important executives play in managing field resources.

17.2   Two Types of Sales Managers

A sales manager's role is best defined by the characteristics of the sales representatives he or she supervises. There are two basic categories of sales representatives:

1. *The account representative*, who primarily services and sells to an assigned group of accounts that are loyal to the company rather than to the individual representative
2. *The entrepreneur*, who acquires and, in effect, controls his or her own accounts

The entrepreneur generally prefers such industries as life insurance, real estate, and financial services, while the account representative usually gravitates to manufacturing and consumer products. See Figure 17-1 for further distinctions between these two categories.

The techniques and skills needed to manage these two types of sales reps are very different. Figure 17-2 contrasts the responsibilities of the account rep and entrepreneur sales managers.

The sales manager in charge of account reps is typically expected to increase overall sales volume, although sometimes his or her goals encompass such other strategic objectives as broadening product mix or increasing gross margin on a specific product. Generally, senior management has imposed the sales organizational structure and marketing plan. This manager is dealing with a fixed resource (number of territories) and can increase its value only by getting the most out of every producer.

Most companies compensate entrepreneur reps with straight commission and low out-of-pocket expense reimbursement. As a result, the companies usually profit from the business of even their lowest producers. The sales manager of an entrepreneur sales force is therefore charged with boosting gross productivity. He or she can accomplish this by effectively training current reps, retaining productive ones, and attracting new producers who will bring additional accounts with them.

Figure 17-1. Two categories of sales representatives.

Account Representative	Entrepreneur
• Services and sells to an assigned group of accounts.	• Sells to a diverse customer base who must constantly be convinced of the product/service need.
• Customers are loyal to the company rather than to the individual representative.	• Customers are at least as loyal to the representatives as to the companies they represent.
• Sells in accordance with company policy, procedures, and culture.	• Employs a high degree of initiative and creative approaches.

Figure 17-2. Responsibilities of the two types of sales managers.

Account Rep Sales Manager	Entrepreneur Rep Sales Manager
• Manage existing resources to achieve company objectives.	• Attract new producers to provide company with new account base.
• Train current representatives.	• Train current representatives.
• Deploy reps efficiently among accounts/prospects.	• Inspire productive representatives to higher levels.

Because it is the individual rep, not the company, who controls the customer, this sales manager is not bound by a fixed (territorial) resource and may hire or fire reps as necessary.

A discussion of the compensation approaches appropriate to each category of sales manager follows below.

17.3 For Account Rep Sales Managers: The "Accumulated Results" Pay Approach

The account rep sales manager's task is to maximize the return on a fixed resource. Therefore, her compensation plan should serve to hold her accountable for the results she achieves through her management of the field force. Usually, the best way for the company to accomplish this is by measuring the collective efforts of the sales reps. Such accumulated results are most often expressed in terms of the aggregate volume of territories supervised. However, volume need not be the only measure.

For example, in a highly competitive market, market share gains may be more important than absolute volume. Therefore, the reps' plan should include some incentive to increase market share, and the sales manager's plan should measure the cumulative result or market share gain.

Ideally, the sales manager's and sales reps' incentive plans should complement each other. Although one plan need not mirror the other exactly, a high degree of synergy is desirable, thereby supporting the company's sales goals at both field sales levels. But it is important to avoid holding the sales manager responsible for account-specific objectives that can only be controlled by an individual sales rep. For example, the company may require reps to sell more of product X than Y because X is more profitable. The only way the reps can achieve this, however, is through their ongoing client contact. The sales manager cannot directly influence each rep's performance, but she *can* be measured according to the aggregate result.

Measuring the sales manager in this way makes her goals compatible with the reps' efforts to sell more of X. A simple equation translates accumulated results into compensation:

> 100% achievement of results
> = 100% incentive payment
> = 100% achievement of target total compensation

If results fall short, the sales manager receives no bonus (or less than the target incentive) and her total compensation remains below the target level. If results exceed the objective, she is paid a higher bonus, bringing her total compensation above the targeted level.

The account rep sales manager's challenge is to improve the company's return (sales volume or profit) on a fixed investment (a number of territories with a specified number of selling hours to be utilized). In doing this, she will effectively increase the average productivity of her sales reps. Because the sales manager can "control" district or region volume through her management of territorial resources, her compensation can be closely linked to that volume.

Given a volume objective to achieve, it is up to the sales manager to parcel out sales rep territory objectives in a manner that will best help her meet her own goals. Clearly the easiest way to achieve this is to follow the "80/20 Rule"; that is, expect the top 20 percent of her reps to produce about 80 percent of her region's objective. She then divides the remainder of the objective among the average or below-average producers.

The company may, however, wish to develop average and below-average reps. In such cases, a compensation plan that holds the sales manager accountable for individual territory results as well as overall performance will require her to concentrate at least some energy on developing less productive reps.

There are two ways to construct such a plan:

1. Pay target compensation only when *both* accumulated *and* individual territory goals are achieved.
2. Pay full target compensation upon achievement of accumulated objectives, with extra bonuses based on individual territory performance goals.

Plans that incorporate individual territory results into the sales manager's goals place a greater burden on the sales manager, but ultimately everyone benefits. The sales manager increases her current income and potential for future bonuses by developing a better sales force. The sales reps improve their productivity, motivational level, and income. And the company enjoys a greater return from its sales organization.

17.4   Illustrative Plans for the Account Rep Sales Manager

The Single Schedule

The single schedule is useful when there is just one key variable on which basis the manager is measured and paid. The example below shows how such a schedule would work when district sales dollars comprise the performance measure and the target incentive is 30 percent of base salary.

Percent Sales $ Quota Achieved	Incentive as Percent of Base Salary
<80%	0%
80	15
90	20
<u>100</u>	<u>30</u>
110	40
120	50
130	55

___ = Target

The single schedule can also work for two or more objectives as follows:

<u>A</u> Percent Objective 1 Achieved	<u>B</u> Incentive as Percent of Base Salary	<u>C</u> Percent Objective 2 Achieved	<u>D</u> Incentive as Percent of Base Salary
<80%	0%	<80%	0%
80	7.5	80	7.5
90	10	90	10
<u>100</u>	<u>15</u>	100	<u>15</u>
110	20	110	20
120	25	120	25
130	32.5	130	32.5

___ = Target

The target incentive is still 30 percent, but in this example the sales manager earns the full amount only if she achieves 100 percent of the performance goal in each category. For three objectives, the incentive for reaching 100 percent in each category should be 10 percent (one-third of the total). Adjusting the percentages in the incentive columns will place greater emphasis on one goal or another.

The Matrix

A matrix is an effective way to compensate a sales manager for performance on two key measures. Figure 17-3 uses district sales and gross margin, both of which can be measured in total dollars relative to an established quota. If both objectives are equally important, they receive equal weight in the matrix.

Note that the amount paid is the same regardless of what combination of sales and gross margin the manager achieves. For example, 80 percent of sales and 110 percent of gross margin, or 80 percent of gross margin and 110 percent of sales, both pay 90 percent of target incentive.

If, however, one objective is more important than the other, the matrix can be structured to reflect a proportional relationship, as illustrated in Figure 17-4.

With this matrix, gross margin is emphasized. The manager earns 110 percent of target incentive at 80 percent of sales and 110 percent of gross margin objectives, but only 95 percent of target incentive at 100 percent of sales and 80 percent of gross margin objectives.

Figure 17-3. Percentage of target incentive earned under various results (two objectives, equally important).

					Sales $ to Goal			
		<80%	80	90	100	110	120	130
	130%	0%	110	120	130	140	150	160
	120	0	100	110	120	130	140	150
	110	0	90	100	110	120	130	140
Gross Margin $ to Goal	100	0	80	90	100	110	120	130
	90	0	75	80	90	100	110	120
	80	0	70	75	80	90	100	110
	<80	0	0	0	0	0	0	0

(Note: Numbers within the matrix denote the percentage of target incentive paid.)

Figure 17-4. Percentage of target incentive earned under various results (two objectives, one more important than the other).

					Sales $ to Goal			
		<80%	80	90	100	110	120	130
	130%	0%	130	135	140	145	150	155
	120	0	120	125	130	135	140	145
	110	0	110	115	120	125	130	135
Gross Margin $ to Goal	100	0	100	105	110	115	120	125
	90	0	90	95	100	105	110	115
	80	0	80	85	90	95	100	105
	<80	0	0	0	0	0	0	0

(Note: Numbers within the matrix denote the percentage of target incentive paid.)

The Multiplier

Another way to structure a dual incentive is to use a multiplier or "kicker." In this type of plan, the sales manager can earn extra incentive by meeting both a primary objective and one or more additional secondary goals. Figure 17-5 exemplifies a typical multiplier plan.

Assume the sales manager reaches both her sales dollar and gross profit dollar quotas. She earns an incentive equal to 30 percent of her base salary (column B) multiplied by 1.15 (column D).

$$30\% \times 1.15 = 34.5\%$$

$$34.5\% \times \text{Base Salary} = \text{Incentive}$$

17.5   For Entrepreneur Rep Sales Managers: The Override Approach

The entrepreneur rep sales manager is concerned with maximizing total productivity. To do this, he must ensure that competitors don't lure away his high producers because the resulting loss of accounts will mean a corresponding drop in overall productivity. In addition, as very few reps walk into the company with pockets full of accounts, the sales manager also spends a good portion of his time training and motivating current reps, especially low-to-average performers. Finally, the sales manager must recruit and train new reps to replace any who do not succeed.

In light of the scope of his responsibilities, the sales manager's performance is best evaluated by his:

- Effectiveness in training current reps
- Ability to attract new producers who can provide the company with additional accounts
- Skill in retaining productive reps

Figure 17-5. A typical multiplier plan.

_A_ Percent Sales $ Quota Achieved	_B_ Incentive as Percent of Base Salary	_C_ Percent of GP $ Quota Achieved	_D_ Multiplier (applied to factor in column B)
<80%	0%	<80%	0
80	10	80	1.05
90	20	90	1.10
100	30	100	1.15
110%	40%	110%	1.25

These measures of sales management are all reflected in the aggregate productivity of the sales manager's subordinates.

Because entrepreneur reps are generally paid largely by straight commission, their income is directly linked to productivity. The aggregate earnings of the sales force, therefore, is an appropriate gauge of the sales manager's success. It follows, then, that a bonus based on a percentage of his subordinates' aggregate earnings or sales—the so-called "override approach"—is the most effective incentive compensation for this type of sales manager.

17.6   Relationship to Business Goals

Because this sales manager's pay is so closely tied to field sales results, it is easy to set up a compensation program that requires him to achieve specified revenue and growth goals before he can attain a "comfortable" earnings level.

Let's assume that such an earnings level is $65,000. If $30,000 is paid as base salary, the remaining $35,000 must come from earned incentive. The sales manager's override, therefore, can be calculated by establishing the dollar value of the measured goal and solving for the percentage that yields $35,000. In the following example, the objective is accumulated sales of $30 million.

$$\$35,000 = x\% \ (\$30,000,000)$$

$$x = .0012$$

$$\text{Override} = .12\% \text{ of sales}$$

If sales fall below $30 million, the manager makes less than his "comfortable" earnings level; if sales exceed the goal, he will make more.

Following this principle, an override can be based on sales, rep earnings, or both.

17.7   Illustrative Plans for the Entrepreneur Rep Sales Manager

Override Tied to District Sales

We have just seen how to calculate the override percentage when sales is the measured goal. Now, here is what a plan keyed to total sales might look like:

Sales	Override
From $1 +	.12% of sales

This can be modified by adding a threshold. For example:

Sales	Override
<$10,000,000	0
$10,000,000+	.12%

A further modification is a graduated scale:

Sales	Override
<$10,000,000	0
$10,000,000–$50,000,000	.12%
$50,000,000+	.14%

Override Tied to Rep Earnings

When the plan focuses on sales rep earnings, the sales manager's override is a percentage of the sum of individual sales rep commissions.

To determine the appropriate percent that will yield $35,000 (the incentive portion of the sales manager's comfortable earnings of $65,000), we begin with the rep's comfortable earnings level of $43,000, expressed as "average" rep commissions. Assuming a sales manager has seven reps, the override percentage is calculated as follows:

$$\text{Average sales rep earnings} = \frac{\$ 43,000}{\$301,000} \times 7 \text{ (number of reps)}$$

$$\text{Target Incentive} = \$35,000$$
$$\$35,000 = x\% \ \$301,000$$
$$x\% = 11.6$$
$$\text{Override} = 11.6\%$$

Assuming the same seven reps, if two earn $25,000 each; three, $40,000 each; and the remaining two, $80,000 each; the sales manager's override is:

$$11.6\% \text{ of } (\$25,000 \times 2) + (\$40,000 \times 3) + (\$80,000 \times 2)$$

or

$$11.6\% \ (\$330,000) = \$38,280$$

A modification designed to encourage the sales manager to develop less productive reps might be:

Average Sales Rep Earnings	*Commission*
<$40,000	0%
$40,001–$50,000	12%
50,001– 60,000	13%
60,001– 70,000	14%

Override Tied to Both Sales and Rep Earnings

If both sales and rep earnings are co-objectives, the plan might be structured like this:

Sales	*Rep Earnings*	*Override*
<$10,000,000	<$40,000	0%
$10,000,000–$50,000,000	$40,000–$60,000	12%
$50,000,001–$100,000,000	$60,001–$80,000	13%
$100,000,000+	$80,000+	14%

17.8   Relationship to Management Compensation Plan

Many companies now use management incentive plans at several levels and for many functions within the organization. If the sales manager is covered under a companywide management incentive plan, the plan should be structured to enable him to participate fully. If his plan is separate, it should offer benefits and opportunities similar to those in the plan that cover other executives. Following are some of the factors to consider in designing the sales manager's incentive program:

   ▪ *Overall organizational climate or culture.* A company will naturally express its value system in its compensation programs including that of the sales manager. For example, a company may be highly risk averse in its compensation philosophy, preferring high base salaries and little or no incentive opportunity. While a sales manager might be allowed more incentive opportunity than are other managers at his level, the increased opportunity would probably be limited to 10–15 percent more than that of his peers.

   On the other hand, a company that has a "commission mentality" with regard to its sales force may pay everyone on a straight commission basis regardless of how appropriate that is to the selling environment. Sales managers for such a company earn most of their income from commissions.

   ▪ *Compatibility with the compensation program offered to peer executives in nonsales functions.* If peers of the sales managers participate in a senior executive bonus plan, the sales manager should also participate. Even though a separate plan might be better suited for the sales manager, excluding him from the plan covering the other executives may convey the message that the sales manager is less important to the organization than his peers are.

If the sales manager participates in the same bonus plan as do his nonsales peers, the plan should have some provision for pay based on achievement of individual objectives. That would allow the sales manager to include field sales goals among his personal objectives. Because this section of the plan would probably be a small proportion of the total incentive, it would be wise to avoid dilution by allowing the sales manager to choose only one or two key field sales objectives.

- *The extent of the manager's incentive opportunity relative to the opportunities available to his field sales subordinates.* A common question is whether sales representatives should earn more than the sales manager does. The answer is, "It depends." What it depends upon is the kind of sales manager being considered. The account rep sales manager should earn more than does the average sales rep under his supervision. This manager formally directs the overall sales effort in accordance with specific company objectives, and his broader responsibility should be recognized through a higher base salary. A smaller incentive opportunity is also appropriate for him, however, because his risk is spread across a larger sales base than is a rep's risk.

That's not to say that sales reps should never earn more than their managers do. An outstanding rep should certainly be compensated for his or her superior individual contribution. But if the average sales rep is outearning the manager, something is wrong with the compensation system.

The entrepreneur rep sales manager's commission percentage is probably lower than the reps' percentage, and the level of talent in his sales reps will vary. Therefore, on average he will earn the same as or less than his highest performing reps do. This makes sense, because in an entrepreneurial structure the rep controls the account.

- *Paying a nonsales manager in a sales environment.* If the sales manager position is occupied by a career corporate manager who may move into and out of the sales organization, the structure of his compensation plan is probably less important than that of a manager who is on an exclusively sales-oriented career path. If the field sales manager position is just one stop on the management training circuit, companies should take care to keep the compensation level of the sales manager spot in line with that of the positions to which individuals will later progress.

18

Special Selling Roles

18.1 Introduction

How simple your life would be if customers bought in ways that allowed you to credit each sale to a single salesperson. The buying process would be much more orderly and predictable. Unfortunately, multiple buyers who need all kinds of information and support (across many sites) are a part of day-to-day business. Furthermore, certain types of accounts, for example, house accounts, sales to governments and institutions, and sales through distributors, require specialized sales roles.

Most sales forces, at one time or another, face situations that do not fit the norm. You should not let the fact that certain markets are different deter you from adopting a field sales compensation program (or other approaches) to better manage the sales process. Just be sure that your sales management process accommodates the needs of the customers in those markets and the sales representatives who serve them.

Let's consider some unusual selling roles—team sales and other situations that might call for split credits, house accounts, and government and distributor sales—in the context of the overall sales management process. We should also examine the implications of special sales roles for compensation and related systems, for example, goal setting, information gathering, and performance measurement.

18.2 Split Credits and Team Selling

A split credit occurs when more than one sales rep plays a role in the sales process. When markets are well segmented and territories properly structured, you can often minimize the crossing of boundaries. Nevertheless, split credits are a fact of life, especially in complex markets. The question is how to deal with them.

In some situations, split credit sales are accidental, and the sales role can be structured to minimize such interactions in the future. But in other, often more critical, situations, split credits and team selling are merely two sides of the same effective approach. Rather than trying to avoid them, you might be better off structuring sales roles and compensation systems to encourage and reward split credits and team sales.

To know which approach to take, you must understand the specific conditions under which the sale occurs. The situations that create overlaps in selling roles aren't all alike.

Hierarchical Accounts

How do you sell to a national chain or a multilocation industry behemoth? With such accounts, the buying process is often divided between a corporate and a divisional (or local) role:

- *Strong corporate/weak unit.* In some chains, the corporate buyer determines which vendor will be used, while the unit buyer merely places the order. Because the size of the order placed is strictly a function of the unit's business, the sales influence occurs entirely at the corporate level. The vendor, however, must make sure that service at the unit level is adequate to maintain the account.

- *Strong unit/weak corporate.* In some franchise operations and many decentralized conglomerates, the corporate function is purely advisory or may not exist at all. Each unit essentially stands alone and makes its own choice of vendor, splitting purchases and so on. In these situations, the sale is made at the unit level. There might be a public relations role to be played at the corporate level, but not much else.

- *Shared corporate/unit.* A third possibility is shared buying responsibilities. Corporate headquarters might develop an approved vendors list (two or three companies), but the decision of which vendor to use is left to each unit. In these situations, sales activities must target both the corporate level (especially to become an approved supplier) and the unit level (to be the selected supplier or to get the largest possible share).

Complex Product/Application/Service Needs

Account structure alone does not determine how many players should be on the sales field. Technologically complex products or advanced applications often require product or market specialists to play a role in the sales effort. Sometimes, particularly in businesses where reliability is a key factor in choosing a vendor, service people also play a special role or may be uniquely positioned to be aware of sales opportunities. Traditionally, these nonsales jobs tend not to be covered by incentives. But if the customer interface team has many members—and success depends on interrelated efforts—it's often wise to find a way to distribute rewards beyond the positions that carry the word *sales* in their titles. However, it's better not to distribute rewards at all than to do it in a way that will be perceived as inequitable.

Internal Staffing and Development Needs

Finally, you may deliberately structure situations where more than one person plays a role in the sales effort, for reasons beyond market or product considerations. Two sales reps may be paired for training purposes; one rep may stand in for another, for example, during an extended illness, or one may take over another's territory. These situations tend to be easier to manage because you create them yourself.

18.3 Split Credits/Team Selling: Noncompensation Issues

The first step in examining a split credit situation is to make sure you aren't creating either too many or too few splits. The nature of the sales role, which is determined by how customers want to buy, will be your primary indicator.

Chapter 6 discussed sales organization and specialization in detail. The issues covered there can help you structure territories to apply team selling most effectively. Useful techniques include:

- Organizing by decision maker rather than by product line
- Defining territories by accounts rather than by geography
- Decentralizing sales support
- Applying national account approaches, where all sales reps who call on a particular national account are covered by the same structure and may have special compensation arrangements

After eliminating the unnecessary splits, articulate the circumstances that call for additional salespeople in the selling process. To help identify the extent to which more than one sales rep should be involved and the nature of the interaction, ask yourself such questions as:

- Is the nature of the overlap accidental (i.e., in a perfect world it wouldn't happen) or deliberate (i.e., necessary to best serve customer needs)?
- What situation generated the need for interaction? Hierarchical accounts (strong corporate/weak unit, strong unit/weak corporate, or shared corporate/unit)? Complex product/application/services needs? Internal staffing and development needs?
- Are the sales reps working sequentially or simultaneously?
- Are the tasks separable (different activities with different measures) or integrated (more than one person working on the same task)?
- Is the overlap long-term or short-term?

The next step is to make sure that the ground rules for splits—in terms of goal setting, information systems, performance appraisal, and compensation—are clearly spelled out.

18.4 Split Credits/Team Selling: Compensation Issues, Goal Setting, and Performance Appraisal

Answers to the following questions concerning team selling will help you set the ground rules for determining split credit situations:

- Should you split at all?
- Should a given sale be "double counted" rather than split?
- Should splits be of the same size incentive fund (e.g., 50-50 or 60-40, for a total of 100 percent) or of a larger fund (e.g., 60-60, for a total of more than 100 percent)?
- Should the rules for making splits be fixed, discretionary, or something else? If the company opts for latitude, who should exercise it? Management? The lead sales rep?
- Should the same measures be used for all positions? What are the implications for goal setting?

You will find the answers within the selling situation itself.

To Split or Not to Split?

Commission splits represent the most common form of compensation in team selling. It is often assumed that commissions will come from a constant-sized fund, the only question being how to divide it. In reality, however, it might be better to ask if a single fund of constant size is the right thing to be dividing, and if commissions are the most appropriate form of compensation at all.

A constant commission fund is most applicable to simple selling situations with high sales prominence, i.e., situations in which the salesperson has a large and direct impact on sales volume. In selling encyclopedias door to door, for example, there's no inherent need for more than one person. Sales are all that count and, of all the marketing variables, the sales rep exerts the greatest influence on the buying decision.

Suppose that the rep decides that it would be more efficient to hire a driver. Should you pay the rep additional commission? No, because in this kind of a high-risk and high-impact selling environment, you care about results, not methods. It's entirely up to the salesperson to determine how to do the job. The rep is free to use a driver, as long as the cost comes out of the original commission fund. Anything else is uneconomical for the company.

Unfortunately, many sales managers use this same compensation structure in situations where it has little relevance. For example, suppose you're dealing with a company that has two sites, one of which does design and prototype manufacturing, while the other does volume manufacturing. You have two buying decisions to make: determining what component to design in and evaluating which components are most cost-effective. However, getting "first print position," that is, getting designed in first, gives a company a significant edge over its competitors in volume manufacturing.

An unexamined commission plan might give the first rep 100 percent of sales on the volume from the design site (which would be close to nothing) and give the second 100 percent of sales on volume from the manufacturing site. But consider the consequences. For one thing, no intelligent rep would "waste" time trying to sell design sites, because the payback would be so poor. On the other hand, if an altruistic rep in another part of the world landed a design-only site, the salesperson on the receiving end would probably spend too much time making absolutely sure this good (and already likely) sale would be landed, and probably not enough time selling developmental accounts in his or her own area.

The design-versus-manufacturing situation is markedly different from door-to-door sales, and the differences show why simple split models don't always work. In the design-versus-manufacturing situation:

- The selling task is complex. Because there is more than one phase, there is more than one sales role (although all roles might be performed by one person).
- You want to direct the sales rep to do something other than simply maximize the ratio of commission dollars to selling time. You care about how the rep spends time, and not just about the superficial measure of result.
- It is not always clear who did what.
- The ratio of time required to get the job done to value of the result isn't constant across all the selling situations from which the sales rep must choose.

In fact, commission or volume-based plans are not the most appropriate in the design-versus-manufacturing selling situation. A split situation that's impossible to resolve indicates that you shouldn't be using commissions in the first place. (Objectives are probably better.) Managing complex selling situations is more than a question of generating sales, although that's still the ultimate objective. The critical decision is how to allocate time to the various customer-interface tasks. In situations that require multiphase and complex selling roles, the simple answers are rarely the right ones.

Size of the Fund

Let's return to our examination of the nature of the sales team interaction. A constant-sized fund is most appropriate if:

- The selling task is relatively simple and self-contained.
- Customer characteristics don't vary.
- The buying process is reasonably short and doesn't involve different phases.
- The company doesn't care how or where the sales rep spends time, as long as sales result.
- There is normally a fixed (and probably relatively high) ratio of sales cost to revenues generated, or other means of controlling the sales rep's time.
- It is fairly easy to evaluate who did what.
- Any overlap is coincidental, not deliberate.
- The share of the fund allocated to each member of the selling team is enough to motivate all to carry out their roles.

The more the situation departs from the above profile, the more advisable it is to make the fund larger if more than one sales rep is involved. For example:

- If two sales reps are involved, the split could total 140 percent, an average of 70 percent each.
- If three sales reps are involved, the split could total 180 percent, an average of 60 percent each.
- If four (or more) reps are involved, the splits could total 200 percent, or an average of as much as 50 percent each.

Try to strike a balance between a number so high that it creates an artificial incentive, motivating more people to participate than necessary, and one so low that the sales rep either risks trying to do it alone or feels inequitably treated. The more complex the situation, the higher the value will have to be. It will also have to be higher the more individual discretion is involved. A closely supervised sales force should require less cash incentive.

In the most complex situations, the pie concept no longer applies at all. Your sales reps' objectives are based on what they're supposed to *do*. In the process of setting objectives, you might count sales dollars in more than one place, so that, in effect, the pie grows by 100 percent each time another person joins the act. This may seem expensive, but it isn't. You are merely using sales volume as one way to direct field attention to what's required to sell most effectively. If you have the right level of deployment and competitive compensation, the approach is self-correcting. And if your company can't afford it, it shouldn't be in the business. A halfhearted attempt to get sales without proper direction is a waste of resources.

Allocating the Fund

If the use of a fund is appropriate in a given situation, how should you divide it?

First of all, examine all the circumstances where splits occur and note the patterns. You might find, for example, that splits happen in two situations: design-versus-manufacturing sales (as discussed earlier) and team sales that require special expertise.

For each category, define the sales roles and determine how time devoted to each sales role compares to time spent on other activities competing for the sales rep's attention. For example, suppose the design sales rep typically averages 200 hours of work in a situation with a 25 percent chance of producing $800,000 in revenues (counting both design and manufacturing together). The expected result is $1,000 per hour ($800,000 times 25% divided by 200). How does this compare to other sales opportunities?

If such sales are as valuable to the company as are other courses the sales rep could pursue, the effective commission rate shouldn't differ much from that earned pursuing alternatives. For example, a split of 75 percent of the normal rate would be acceptable, if other sales would bring $1,500 per hour with about the same risk and time horizon. If the alternatives were less risky or took place sooner, a higher figure would be required.

If you looked at the manufacturing role and also came up with 75 percent, that would indicate that you would need a larger-than-normal fund and that the shares ought to be about equal.

Evaluate the importance of each role with respect to the end result. Does getting design in require a scarcer talent? Is it a more difficult task than maintaining sales in a manufacturing site once design is established? If so, the design sale probably ought to get more of the pie, even though it generates fewer dollars directly.

Finally, take into account sales expectations and past precedents. If what you've done before has been reasonably well received, you should institute changes gradually.

Rules: Fixed, Contingent, or Discretionary?

How much should the rules change over time or from situation to situation? If you've got only one situation—or several, but with roughly equal splits—then you're best off with a fixed set of rules.

If you've objectively identified several patterns, and the nature of the sales role varies in each, then the patterns will determine how to apply the splits. If neither of the above applies, then consider a discretionary split. But try the numbers out; if the difference between an ideal discretionary split and the standard rule is small, stay with the rule.

If a discretionary split is appropriate, there are several ways to approach it. Establish some kind of rough determination of the split beforehand. If one sales rep will be taking the lead in the project and controlling who else is brought in, that person might recommend the split.

18.5   Government Sales

Sales to governments—federal, state, local, or foreign—frequently require skills and degrees of influence far different from those employed in sales to the private sector.

Distinctive Market Characteristics

Sales to governments involve a process of competitive bidding that begins with a request for proposal (RFP) and concludes with the selection of a choice from among a list of "best and final" contenders. Selling is usually a team effort, requiring a variety of skills (several of which may be expected of a single sales rep). The selling process generally includes two phases:

1. Obtaining information in advance from sources in government. This allows the employer to respond to the RFP based on a knowledge of the factors that will influence the selection.
2. Presenting the proposal, revising it, and redefining the scope of the project. If awarded the contract, the employer oversees its execution.

Sales to governments are predictable in one sense: The date that a contract will be awarded is often known far, sometimes years, in advance. These sales do not, however, follow predictable chronological patterns and do not occur at regular intervals. Therefore, in most months no current sales will be recorded, but work will be under way to secure sales in various stages of the proposal process. Conversely, sales results in a month simply reflect the data a contract is awarded, not the consequential sales activities undertaken in that month to improve the chances of securing contracts to be awarded in the future.

The role of field sales reps in this process is very prominent (although the value of contracts and knowing one's way through bureaucracies should not be underestimated). Most conventional approaches to sales compensation do not fit government sales because:

- Conventional plans assume that there will be results within a year, but government sales frequently take more than twelve months to complete.
- Given the "big ticket," random incidence of sales, sales goals cannot be set with confidence. Selling skills may influence whether a sale is made, but the timing and size of the sale are almost entirely beyond the influence of the sales rep.
- Any measure of results must await the awarding of the contract. However, one can see why an incentive based on current sales would be at best incomplete and at worst a totally misleading measure of sales effectiveness. The principal accomplishments of the sales force in a given month relate not to contracts awarded that month, but to work on contracts pending in various stages of completion.

Compensation Approaches

Because conventional compensation measures are inappropriate for government sales forces, you might consider specific pay plans for dedicated government field forces that include:

- Straight salary (a common approach, even where commercial reps are on incentive)
- A higher proportion of salary in the salary/incentive mix
- A maximum on the incentive to be earned from any one transaction

Two other approaches recognize that, with respect to government sales, the calendar has less meaning than does the event of the sale. They are the "event-driven" and "line-of-credit" approaches.

The Event-Driven Approach

The incentive period of the event-driven approach is neither a year nor a quarter but rather the life of the contract. The sales rep receives simulated equity in the contract itself, consisting of any or all of the following:

- A front-end bonus for securing the sale, paid when the contract is awarded. This approach could be applied to award incentive payments before the sale as well, based on achieving certain milestones (e.g., reaching "best and final" stage) that signify progress toward securing the contract.

- A continuing share of revenue or profit, if the sales rep played a significant role in defining the project secured from the contract, with awards paid on anniversary dates of the contract's acquisition.

The Line-of-Credit Approach

The line-of-credit approach recognizes that a rep may have no sales in a particular month (or even year), but that eventually some revenue must be generated. The rep receives a salary, part or all of which is treated as an advance against a compensation "line of credit." For example, the salary may be $80,000 per year, and the credit "limit" $300,000. Whenever a sale is made, part of the line of credit is repaid, according to the plan's commission schedule. Excesses, that is, accumulated commission in excess of accumulated salary, are paid to the individual on a quarterly or annual basis. Thus, all sales are credited toward earnings, but the timing of sales has no impact on compensation. Should the accumulated excess of salary over commission exceed the "credit line," you would inform the rep that his productivity no longer justified the high salary (or even, perhaps, his continued employment).

The line-of-credit approach applies the commission principle in a nonchronological, event-driven context. As with any commission approach, its validity rests upon a close linkage between sales influence and revenue results. As noted earlier, with government sales, there is often a very distant relationship between the sales rep and the revenue. In such cases, you might use the line-of-credit approach in those (relatively few) situations where the sales rep can parlay his or her unique skills or personal relationships with government decision makers into government contracts.

18.6   Distributor Sales

Selling to distributors can also require specialized skills. For example, the sales rep can function as a consultant to the distributor in all facets of the latter's business. Orchestrating a mutually beneficial relationship between a manufacturer and its distributors can be a delicate balancing act, but you can usually use conventional compensation techniques both for the rep specializing in managing distributors and for the distributor organization itself.

A manufacturer sells through reps or distributors to secure sales that could not otherwise be obtained within the financial constraints of the manufacturer's business. Therefore, the role of the distributor is analogous to that of the commission rep, whose influence over volume is so pervasive, if not exclusive, that current volume is a complete and accurate measure of worth. Hence, the commission mode of compensation, historically the preeminent way companies pay their distributors, is appropriate in this context.

You may use variants of the commission approach in dealing with distributors, but in principle, current volume should be the cornerstone of the program by which a manufacturer pays its reps. The role of the individual who is responsible for sales to distributors is more multifaceted but can still normally be accommodated by a conventional sales compensation program.

Such an individual functions as an overall business adviser to the distributor, helping the distributor manage its sales force and, in the process, obtaining a greater share of the attention of the distributor rep toward the manufacturer's products. The rep may even aid the distributor in selecting, motivating, and training distributor sales and service personnel. At times, the responsibilities of the distributor rep extend to selecting and replacing distributors as well. Although all these functions are more business management than sales, they are nevertheless undertaken for a single purpose: to maximize the flow of the manufacturer's goods through the distributor organization. That being the case, a compensation system based on volume secured from assigned accounts (perhaps relative to a quota) should determine incentive compensation for the distributor sales specialist.

19

Internal Equity

19.1 Introduction

The vice-president of sales of a large material handling company designed a new incentive plan for the sales force. The plan, consisting of a base salary and a commission on total sales volume, provided unlimited earnings potential for the sales representatives. Corporate management reviewed and approved the plan, which was implemented and operated successfully for two years.

The company's chief executive officer received a report each March listing the previous year's twenty-five highest-paid employees. The list named the CEO, other officers, and a few group vice-presidents.

One year, a new name, one the CEO did not recognize, appeared on the list: that of an employee whose earnings exceeded those of a number of the officers. Payroll verified the figure and identified the employee as a sales rep in Detroit. The vice-president of sales confirmed that the sales rep had indeed earned the amount shown on the list. He explained to the CEO that one of the rep's customers, a major automobile manufacturer, had decided to replace more than one-third of its lift trucks that year. The order resulted in a commission that moved the rep up to the CEO's list.

The CEO met with the vice-president. After a lengthy discussion on internal equity of pay, they decided to amend the plan by adding a cap on total earnings.

19.2 Pay Comparison

A sales incentive plan that enables a rep to earn as much as, or more than, some of the top executives may be approved when first discussed. Not many executives disagree with the concept that sales reps should be rewarded for results—with no limit on their potential earnings. When the payment comes due, however, some executives doubt that a sales rep is worth as much money as one of the company's top officers.

Some managers, in fact, will question the validity of the compensation plan if a sales rep outearns his peers in engineering, manufacturing, or finance. The managers understand that sales reps should be paid differently but feel something is wrong if the reps are paid more.

These attitudes can be attributed to a number of factors, including the company's culture and salary management policies and a lack of understanding about how sales incentive plans are designed.

Company Culture

Using the concept of company culture introduced earlier, determine whether your company is sales, manufacturing, engineering, or finance oriented. The company's culture influences the issue of pay equity between sales reps and other employees. In some sales-driven companies, where reps have a high prominence in creating sales in new or rapidly changing markets, the reps virtually are the company. Without the sales reps' continued efforts and success, the company would not stay in business.

If you manage a sales-driven company, you probably review the compensation program continually in response to changes in selling requirements, but you are rarely concerned with the relation of the reps' pay to that of nonsales positions. Conversely, if you are in a manufacturing- or engineering-driven company, where the sales rep is seen as an adjunct, you will probably want the reps' pay to be in line with that of peer positions in manufacturing or engineering.

In companies where team selling prevails or in markets where the reps have little prominence, there may be good reasons for paying reps the same total compensation as you pay employees in peer positions. But be sure to review your reasons before you introduce a common pay program.

19.3 Job Evaluation Programs and Questions of Equity

How do you define peer positions? Peer positions are usually identified by a company's job evaluation program. The program quantifies differences in the internal value of various positions on the basis of factors defined as important to the company.

The job evaluation program has established an internal hierarchy. Unfortunately, some companies go further, mandating equity in compensation on the basis of the internal evaluations. Equity in pay between peer level positions often ignores differences in the jobs or in the form of compensation.

As noted earlier, designing pay programs for sales reps is not so simple. There is no direct correlation between a position's internal value and the amount and form of pay. Pay programs for reps must consider marketplace pay levels and customized incentives to align the reps' compensation with company objectives.

Addressing Questions of Equity

During a presentation to a group of sales managers, the question of internal equity was raised. When asked whether they had heard complaints from nonsales employees about job equity, the managers responded with loud groans.

One sales manager replied that she continually heard complaints from nonsales employees about the equity between their jobs and the sales reps' positions: "'The reps set their own hours; no one looks over their shoulders; they entertain clients, eat at fancy restaurants at company expense, etc.'" "However," the sales manager added, "all complaints about job equity cease when I ask them: 'How would you like to take this product catalog and list of prospects and start making calls in this territory next week? We expect a minimum of ten calls per day. Here is your per diem rate for travel and entertainment. We expect these forms to be completed and mailed to the home office at the end of each day. Here is your incentive plan, which details the rewards you can earn for sales at various profit levels. Oh, and by the way, your base salary will be cut tomorrow to one half of what it was. Good luck.'"

When you point out some of the trade-offs—the comfort of an office, working with familiar people, someone nearby to answer questions, and the guarantee of a monthly paycheck—you illustrate the concept that equity neither means sameness nor implies parity.

19.4   Introducing Risk

Most compensation programs provide for employees to receive all, or a major portion, of their pay as base salary. It is very unlikely that pay will be reduced in such programs.

Companies grant base salary increases but rarely take away an increase or reduce an employee's base salary. If you pay all your employees, including sales reps, according to a straight salary program, your program can reflect marketplace pay levels and internal values as well. The reason for paying your reps a straight salary, however, should not be to maintain equity with their peers in the company.

The sales reps' work habits tend to set them apart from other employees. Therefore, a compensation plan that focuses your reps' attention on what you want accomplished provides them with the same direction given nonsales employees. When a portion of their pay is incentives, your reps' compensation will be related to achieving specific results.

By tying a portion of the reps' pay to the achievement of specific results, you also add an element of risk to the compensation program. If the reps do not achieve the anticipated results, they could receive less total compensation than they did in previous years. Recognizing their added element of risk, most plans typically build in some opportunity to increase earnings by attaining certain goals.

Additional Risk

Most sales reps are directly responsible for achieving results through their own efforts. In other positions within a company, individual results are rarely so visible. More often than not, increases are granted annually to nonsales employees and usually vary slightly depending on a number of factors, only one of which is the individual's performance for the year.

So, while two positions within your company might have the same internal value, the form of compensation and the total earnings opportunity might be different. These differences might result in the total compensation also being different, and this must be taken into account in your pay plan.

Many pay programs recognize additional risk and reward the reps for it. For example, a pay program for three positions with the same internal value could be designed as follows:

Position	Base Pay	Total Pay
Company job A	$45,000	$45,000
Company job B	45,000	45,000
Sales representative	35,000	49,500

The targeted total compensation of the sales rep is 10 percent more than the other two; however, the rep has almost 30 percent of his total sales compensation at risk and, if the sales goals are not reached, could earn less than 80 percent of the pay received by the other two.

Remunerating this additional risk can create total income levels for some salespeople that reach those of middle management employees and even of some executives. The additional pay is usually found only among the very top performers, but even with the risk variable a rep's average pay rarely rises above that of managers or executives.

All-Commission Plans

In most cases, the sales rep paid totally on commission should be considered separately. The value of the position might be equal to that of others within the company, but the sales rep's pay depends entirely on the structure of the sales plan and on the sales rep's results. In an all-commission plan, all of the rep's pay is at risk, but there is essentially no limit on the amount the rep can earn.

With such a plan, the pay for four employees could be as diverse as follows:

Position	Base Pay	Total Pay
Company job A	$45,000	$45,000
Company job B	45,000	45,000
Sales rep A	0	34,000
Sales rep B	0	75,000

Although the two reps' average pay is $54,500, their incomes vary significantly.

19.5   Equity With Management

In the above case, sales rep B might earn more than the company's middle manager does; on rare occasions, the rep might, depending upon the sales incentive plan, earn more than some executives. It is not unusual for the total compensation of an excellent sales rep on a commission compensation program to equal that of middle management. It is unusual, however, for the sales rep's average pay to equal the middle manager's pay.

The exceptions are companies where a career progression has been devised for the sales force. Acknowledging that not all excellent salespeople make good managers, some companies have established career progressions for sales reps that allow them to earn as much as managers do without requiring them to manage people. The career progression can be viewed as a ladder with the right side indicating levels from sales representative to sales management, and the left side, levels from sales representative to higher sales positions. The *rungs* of the ladder illustrate the comparability of positions within the organization. Figure 19-1 is an example of such a career ladder.

After attaining the position of senior sales representative, the sales rep can advance into management—the district sales manager position—or stay in sales and advance to the sales specialist position.

Figure 19-1. Sample career ladder.

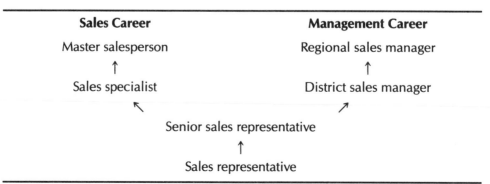

As a rule, reps are promoted to the sales specialist and master salesperson positions only for continued outstanding performance, not in recognition of service or experience. The number of employees in these positions tends to be limited, just as the number of managers is limited.

It is easy to understand why, in a company with a dual ladder organization track for sales reps, you might pay the reps more than you do middle or upper management. In other companies, the characteristics of the marketplace often dictate the type of sales plan and reward opportunities for the reps.

19.6 Team Selling

In situations in which the selling is a team effort—involving engineering, product management, product development, manufacturing, merchandising, or other functions—questions of equity would arise if the sales rep alone received an incentive or commission award. In such situations, other members of the team should participate with the salespeople in an incentive award, for example, a team bonus. The award for the reps might be slightly more than that earned by the others, but it cannot be too much larger without creating inequities.

Do not include, in an incentive plan, every employee who played a minor part in a sale. Compensate only those employees who performed specific, observable roles in concluding the sale.

The sales manager in a company in the electronics industry believed that sales were made by teams. When faced with selecting incentive participants, he protested that he did not want to discourage any employees, so he named almost all of his employees as participants. At the end of the first year, allocations of awards from the plan were made to almost every employee. The result? Employees who had made the greatest contributions complained that the "incentive" was a joke, that people were rewarded not for achieving results but for simply being there. A properly designed sales incentive plan is a communication mechanism that will change behavioral priorities. The plan will operate most effectively when the participants are the employees who can produce results.

Besides selecting the participants, another part of the construction of a team incentive is allocating awards. You must decide whether all participants will share in the award equally, or whether some, such as the sales reps, are more instrumental than others in making the sale. Although you might be able to note differences in the participants' contributions, unless they are fairly obvious to all, a conservative approach is to pay all of the participants identical awards and recognize performance differences in the base salaries.

Matrix Organizations

Companies with a matrix organization face additional difficulties when they introduce team incentive plans.

An engineering company providing high-tech services to a limited market niche used a matrix organization for two years. This allowed the company to assign engineers and draftspersons on a project-by-project basis. Although the project manager and site engineers were generally responsible for one or two projects, the project staff might work on as many as ten projects at once.

In an attempt to improve the productivity of the staff groups, the company introduced an incentive plan that rewarded profitability and timely completion of individual projects. After one year, however, a number of clients were complaining about delays, and profitability had decreased.

The incentive plan was designed to change behavior, and it did: Because payments were made for each project, the engineers and draftspersons quickly learned which project managers were outstanding at bidding on projects and getting them completed on time. The staff focused on the projects run by the outstanding managers, to the complete detriment of the other projects. Projects run by marginal or poor managers were completed late and inadequately, so that they required rework.

The cost of the incentive program was higher than expected. The awards for some projects reached the maximum because those projects received the most attention. Yet overall performance declined. Not quite the results the company had expected. The plan was canceled after one year.

Incentive plans, whether well designed or poorly designed, will change behavior. When you structure a team incentive plan, stop and consider what questions the plan might elicit from the employees. Asking these questions during the design stage will prevent many future problems.

19.7   Potential Compensation Problems

If the sales reps' peers demand to be included in an incentive plan, it may indicate the following problems with the company's other compensation programs:

- Employees may believe their base pay to be inadequate and perceive the incentive plan as a source of additional income.
- Employees who feel the need for more discussion of their performance and more information about the company's salary management program may see an incentive plan as a substitute.

- The most productive employees may view an incentive plan as an opportunity to be recognized with additional pay for outstanding performance.
- The job evaluation program may be outdated, its position levels no longer suited to changes in responsibilities.

An incentive compensation plan is not a substitute for a comprehensive salary management program. You can use the two programs to complement each other.

Expanding Plan Participation

There are times when you will want to expand participation in an incentive plan to include employees as well as the field sales force. The following are a few such cases:

- When the product or service is highly technical and the sales rep does not have the experience or education to answer all the client's questions
- When service plays an important part in the initial or follow-up sale and the sales rep is not responsible for service
- When products or services are grouped to fit the specific needs of a customer and the rep does not have experience or education in all areas
- When the financing of a sale is so complex or otherwise unique that an expert is needed to formulate new or special terms or discounts

In the many situations where a sales rep needs the assistance of one or more fellow employees to close a sale, consider including the rep's colleagues in some type of incentive plan. As previously noted, however, extend participation only to those employees who play specific roles in creating and closing the sale. If part of a service rep's responsibilities is to watch for additional sales opportunities, the service rep should participate in an incentive plan. Similarly, participation in an incentive plan can motivate an engineer, for example, to help a sales rep meet a customer's needs with a service or product.

20

Is The Plan Working?

20.1 Introduction

Companies spend a great deal of time and money developing or revising a sales compensation plan. Naturally, after an initial "trial" period, they want to know if the new plan is effective. (How long the trial period should be depends primarily on the length of the selling cycle. For example, if the selling cycle is from eighteen to twenty-four months, it would be unreasonable to attempt to analyze the impact of the plan change after one year.)

20.2 Plan Objectives

To determine if a new plan is working, companies should, after the appropriate interval, review the program in light of their legitimate expectations of it. Over the years, companies have adopted an assortment of criteria for evaluating the effectiveness of a sales compensation plan. Among the objectives a new or revised plan might be expected to achieve are:

- Increased revenues
- Decreased sales cost as a percentage of sales
- Reduced turnover
- Better retention of key sales talent
- Additional penetration of current accounts
- Enhanced new account development
- Improved price realization or profitability
- Increased percentage of salespeople exceeding quota
- Less complaining about the plan
- Broader product line selling

In addition to its other objectives, the plan should strengthen the important sales management process. Three types of qualitative and quantitative tests can be applied to "test the strength" of the sales management process. These tests can help determine whether a new or redesigned field sales compensation plan did the company any good. The tests are sales management analysis, correlation analysis, and behavioral analysis.

20.3 Sales Management Analysis

If the management process has been enhanced, then the new sales compensation plan has had some positive impact. The term *management process* means the process by which sales managers plan, organize, and direct the sales force in executing the company's marketing and sales strategies.

Some specific ways that an incentive plan can strengthen the sales management process are:

- By forcing field representatives and supervisors to identify and discuss the goals on which incentives will be based, thus imparting discipline to the territory management process.
- By requiring field sales representatives to collect more information about current and prospective customers and their potential. This, in turn, should give sales managers a solid foundation for making important decisions about expanding coverage within a territory, consolidating territories, or creating new territories.

As an example, consider the case of an East Coast trucking company that changed its sales compensation plan from a commission-centered one to one that based incentive earnings on the measurement of a sales person's performance against an established goal or quota. In years 1 and 2 of the plan, trucking company executives found it very difficult for them and the field salespeople to derive an equitable and fairly straightforward quota. No one felt completely comfortable with the process that had been used in determining these important figures. Yet the company continued with the incentive plan while improving its territory and account-specific data collection and analysis process.

In year 3, however, trucking company executives believed that the quota-setting process helped field sales representatives become more disciplined in their thinking and sales managers become more analytical in their decision-making process. After five years, the new incentive plan is working well for this company, even though it took three years for the underlying quota-setting process to be implemented successfully.

Although sales management analysis can be undertaken in a number of ways, generally it is done by surveying first-level field sales managers. In the survey, home office executives solicit field managers' opinions about their ability, under the new sales compensation plan, to communicate with and direct their field representatives effectively. If the field managers think their ability to manage their sales force is no better than before, then the plan change may not have had the desired result even if sales statistics are improved. If the plan change made the management process less effective, then the change was probably poorly thought out.

20.4   Correlation Analysis

The second analysis is a comparison of earnings before and after the plan change. In this analysis, field sales representatives are subjectively ranked by management according to their skill levels. These rankings are intended to capture the representatives' nonquantifiable contributions (for example, professionalism, initiative, adaptability to change).

Ranking by Skills Level

1. Susan S.
2. Jim P.
3. Peter T.
4. Tom L.
5. Joe H.
6. Alicia S.
7. Bob K.

Next, the rankings are correlated according to earnings. First, managers calculate one year's incentive earnings generated under the plan *prior* to the change. Then they correlate these figures with one year's incentive earnings under the *new* plan (see Figure 20-1). This can be done either with a calculator (in the case of a small sales force) or a software package and a microcomputer (for large sales organizations).

If the plan change has increased sales effectiveness, the correlation

Figure 20-1. Comparison of earnings before and after plan change.

	Incentive Earnings	
Ranking by Skills Level	Prior to Change	After Change
1. Susan S.	$4,500	$4,700
2. Jim P.	5,900	6,500
3. Peter T.	5,800	6,100
4. Tom L.	4,700	5,000
5. Joe H.	6,100	6,800
6. Alicia S.	5,100	5,400
7. Bob K.	5,200	5,500

between rankings and earnings should show significant improvement. It will not be perfect because sales representatives are ranked by both subjective and objective criteria, and any distribution of earnings may be affected by events outside the organization. If those who are known to be the best performers earn more after a change in the sales compensation plan, then management knows its efforts to restructure the plan have been successful.

20.5 Behavioral Analysis

As a third test of effectiveness, companies should examine the time allocation of plan participants prior to and after the plan's implementation. If the time allocation has been altered to conform with the company's marketing and sales strategies, then the plan can be presumed to have had an impact.

Very few salespeople are good time-and-motion engineers. As a result, one often finds excellent salespeople spending very little of their time selling. Instead, they stock shelves, train retail salespeople, run down orders, and handle other important tasks. But these tasks do not necessarily constitute the best use of a large block of their time. If the new compensation plan emphasizes some strategic sales objectives, for example, key account penetration or new account development, then a salesperson's time allocation can be modified accordingly. The nonselling tasks will not disappear, but they may be handled more expeditiously or properly.

The test, therefore, is to see if the time allocation of the sales force has been positively altered with the implementation of the new pay plan.

Figure 20-2. Survey of time allocation before and after new plan.

Primary Tasks	Time Allocation	
	Preplan (%)	Postplan (%)
Selling to established customers	_____%	_____%
Prospecting and selling to new customers	_____	_____
Training and supervising	_____	_____
Internal coordination, customer service, problem solving	_____	_____
Administrative, paperwork	_____	_____
Travel	_____	_____
	100%	100%

A simple pre- and post- new plan survey of time allocation can be used to measure such a change (see Figure 20-2 for an example survey).

Summary

Often, companies choose not to undertake these diagnoses, but instead rely on their internal "comfort" level with the new plan. Although this type of subjective analysis can yield some fruitful observations, the proposed analyses may assist all interested parties—marketing, sales, and human resources departments—to reach a consensus more readily.

21

Do We Need Another Change?

21.1 The Only Right Answer: It Depends

Sales compensation is a discipline in which there are few, if any, absolutes. Almost any approach will prove valid in the right context. Sales compensation is the art of understanding, in the particular situation, what the right answer "depends on," as exemplified in Figure 21-1.

Figure 21-1. Guide to plan design alternatives.

Decision		Appropriate Situations
Incentive Plan		• Sales rep has medium/high prominence. • Industry practice is to pay incentive. • Sales is a career commitment.
No Plan		• Sales rep has low prominence. • Company culture is anti-incentive. • Sales is a "pass-through" position.
Commission Plan		• Rep, not company, "owns" accounts. • Volume is complete indicator of sales effectiveness.
Bonus Plan		• Company owns accounts. • One rep is substitutable for another. • Volume alone does not demonstrate sales effectiveness.
	% Base	
Mix of Base	80+	• Sales rep has low prominence.
and	60–80	• Sales rep has medium prominence.
Incentive	0–60	• Sales rep has high prominence.
Payment Frequency	Monthly	• High percentage of incentive is at risk. • Sales cycle is short.
	Quarterly	• Incentive is commission. • Financial goals are quarterly.

(continues)

277

Figure 21-1 *(continued)*

Decision	Appropriate Situations
Semi-Annually	• Account planning is done twice a year. • There are two selling "seasons."
Annually	• Low percentage of incentive is at risk. • Sales cycle is long.
By event	• Sales are usually large. • Few transactions occur. • Timing of sales in unpredictable.

Glossary

accelerating incentive rate   An incentive rate that increases after a certain level of performance is achieved.

at the margin   The point at which sales reps make active trade-offs among various priorities.

barrier to entry   Credentials that a candidate must possess to be considered for a particular position.

barrier to exit   The combination of cash compensation, noncash awards, and career opportunities designed to retain qualified employees.

bonus   An opportunity to earn a percentage of salary or a set dollar amount or range in exchange for attaining specified results.

buying group   Independent entities aligned for the purpose of purchasing goods under more favorable terms.

cap   Maximum earnings realizable from an incentive plan.

combination rate plan   A plan that uses two or more incentive rates to compensate sales reps.

commission   A predetermined proportionate sharing of revenue arising from a discrete unit of sales.

cost-of-sales ratio   Sales costs divided by sales volume.

decelerating incentive rate   An incentive rate that decreases after a certain level of performance is achieved.

direct compensation   Compensation in the form of cash or cash equivalents, including salary, bonus, and commission.

disguised base salary   Level of income above base salary that is highly likely to be earned regardless of the individual's effectiveness.

distribution channel   The conduit by which a commodity is marketed or merchandised.

draw   Cash advanced against future income.

draw, nonrecoverable   Minimum level of income guaranteed for a specific period of time regardless of sales results.

draw, recoverable   Strict cash advance for which a sales rep must forfeit any portion not covered by calculated incentive earnings.

end user   The ultimate consumer of a finished product.

entry-level threshold   Performance level at which an incentive plan payout begins.

event-driven approach   Incentive whose payment is made at the date of accomplishment rather than at chronological intervals.

experience approach   Same as maturity ladder approach.

gunslinger   Sales rep whose only concern is maximizing the number of sales and who is not responsible for client service.

high-risk compensation   Income that the sales rep may receive none of, unless warranted by results.

house accounts   Customers buying very large volumes who are managed, serviced, and "sold" by management rather than by the field sales rep.

implicit quota   Unspecified patterns of performance that create high income for the sales rep.

incentive compensation   Payment received to reward current productivity (may be commission, bonus, or combination).

leverage   The proportion of the pay package that is represented by high-risk compensation.

line-of-credit approach   Program in which part or all of the sales rep's salary is treated as an advance against future incentive earnings.

longevity approach   Base salary increases as years of internal sales experience increase.

low-risk compensation   Compensation a sales rep is virtually assured of receiving, regardless of effectiveness.

market segments   Groupings of accounts whose buying characteristics are similar.

marketing strategy   A statement of the focus and priorities of a company's business.

maturity ladder approach   Base salary increases as years of sales experience increase.

moderate-risk compensation   A package that combines assured income with high-risk compensation.

NER (net expected return)   Expected return (return times probability of return) minus expected cost (cost times probability of cost).

OEM   Original equipment manufacturer.

percentile   Measure of location in a distribution of numbers that defines the value below which a given percentage of the data fall.

perforated cap   Restrictions on maximum incentive plan earnings that allow partial credit for a windfall sale.

perquisite   A benefit tied to a specific key or management-level job (e.g., a company car).

principle of sufficient difference   The difference in economic return sufficient to make a sales rep actively pursue one course of action over another.

progressive commission rate   A commission rate that increases in steps after certain levels of performance are achieved.

prominence   Degree of the sales rep's influence on the buying decision.

quota "kicker"   Increase in commission rate resulting from quota attainment in each product line.

recognition program   Program that provides material recognition to employees for meeting defined criteria.

regressive commission rate   A commission rate that decreases after a certain level of performance is achieved.

RFP   Request for proposal issued by an organization soliciting bids for a project.

risk-averse   Incentive compensation with little true variability based on sales results.

risk compensation   Income that a sales rep may not receive.

Risk Preference Factor (RPF)   Ratio reflecting balance between a sales rep's tolerance for income uncertainty and the desire for high earnings potential.

sales contest   Event entailing short-term sales effort to maximize results for a nonrecurring purpose in an effort to win a prize.

sales information system   Formal compilation of the collective knowledge of the markets, together with systems for disseminating the information.

single rate base salary   All sales reps receive the same base salary.

split credits   Sharing of sales credit between two or more sales reps.

stack-ranking   Salary increases are taken out of an allotted budget based on the ranking of each sales rep's performance.

tenure approach   Same as longevity approach.

validation factor   That part of a sales rep's guaranteed income that must be covered by computed incentive earnings before incentive is paid.

variable pay   Nonguaranteed portion of total compensation.

windfall   A sale created by fortuitous conditions beyond the influence of the sales rep.

Index

[Italic page references refer to figures and tables.]

About the Editor

John K. Moynahan is one of the nation's foremost authorities on sales force management. He has been a management consultant for over twenty-five years and recently retired as a vice-president of TPF&C (a Towers Perrin company). Mr. Moynahan has worked with clients on a wide range of sales and human resources issues. He has assisted clients with sales force role definition, account analysis and classification, goal and quota setting, base salary administration, career planning, and compensation. He has designed sales incentive (commission and/or bonus) plans for over 150 companies.

His consulting specialties have included, in addition to sales force management, executive compensation, compensation surveys, compensation communications, and multinational compensation. His clients have included many Fortune 500 companies, as well as numerous major banks and insurance companies.

A frequent writer and lecturer on compensation issues, Mr. Moynahan is the author of *Designing an Effective Compensation Plan* (AMACOM, 1980), and *Incentive Compensation Workbook* (Bank Marketing Association, 1981). He has also written numerous articles published by *Sales and Marketing Management* and *Compensation and Benefits Review* magazines.

In addition to his consulting activity, Mr. Moynahan has conducted training sessions for sales, marketing, and human resources executives for numerous companies, trade associations, and educational institutions in the United States, Europe, and Australia.

He served for two years as course coordinator for the American Compensation Association certification course in sales compensation. Previously, he was an instructor in sales compensation for American Management Association, Management Centre Europe, and Canadian Management Association.

He received his B.A. from Williams College in 1962, and an M.B.A. from New York University in 1969. Mr. Moynahan resides in Treasure Island, Florida.

About the Contributors

Gordon Canning, Jr., is a partner in Easton Consultants, Inc. He concentrates in the areas of strategy and marketing. For many years, Mr. Canning served as a senior vice-president of Hayes/Hill, Inc., the predecessor firm to Easton. Prior to joining Easton, he was a vice-president of Cresap, a Towers Perrin company specializing in general management consulting.

Stockton B. Colt is a vice-president in the Los Angeles office of TPF&C, a Towers Perrin Company. He is the practice leader of the firm's sales management consulting practice. Mr. Colt has conducted and managed a wide variety of client assignments in sales compensation, marketing, time and territory management, and merger and acquisition planning. Before joining TPF&C, Mr. Colt was with Litton Industries, where his responsibilities included industrial relations, corporate communications, and business development. He is a frequent speaker on sales productivity and compensation, and periodically conducts American Management Association courses on these topics.

James R. Deach is a principal in the Atlanta office of TPF&C. He advises companies on sales management processes, including goal setting, performance planning, organization, personnel development, and sales force compensation. Prior to joining TPF&C, Mr. Deach was vice-president of human resources at White Consolidated Industries, Inc., a Fortune 500 major appliance company. Before joining WCI, Mr. Deach managed the compensation and organization department at Eaton Corporation.

Frank X. Dowd III is a principal in the Stamford office of TPF&C. He has conducted executive and sales force compensation assignments in a broad range of industries. Before embarking on a consulting career, Mr. Dowd held logistics and sales force management positions at Johnson & Johnson, Xerox Corporation, and the Wilson Sporting Goods division of PepsiCo. With Wilson Sporting Goods, Mr. Dowd served as director of sales planning and analysis, as well as director of materials and distribution.

Marla J. Forbes is a consultant in the Chicago office of TPF&C. She specializes in sales force management and compensation consulting. Ms. Forbes has conducted assignments in a variety of industries, including health care, financial services, publishing, and manufacturing. Her experience includes auditing sales compensation plans, designing incentive plans, and training sales management in the use of compensation and appraisal systems. Before joining TPF&C, she held sales and marketing positions in publishing and telecommunications.

Edward A. Francisco is a principal in the Dallas office of TPF&C. He has more than ten years of consulting experience in strategy, organization, and sales management with companies in many major industries. In addition to his consulting work, Mr. Francisco speaks and writes frequently on issues of sales effectiveness. He is the author of *Sales Compensation in the Contemporary Firm*, a TPF&C publication, and is the developer of Compmix, a TPF&C software tool for market pricing sales jobs. Prior to joining TPF&C, Mr. Francisco was associated with Booz, Allen & Hamilton, Hay Associates, and Sibson & Company.

Robert J. Freedman is a principal and vice-president in the Stamford office of TPF&C. He has conducted sales and compensation assignments in a broad range of industries covering communications, consumer products, durable and nondurable manufacturing, financial, and service organizations. Mr. Freedman has been consulting for over fifteen years; this has provided a basis for him for linking strategy, organization, and compensation. Most recently, in the area of sales management, he has broadened his focus to include sales teamwork and account coordination issues in national account selling situations. He speaks regularly on the design and development of sales and executive compensation programs. He has also written articles for *Harvard Business Review, Compensation Review, Directorship,* and *Sales & Marketing Management.* Prior to joining the Stamford office of TPF&C in 1989, Mr. Freedman spent fourteen years at the firm's New York office and one year as a partner with Personnel Corporation of America.

Steven H. Grossman is a principal in the Chicago office of TPF&C. He specializes in sales force management. His consulting experience includes numerous assignments in international and domestic marketing and strategy, as well as compensation and organization. Mr. Grossman is a member of The American Marketing Association, and Sales and Marketing Executives of Chicago.

Mark R. Hurwich is a vice-president of the Wilkerson Group, a New York-based marketing and strategy consulting firm, exclusively serving pharmaceutical, medical device, biotechnology, and related health care companies. Mr. Hurwich focuses on sales management, organization, and similar marketing implementation issues. Mr. Hurwich was previously a principal with TPF&C, where he practiced in general management and sales, along with executive compensation. He has also held technical positions with two electronics companies.

Jay C. Knoll is a vice-president in the Philadelphia office of TPF&C. He leads that office's compensation consulting function and specializes in executive compensation, sales compensation, and salary administration. Mr. Knoll joined TPF&C in 1977, after spending eight years in commercial banking. He is a member of the American Compensation Association and the board of directors of Horizon House. He is a graduate of The Community Leadership Training Program, and is a past treasurer of The Philadelphia Industrial Relations Association.

Gary M. Locke is a consultant in the Minneapolis office of TPF&C. He leads that office's compensation consulting function, and he specializes in executive compensation, salary management, and sales compensation. Mr. Locke has coauthored compensation articles for *Compensation and Benefits Management* and Prentice-Hall. He is a member of The American Compensation Association.

Eric L. Sawyer is a senior specialist in the Valhalla office of TPF&C. As a member of the firm's compensation survey unit, he has managed or served as a project staff member on various compensation projects and surveys. Prior to joining TPF&C, Mr. Sawyer was a senior compensation analyst for American Standard Corporation, and an internal compensation consultant for Citibank, NA.

David N. Swinford is a principal in the New York office of William M. Mercer Meidinger Hansen Incorporated. He specializes in executive compensation, sales force management, and incentive plan design. Mr. Swinford is a member of the *Compensation and Benefits Review* Editorial Advisory Board and the American Compensation Association. He is also a frequent speaker to professional and industry groups, including the American Management Association, the American Bar Association, the American Electronics Association, and the Conference Board.

Timothy J. Weizer is a manager in the business and marketing strategy group of A. T. Kearney, Inc., an international management consulting firm with worldwide headquarters in Chicago. Mr. Weizer has more than ten years of broad-based consulting experience in organizational design and effectiveness, sales force effectiveness, incentive compensation, and performance measurement. He has conducted projects in a wide range of industries, including telecommunications, manufacturing, aerospace and chemicals, direct sales, automotive, building products, and consumer packaged goods.